CH00842943

The Bro ˇˇˇˇ of Saudi Culture

Describing the Saudi from Head to Toe

Abdul Al Lily

allili55@hotmail.com
WhatsApp: +966540015997
https://abdulallily.wordpress.com/

Indie-Published
2020, Al Khobar, Saudi Arabia

© Author
9th edition
ISBN-10: 1532830130
ISBN-13: 978-1532830136
https://brocodeofsaudiculture.wordpress.com

Praise for the Book

This book is available in Spanish and Chinese. It is featured in different languages. It is added to the reading list of the *Saudi-British Society*, declaring it to have 'gained a lot of interest and attention'. It 'breaks significant new ground', stated the *British Foundation for the Study of Arabia*. It 'made me laugh and cry', said a Saudi female reader. It 'provides guidance far beyond the other guidebooks', said a US reader. It helps to understand Saudis 'from every facet of their lives, literally!' (UK reader). It 'presents quite unique material' (Polish reader). A Romanian praised the book for taking the reader 'from *"oh ok, it makes sense"* to *"omg, are you serious???"*'. While reading the book, an Australian 'was smiling and nodding'. One 'read the whole book in one night!'.

The book is 'like my best friend accompanying me every step in exploring the [Saudi]' (Chinese reader). It 'represents a masterpiece in its style and gender' (Uruguayan professor). It 'can be used as a "training manual" for expats' (Jordanian reader). It is 'hilarious' (Spanish reader), 'honest' (Filipino reader), 'entertaining' (Canadian reader) and 'suitable for intercultural communication' (Gambian reader). It 'hits the nail on the head with Saudi culture' (UK reader). It 'would have been gold to me when I first arrived' (US reader). It 'should not only be given to non-Saudi people, but also to the Saudis so they can be more aware of their cultural characteristics' (Saudi female reader). A Saudi male reader said: ' *"yeah we do that"* was a constant feeling throughout the book'. The author 'doesn't defend or criticize his Saudi culture, he factually explains it in a non-biased way' (US reader).

Contents

Opening

Every culture is governed by an internal code of conduct, and this publication captures the code of Saudi culture. Most Saudi norms have long been unwritten and only orally communicated among citizens. As a result, visitors to the country have been unable to read about these norms. For this reason, this book spells out these norms in bold print. It provides bite-sized descriptions of 'the Saudi'. It is informed by around 2,000 interviews with nationals and expats. It is the first to talk about the culture in a purely descriptive (and therefore non-judgemental) manner.

Writings about Saudi culture tend to be too serious; however, this publication is meant not to be taken too seriously. It is, rather, intended to be entertaining (and, surely, informative). It is written mostly on the toilet (and is, likewise, meant to be read on the toilet). It avoids being biased, recording both 'negative' and 'positive' norms. It tries to avoid using such sensitive words as 'religion' and 'politics', since it is written entirely for cultural orientation (not for religious or political matters).

The book is the first to be written by a male Saudi who was born and raised in the country, who is still based there, who is a former officially-recognised 'imam' (i.e. a worship leader) and who comes from a working-class family. Yet, he is a traveller, professor and Oxford graduate. He has been with people from different ethnicities. He has published in different languages and with globally known publishers. Hence, he has shown an ability to communicate with international readers and convey information to foreign mentalities.

Introduction

Domestic–Public Separating

1. Traditionally, the house door divides the entire nation into two domains: the female inside-the-house domain and the male outside-the-house domain. The house door has the following features:

2. **Door Design**: First, the house door tends to be elaborate, even when the rest of the house is in bad condition, indicating the house door as being the most important component of the building's façade. Second, the house door is traditionally made of wood or metal and, at times, decorated with carvings, cut-outs and/or a gold colour. Households express their identity and wealth by applying distinguishing patterns and decorations on their house door. Third, the house door is painted in dark colours to contrast the light-coloured walls, therefore highlighting its presence.

3. **Door Thickness**: A *heavy* house door is a common feature. This heaviness is intended mainly to stress the sharp line between the external public and internal private domains.

4. **Door Position**: A wall is sometimes added behind the house door to prevent a knocker from having a direct view into the house when the door is open. At times, such a wall does not exist; hence, a knocker is culturally advised to stand on the right or left of the door to avoid having a direct view into the house when the door is opened. In addition, the house door may be positioned at

the corner of a house to avoid exposure of the house's core middle space and yard to a knocker.

5.   Neighbour's Door: House doors tend not to face one another, to avoid exposing the inner spaces of homes to one another. In short, the house door is physically designed and culturally configured to be in a strong and defensive position and to generate a 'defensible system'.

6.   Walls: The house door encompasses not merely the entrance to a home, but also high concrete walls that surround the entire property. These walls contain no holes, preventing passers-by from seeing through these holes. Some households use cladding sheets to expand the length of walls surrounding their house, effectively doubling the walls in length and making them much higher. In brief, the house exists as a 'compound' with secure, high, wide doors and walls, effectively turning towns into 'municipalities of closed spaces' and 'cities of walls'.

7.   Door Frame: The house door has an elaborate concrete frame that is higher and thicker than the walls in order to stress its existence.

8.   Stairs: There are generally (unnecessary) stairs by the house door, existing as a cultural sign to underline the transition from one domain to another. That is, the act of having to go upstairs to enter the inside-the-house domain reinforces an implicit sense of going up from a low-status (outside-the-house) domain to a higher-status (inside-the-house) domain.

9.   Windows: When building a house, the owner will ensure that windows are designed in a way that prevents neighbours from seeing into the house, implying that windows are part of the house door.

10. **The house door creates certain cultural norms. These norms show the act of 'crossing the doorstep' to constitute a fundamental transition in social roles, configurations and settings.**

11. **Norm one**: While stepping over the threshold to leave the home, one is expected to articulate: '*In the name of God, I place my trust in God, and there is no might nor power except with God. O God, I take refuge with You lest I should stray or be led astray, commit or be made commit a sin unintentionally, oppress or be oppressed, behave foolishly or be treated foolishly*'. The wording of these sentences provides some insight into how much the house door exists as a transitional borderline.

12. **Norm Two**: While entering through the house doorway, one is culturally expected to say to residents '*peace be upon you*', a practice that highlights the house door as representing an essential shift from a non-peaceful 'territory' to a peaceable zone. Some nationals subscribe to the belief that what lies behind the house door, in the public domain, represent vice, sin and wickedness.

13. **Norm Three**: Men are associated with the outside-the-house domain, and women with the inside-the-house domain. This means that the house door originates from the power relationships between inhabitants, namely, men and women. The association of women with the inside-the-house domain is well- established, to the extent that it is thought that, once a woman steps outside the home door, the devil, immediately, starts escorting her until she returns home.

14. **Norm Four**: Before a woman opens the house door to leave the house, she may take certain actions, including gaining oral permission from a 'male guardian' and/or being escorted by a male relative.

15. Norm Five: When a woman goes outside the domestic domain to the public domain, she covers her body with a loose cloak. Some, moreover, believe that, when entering the public domain, women should be escorted by a (related) man.

16. Norm Six: Sports facilities belong to the public domain; hence, such facilities are, mostly, for men. An initiative was taken in 2018 to legally allow women into sports arenas. There were, however, social campaigns against such an initiative.

17. Norm Seven: An outsider may think that women, who are culturally responsible for domestic domains, should buy supplies for the house. This is, however, not the case in some towns where men are the ones responsible for purchasing decisions, given that everything in the public domain is a male responsibility.

18. Norm Eight: It is not part of the culture that one's laundry is left to dry by being hanged on windows or balconies, as laundry is culturally seen to belong to the domestic domain and therefore not to be exposed to the public domain.

19. Certain cultural values are 'inscribed' on the house door. In other words, the house door exists as a cultural 'representation' and 'concept', which women 'carry' with them and sustain outside the house. The following represent some examples accordingly.

20. Example One: When outside the domestic domain, women wrap their entire body (including hair and face) with loose fabric, utilising this fabric as a form of a mobile 'house door'.

21. Example Two: Many restaurants are divided into small rooms with closed doors (with one room per family), creating a temporary house door. Other restaurants have no such rooms; alternatively, they offer female customers movable, flexible, non-transparent and long partitions with which to border themselves and their dining table, thus replicating the house door.

22. Example Three: The windows of some cars are covered with one-way film, through which passengers can see out, but passers-by cannot see in. The film prevents men on the street (i.e. the public domain's members) from seeing female passengers (i.e. the domestic domain's members). This film is culturally applied to serve in the role of house door, turning the car into a 'domestic private domain'. Despite the application of this film, women still veil inside cars because this film covers only windows on the sides but not windows at the front and back.

23. Example Four: On beaches and in deserts, some women build temporary fabric walls (or use their cars) as borders between themselves and the public domain, thus 'self-enforcing' the concept of 'house door'.

24. Remark: Bearing these four examples in mind, the house door can be viewed as permanently 'attached' to women, even when they are physically in motion (e.g. while going for a walk or being in a car).

25. Various instances highlight the house door as transcending its basic physical presence to take an immaterial and 'metaphysical' form.

26. Instance One: A man may be notified if his neighbours have workers on the second floor or rooftop of the house, since these workers may be able to overlook the courtyard of the neighbour's house, see his female family members and therefore undermine what house doors and walls are made for. When he receives such a notification, he will ask his female family members to close the curtains and to not go out into the courtyard. This implies that the house door exceeds its physical presence and ascends into the air limitlessly, constituting an immaterial concept and taking on 'metaphysical' form.

27. Instance Two: For some residents, female contact information is private, confidential and not to be released to the public domain. In situations where female contact details (e.g. a mobile phone number) must be given, some women instead provide the contact details of their male relatives. In this case, the mobile phone is culturally configured to entail a 'house door', which members of the male public domain cannot access or breach. In other words, in this instance, the house door has been digitised. In some cities, a man is not supposed to know the names of his friends' wives, mothers or any other adult female relatives, as these names are part of the domestic domain. That said, it is fine to publicly release the names of female children.

28. Instance Three: Going online is viewing as 'crossing' the house door to the public domain. For this reason, some households impose certain restrictions on their female family members. In this case, the house door takes on a virtual form. Some women wear a veil when using a webcam to talk to others, even family members. When not in use, they cover the hole of the webcam with tape, thus 'closing' the digital house door.

29. Remark: Despite the division between the domestic and public domains, digital technology has enabled some women to digitally access the outside world without physically being an integral part of it.

Male–Female Separating

30. Gender separation can take place *inside* houses (and other private spaces such as private farms). Inside houses, there can be male-only and female-only living rooms. This separation has led to certain consequences:

31. **Hosting:** In some houses, male hosts do not go to female guest rooms. Likewise, female hosts do not go to male guest rooms. Put differently, in some households, men invite only men, and similarly, women invite only women. Male children can enter both male-only and female-only guest rooms and therefore are used as 'go-betweens' who deliver messages and transfer food between the two rooms.

32. **Communicating:** In some WhatsApp family groups, siblings-in-law are not included, for various reasons. First, siblings-in-law are perceived not to be actual family members. Second, brothers are not to know the phone numbers of sisters-in-law. Third, brothers are not to socialise and communicate freely with sisters-in-law.

33. Gender separation can happen *outside* houses (i.e. in public spaces such as universities, schools, wedding venues, barbershops and workplaces). In these spaces, there are male-only and female-only buildings. This separation has brought about certain consequences:

34. **Building:** First, one is not permitted to access the other gender's building. The female-only building is private, sheltered and bordered by long, concrete walls. A clear sign is placed by the door of the single-gender

building. This sign specifies the gender that is allowed in that building. <u>Second</u>, some female-only buildings (e.g. female beauty salons) are protected by security guards. These security guards tend to be elderly and/or 'unattractive' men who sit by the entrance. <u>Third</u>, there are shops and markets run by women only. At times, men are allowed in these places but only if escorted by women.

35. Socialising: <u>First</u>, in some towns, wives socialise alone (and therefore may/can act in a feminine way). Likewise, husbands socialise alone (and thus may/can act a masculine way). Hence, in coffee shops and restaurants, it is common to see male-only or female-only groups hanging out. <u>Second</u>, some friends do not socialise in their spouses' company. They do no double-date and do not even introduce their spouses to their friends. In short, they do not meet their friends' spouses. <u>Third</u>, for some, non-related people of different genders must not meet, whether individually or collectively, privately or publicly. They believe that cross-gender friendships, colleagueships and non-marital relationships must be prevented. <u>Fourth</u>, in some workplaces, there are no work-related occasions and parties where colleagues bring their partners. <u>Fifth</u>, 'tradition authorities' (who used to freely drive and walk around to ensure cultural and traditional discipline) used to stop 'suspicious' couples (e.g. who were too romantic, very happy or too young), asking them for proof of a marital relationship. It should be remarked that the activity and power of tradition authorities are now considerably limited due to recent changes. Besides, tradition authorities exist only in main cities. <u>Sixth</u>, in some districts, if friends (and their spouses) have a picnic, husbands sit on their own, and wives sit on their own, with a distance of approximately four metres between the two groups.

36. Schooling: Gender separation can occur in two educational settings. Setting 1 is schools, with there being male-only and female-only schools. Male relatives, employers and employees cannot access female-only schools (and vice versa). This reportedly presents a struggle for single parents. Some fathers avoid phoning the female teachers of their daughters to enquire about their daughters' performance, for example. Setting 2 is universities, with there being male-only and female-only campuses. The female-only campus, including its gossip, is mysterious to men. Likewise, the male-only campus is unknown to women. That said, some men and women have started sharing their experiences (experiences that take place inside their gender-specific campus) on the Internet (e.g. through Twitter and web-based forums), therefore digitally exposing their campus to the other gender.

37. Transporting: The windows of some female school buses are covered with one-way film, through which people inside the car can see out while those outside cannot see in. The film prevents people on the street from seeing female passengers.

38. Events: In ceremonies, there is gender separation, meaning the existence of male-only and female-only ceremonies. Hence, a daughter cannot bring her father, husband or brother to their graduation ceremonies.

Male–Female Mixing

39. There are certain *digital* spaces where gender separation has a limited effect (or no effect). In other words, although gender mixing normally does not take place in offline settings, it, at times, occurs in

online settings. Here are some of these online settings:

40. Teaching: In some higher education institutions, men do not teach women face to face unless this teaching is done under one of the following conditions. First, men can teach women if this teaching is done through a video-network. That is, male teachers and female students are on the same campus and yet are in separate rooms and communicate through an internal video-network. Male teachers can only hear female students whereas female students can both see and hear male teachers. A female coordinator is present in the female students' room, assisting male teachers with class management. Second, men can teach women if this teaching is conducted through a 'glass wall'. That is, male teachers and female students occupy a single classroom, with a glass wall separating the two parties. This glass is one-way, enabling female students to see male teachers while preventing male teachers from seeing female students. In the glass wall, there is a hole through which male teachers and female students exchange documents. Third, men can teach women if this teaching is done through online education. Fourth, a man can teach women face to face if he is blind.

41. Supervising and Examining: First, in some universities, men do not supervise women for their higher degrees, unless this supervision is done virtually through technologies, such as postal exchange, telephone, email and WhatsApp. Women normally do not supervise men, even if this supervision would happen only virtually. Second, in some universities, PhD oral examinations (aka defence or viva) are public events. They are moreover used to be broadcasted on a national radio channel, with only male examinations being broadcasted. Men do not exam women for their oral examinations unless this is done through an internal video-network. In contrast, women normally do not exam men by any means.

42. Managing: In some universities, if a department has only female members, the head can be male or female. If, however, a department has both male and female members, the head must be male. Although a man can be a manager of women, he cannot meet them in the flesh and cannot moreover access the female wing during working hours. He can communicate with the female members of his team only by means of technologies, for instance, telephone, email, WhatsApp and video-networks.

43. Learning: In some universities, female students share classes with male students, but only through internal video-networks. That is, the male-only and female-only classrooms are connected through these networks. Teachers can only be male, who are present in the male classroom. Male students and male teachers can only hear female students, whereas female students can both see and hear male students and male teachers.

44. Parenting: Some mothers communicate with the male teachers of their sons via WhatsApp to enquire about their children. This has resulted in emotional relationships between mothers and male teachers. Some male teachers show so much care of the student whose mother they are interested in, until the mother notices them. They may hold a party for the child, make a video of his academic achievements and/or visit him if he is having surgery. All this is intended to show his mother that they are caring and outstanding individuals, therefore attracting her attention.

45. Entertaining: Before the existence of technology, a man used to write his number on a small piece of paper.

Then, he would walk or drive by a woman, wink at her and throw the piece of paper on the floor, hoping that she would collect it when no one was watching. Another old-school way is that a man might write his number on a piece of paper and ask his little brother to pass it on to a nearby female stranger, in the hope that she might contact him. Yet, the existence of technology has led to new strategies. For example, some men use apps (e.g. Tango, WeChat, Tinder, Azar, eHarmony, OkCupid, happn and MeetMe) to find and communicate with female users within the area.

46. There are certain _non-digital_ spaces where gender separation has a limited effect (or no effect). Here are some of them:

47. Volunteering: In the past, mostly religious people were interested in voluntary work, as they believed that this would bring them religious rewards and gains. Currently, some non-religious men have also become interested in voluntarism (e.g. the organisation of book fairs), partly because voluntary work at times involves gender-mixing. Hence, these men see voluntarism as an opportunity to meet and be around women.

48. Writing: Journalism is one of the few domains on which the norm of gender separation has a limited effect. For this reason, some men have joined the journalism sector with the intention of socialising with the other gender.

49. Medicating: First, medical colleges, unlike other colleges, experience various forms of gender mixing. Second, hospitals are places where there is hardly any gender separation, enabling one gender to talk with the other. Moreover, some women work as receptionists. A male patient may hit on a female receptionist. A man may visit the hospital for no real medical reason, but only to talk with female receptionists. A man may call the reception desk to hit on female receptionists.

50. Painting: Those women who are open to the idea of talking to men can be seen in such places and events as art galleries and exhibitions, where there is no gender separation.

51. Reading: Some go to national book fairs, for two reasons that have nothing to do with reading. First, some go to book fairs because they are places where they can meet and be close to the other gender. Second, many go to the book fair because it is one of the few 'fun' formally-organised outdoor activities and events.

52. Transporting: First, in the VIP section of the train, there can be gender mixing. That said, some women do not allow an unrelated male passenger to sit on the seat next to them or even the seat facing them. They, moreover, do not allow him to share with her even a four-passenger table. Second, on the train, there are many groups of female students who commute from one city to another. There are male passengers who walk through the train, looking for loud groups of women. For these men, being loud women equals being 'bad girls' who are willing to talk to men. Third, a man may write on a sticker the statement '*Car for Sale*' and attaches his phone number. He then puts this sticker on his car window, pretending that he wants to sell his car, but the intention is that a woman might get his number and call. That said, nowadays, a man may have his number as his *Bluetooth* or *Personal Hotspot* name, in the hope that a woman calls him. Alternatively, some men put their phone number on Twitter, BB, Facebook, WhatsApp, or through Keek, or attach it to YouTube videos, hoping that a woman might call.

53. Taxiing: <u>First</u>, there is no gender separation inside taxis, in the sense that a male taxi driver drives a female passenger. Hence, some men have jobs as private drivers who are employed to drive women to where they would like to go. While driving women, some of these drivers start talking with them and eventually get their numbers. <u>Second</u>, some men have signed up as ridesharing drivers, not because they are interested in money and further income, but rather to meet women. They have fancy cars and fancy mobile phones, dress up and keep their cars clean and shiny, not necessarily because they take their job seriously, but because they want to impress female passengers. Some have fancy phones dedicated to ridesharing alone. Some, moreover, pass their female customers' mobile numbers (displayed automatically on ridesharing apps) to their male friends. Moreover, a man may connect his male friend with a female friend of his lover.

54. Shopping: Some men drive their female family members to a shopping mall, drop them there and pick them up later. For some women, this is the only time when they are alone and away from the censorship of their male family members. So, they start talking with men, especially given that there is no gender separation in shopping malls. For this reason, some mothers do not let their single daughters go to shopping malls without being accompanied by their *married* sister who is expected to be a 'moral supervisor'. In these malls, if a man senses that a woman is interested in him, he may walk by her and pretend to be on the phone, telling the fake caller his number loudly in the hope that the woman overhears the number and writes it down. Some women do not write it down, as they have the ability to memorise it.

55. Sporting: *'Walking Areas'* have been recently established for those who would like to go for a walk.

Some men have reported finding these areas a good opportunity to talk to women.

Interval

In an anonymous survey of 25 male married nationals, they were asked the following question: '*What would be your reaction if you came to know that your wife was in an intimate relationship before she married you, and that this relationship completely ended before she agreed to marry you?*'

One 'could not think of any answer'. For another, 'it is a complicated question'. One 'would murder her'. One would be 'angry'. One 'would leave her'. One 'would divorce her immediately – why didn't she confess and why was she not honest with me when I first proposed to her?' One answered: 'God forbid – divorce, or perhaps even a stronger reaction than just divorce'. One 'may divorce her or at least never sleep with her'. One 'would forgive her, but I would be careful. I would check her phone regularly. I would ask her to let me check her phone and personal stuff at any time. If she does not agree, divorce is better'.

One said: 'Thank God; there is no such a situation in the society where I live'. For another, 'she would always remember her previous relationship and would compare it to her current relationship with me'. One 'would talk to her and then judge'. One 'would do some tests to see if she really ended her past'. One 'would forgive her, and my forgiveness would depend on her faith, morality and sensible behaviour and on how devoted she is to her married life and to her children'.

Face and Hair

Dressing

56. In public, men wear one of the following combinations of fabric:

57. Very Conservative: Some men wear a cloak from the shoulders to *above* the ankle. They cover the hair with a headwear. They *do not* wear a black 'cord' (i.e. a cord that is intended to hold the headwear). This way is rare.

58. Medium Conservative: Some men wear a cloak from the shoulders to *below* the ankle. They cover the hair with a headwear. They *wear* a black cord to hold the headwear. This way is common and standard.

59. A Bit Liberal: Some men wear a cloak from the shoulders to below the ankle. They *do not* cover the hair with a headwear. This way is not common.

60. Liberal: Some men wear no cloak, no headwear and no cord. Instead, they wear shorts *below* the knee and t-shirts. This way is not common.

61. Very Liberal: Some men wear no cloak, no headwear and no cord. Instead, they wear shorts *above* the knee and t-shirts. This way is rare.

62. Exceptionally Liberal: Some men wear no cloak, no headwear and no cord. Instead, they wear shorts above the knee and *tank tops*. This way is very rare.

63. The male outfit consists of the following components:

64. Cloaks: First, male individuals, despite their age, wear the traditional cloak. They are supposed to wear the traditional cloak when visiting governmental departments and, at times, when visiting the places run by the state (e.g. some hospitals, schools or universities). In other words, one's access to such places can be denied for not wearing the traditional cloak. Wearing the cloak for work is the equivalent to wearing a suit in some other countries. That said, foreign men are not required to wear the traditional cloak. Some citizens voluntarily wear the traditional outfit everywhere, whether in formal or informal settings, for example, on the beach, while chilling out in the desert and moreover at times while playing football. Second, some men do not buy ready-made traditional cloaks, as they see it as shameful to wear ready-made cloaks. Rather, they go to tailor shops where careful measurements of their body are taken. Based on these measurements, cloaks are made to perfectly fit their body. These tailor shops are spread throughout the country. Third, men are culturally not allowed to wear cloaks made of pure silk.

65. Pockets: The male cloak consists of three pockets. One is located in the area where the heart is. One is on the right side of the hip. One is on the left side of the hip. At times, inside these pockets, there are mini-pockets. Partly because of having these pockets, many men do not carry handbags (particularly backpacks). Actually, some do not like to have backpacks because they can be looked down at (or even laughed at) for carrying backpacks. Backpacks are not part of the culture.

66. Underwear: Underneath the male cloak, there are three pieces of underwear: a short, trouser and shirt. Normally, men wear light, loose white underwear in summer. In winter, however, they wear thick, tight white underwear (similar to white 'skiing wear').

67. Headwear: <u>First</u>, the male headwear is a piece of loose fabric that has a length of around one metre and a height of around one metre. It is folded to look like a triangle. It can be either purely white, or a checkerboard of white and red. For some, choosing the colour of the headwear is based on what they think suits them best. For others, choosing the colour of the headwear is informed by ideological reasons and is a reflection of their spiritual school of thought. <u>Second</u>, some leaders of a faith-based minority wear a (white or black) 'turban' (which is a type of headwear based on cloth winding). <u>Third</u>, because of the headwear, it is unpractical to use headsets. For this reason, the wearers of the headwear are forced into using earbuds since they do not conflict with the headwear.

68. Necklaces: Wearing any kind of necklaces, bracelets or earrings for men is socially unacceptable, as these are for women.

69. Nightdress: Inside houses, some men wear a different kind of cloaks, namely '*House Cloak*' or '*Night Cloak*'. House cloaks are loose and long. They are similar to the cloaks that men wear in public. The only difference is that public cloaks are in one colour whereas house cloaks are colourful with elaborated patterns.

70. There are certain gains and limitations when wearing the male outfit:

71. Health: <u>First</u>, when wearing the cord, one needs to keep up right his head and his back, as otherwise the cord will fall down. So, wearing the cord forces one into keeping one's head up and one's back straight. <u>Second</u>, if the cloak is below the ankle, the lower part of the cloak gets very dirty since it touches the ground, making this lower part dark and very difficult to be washed and cleaned, especially given that the cloak is white.

72. Beauty: <u>First,</u> because the male cloak touches the ground, it can easily get stuck in escalators. <u>Second,</u> because the male cloak is loose, it is difficult to know the shapes of men's buttocks.

73. Architecture: That male cloaks are long has two implications. <u>First,</u> male wardrobes are (and must be) long. <u>Second,</u> when the street is wet (because of rain), people grab up the bottom of their cloaks.

74. Mobility: The male cloak (which wraps the whole body) limits one's mobility, preventing one from doing many activities.

75. In public, women wear one of the following combinations of fabric.

76. Very Conservative: Some women wear a cloak *from the top of the head* to the bottom of the feet. They cover the hair with fabric, cover the face with fabric and wear gloves and socks. This combination is rare.

77. Medium Conservative: Some women wear a cloak from the top of the head to the bottom of the feet, cover the hair with fabric, cover the face with fabric and *do not* wear gloves. This is very common.

78. A Bit Liberal: Some women wear a cloak from *the shoulders* (not from the top of the head) to the bottom of the feet, cover the hair with fabric, cover the face with fabric and do not wear gloves. This is very common.

79. Liberal: Some women wear a cloak from the shoulders to the bottom of the feet, cover the hair with fabric, *do not* cover the face with fabric and do not wear gloves. This is *rare*.

80. Very Liberal: Some women wear a cloak from the shoulders to the bottom of the feet. They *do not* cover the hair with fabric. They do not cover the face. They do not wear gloves. This way is *very rare* and is done mainly by foreigners.

81. The female outfit consists of the following components:

82. Cloaks: First, Saudi society is a black and white community. Men, mostly, wear white cloaks. Women, typically, wear black cloaks. Second, female cloaks (and dresses) are long; hence, female wardrobes are long. Third, the female cloak goes *below* the ankle (so as to totally cover the female legs), to the extent that the cloak touches the ground. Fourth, because the female cloak is loose, it is difficult to know the shapes of women's buttocks.

83. Pockets: The female cloak tends to have no pockets, since women normally carry handbags.

84. Underwear: Women are not naked under the traditional cloak. They wear bras, panties and dresses (or trousers and t-shirts).

85. Face Cover: Although the faces of many women are covered with fabric, there is a hole around the eyes that helps them see better.

86. Typically, an adult woman covers herself in the presence of anyone with whom she is eligible to be in a marital relationship, including an adult immediate cousin, brother-in-law or adoptee:

87. Cousins: Many adults do not socialise with their immediate cousins of the other gender.

88. Brothers-in-Law: <u>First</u>, many men do not know how their adult female cousins or sisters-in-law look like. <u>Second</u>, a man can marry the wife of his dead brother. Some hold the belief that marrying the wife of one's dead brother is good, as the alive brother is expected to be the one who can best care for his dead brother's wife, children and general affairs.

89. Adoptees: When an adoptee reaches the age of maturity, his adopted 'mother' will start veiling in his presence as he is, theoretically, eligible to be in a marital relationship with her. To avoid the problem of the mother veiling in the presence of her adopted son, she may breast-feed him and therefore become a 'real' mother, given that one is considered a mother for anyone whom she breast-feeds. Alternatively, the adopted 'mother' may ask a sister of hers to breast-feed the adoptee, and thus the adopted mother will become considered to be related to the adoptee (i.e. his 'auntie'). By becoming an 'auntie' of the adoptee, the adopted mother will lose her eligibility to have a marital relationship with the adoptee and, therefore, she will not have to veil in his presence.

90. There are certain types of people who are eligible to see women unveiled:

91. Other Women: All women can see each other unveiled. When they swim collectively (at female-only swimming pools in private farms), some wear loose trousers and shirts. There is normally only one swimming pool. The swimming time is, for some families, divided into two sessions: one for men, and one for women. Women are normally not good at swimming, partially because there is hardly any place where women can receive professional training in swimming.

92. Relatives: Women can be seen unveiled by their very close male relatives, such as husbands, brothers, sons, grandsons, fathers, grandfathers, uncles, granduncles and the like, but *not* cousins. That said, after a woman divorces, she must veil in the presence of her ex-husband and is no longer allowed to even be in a place alone with him.

93. Sons-in-Law: Women can be seen unveiled by their sons-in-law.

94. Potential Husband: A woman can be seen unveiled by a man who is considering proposing to her. This man will be allowed to see this woman only once in the presence of her male relatives, so as to decide whether to go ahead and propose.

95. Doctors: In hospitals, female patients can be seen unveiled by their doctors. That said, there were social campaigns against this practice.

96. Brothers-in-Milk: Women can be seen unveiled by their 'brothers-in-milk' or 'sons-in-milk'. The concept of 'brothers-in-milk' or 'sons-in-milk' means that two total strangers are perceived as 'brother' and 'sister' if they are breast-fed by the same mother. This has three implications. First, if this mother is unrelated to these two strangers, she will become considered their 'mother', and also the siblings of this mother will become their 'aunties' and 'uncles'. In this case, the 'mother', 'aunties' and 'uncles' will all lose their eligibility to have a marital relationship with this male stranger and therefore will not have to veil in his presence. Second, although the two strangers of different genders are biologically unrelated, they are socially considered to be relatives and therefore will lose their eligibility to have a marital relationship with one another. Moreover, she will not have to cover her face in his presence. <u>Third</u>, if two unrelated individuals get married, and then it is found that, when they were children, they shared the breast-milk of the same mother, the marriage is no longer valid as they are now considered 'siblings'.

97. Everyone: There is an argument that it should be OK if an elderly woman is unveiled in public since no one is attracted to her anymore. That said, hardly any veiled woman will suddenly become unveiled just because of being elderly, since she has grown up with the veil, and therefore the veil has become an integral part of her character.

98. There are certain laws, norms and practices regarding the female outfit:

99. Warning: <u>First</u>, when a man wants to open the door of a room where there could be women who veil in his presence, he makes loud nose (e.g. shouting '*HAY*'), so that the women notice him and therefore veil. Once women are veiled, he will be given the OK to get into the room. <u>Second</u>, when the TV innovation entered the country, some women used to veil in the presence of the TV, thinking that those on the TV can see them. <u>Third</u>, because some women cover their face in the presence of non-related men, men are not supposed to know about (and be informed of) the features of non-related women. So, sisters would not tell their brothers about non-related women's looks.

100. Outing: <u>First</u>, for many families, when having a picnic, their female members remain fully covered, since a picnic happens in public. <u>Second</u>, many women do not allow their spouse to check out other women even if these other women are fully covered with the cloak and veil. <u>Third</u>, it is normal in public places to see a man wearing a short and t-shirt, accompanied by a woman who is fully covered from head to toe.

101. Finding: <u>First</u>, because some mothers cover their face in public, their small child may get lost and become unable to identify their own mother among all the other veiled mothers and therefore start crying and shouting '*mum, mum, mum, waah*'. Then, the mother will respond and say: '*I'm here*'. <u>Second</u>, some women have an exceptional ability to realise their female friends in public, despite all of them having their faces covered.

102. Guessing: <u>First</u>, some men assess the beauty of their (male) friend's veiled wife by observing his children. For them, if a child of his does not look like the father, he must then look like the mother. <u>Second</u>, some men guess the beauty of a single veiled woman by observing her brothers. For them, if the brothers are good-looking, their sisters must be good-looking too.

103. Consistency: Some women are inconsistent in terms of wearing the cloak. Sometimes, they wear it, and at other times, they do not. For example, they may go into the cinema wearing the veil and yet leaving the cinema not wearing the veil.

104. There are various safety, health and hygiene issues that are associated with the female outfit:

105. Hygiene: <u>First</u>, because the female cloak touches the ground, it gets dirty quickly from the bottom. The ends of the cloak catch objects on the ground. <u>Second</u>, when sneezing, a veiled woman passes tissues underneath the veil to blow her nose.

106. Pollution: The veil helps, to some degree, filter traffic pollution (or, at least, sand).

107. Safety: <u>First</u>, if one walks close to a woman, one can easily step accidentally on her cloak because it is so long and touches the ground. <u>Second</u>, women may trip over the cloak when climbing stairs. <u>Third</u>, women may get the cloak caught on sharp items. Because the female cloak touches the ground, it can easily get stuck in escalators. This is why next to some escalators, there is a sign asking women to watch the bottom of their cloak. <u>Fourth</u>, when women get into the car and close the car door behind them, some of them forget to pull the lower part of their cloak inside the car. This is why, at times, while cars are in motion, the lower part of the female cloak is seen to be looking out of cars and to be waving because of the wind.

108. Vision: Wearing such a veil at night is like wearing sunglasses at night, limiting one's vision to a significant degree.

109. There are some travelling issues associated with the female outfit:

110. Road-Trips: While being in the car on highways, some women (who veil their face in public) reveal their face, for two reasons. <u>First</u>, some car windows are covered with one-way film through which people inside the car can see out while those outside cannot see in. <u>Second</u>, on highways, cars pass by each other quickly, meaning that it is difficult for others to spot the face of those face-uncovered women in cars.

111. Airports: <u>First</u>, at the airport (including its taxi area), foreigners are allowed *not* to wear the cloak. The airport zone is off-limits. <u>Second</u>, airports have a private female-only room. Inside this room, a female officer checks the identity of those female travellers covering their face. That said, these travellers, at times, get through the customs without their face being checked.

112. Travel Companions: It is difficult to travel abroad with some Saudi women for three reasons. First, while travelling, they want to maintain many detailed traditional values and norms which are difficult to be maintained outside the country and which are very distinct from the values and norms of other countries. Second, they are not good at being independent, and therefore they rely on their travel companion. Third, the veil prevents them from eating everywhere and on the go, which is an important aspect for backpackers.

113. Overseas: When travelling abroad, many Saudi women want to be allowed to wear the traditional cloak and veil. That said, when foreigners come to Saudi Arabia, Saudis enforce wearing the cloak.

114. There are certain gains that one gets when wearing the female outfit:

115. Imagination: In women's boutique stores, there come female customers completely covered in black holding stylish pieces against their body while looking in the mirror and judging whether these pieces suit them. They have developed a good sense of imagination for this judgement to be effective.

116. Self-Steam: Wearing the veil is a manifestation of power for some women. When a female child reaches adulthood, she may feel excited to wear the veil, not necessarily because she is convinced of its value but because it is seen by her and by wider society as a sign of being a grown-up woman and a sign of entering adulthood. As she grows older, this veil gradually becomes part of her character, identity and being, for which would fight any critic. Some Saudi women report feeling shy to reveal their face even outside the country because they are used to it. Some women, studying abroad and being unveiled, report missing wearing the veil.

117. Respecting: In workplaces, some women report feeling particularly more respected and appreciated by male colleagues because their bodies are covered. That is, this covering encourages male colleagues to pay attention to their words, instead of paying attention to their clothes and bodily features.

118. Convenience: Some foreigners fall in love with the black cloak because they found it convenient. That is, one advantage of wearing the black cloak is that women do not have to worry about what to wear when going out and going outside the house. Some women go out in pyjamas (or even, yet not very likely, nude) under the black cloak.

119. There are certain limitations caused by wearing the female outfit:

120. Misjudging: <u>First</u>, since some women cover their face, a man may hit on women who turn out to be, for example, his sisters, friends of his sisters or aged women. <u>Second</u>, it is difficult to tell the age and liberalism of a totally veiled woman. Yet, one can tell from the type of the fabric of the cloak and veil and from the way she wears them. Older and conservative women are more likely not to wear flashy cloak and veil.

121. Eating: When eating, the veiled woman delivers food or drink to her mouth from under the veil. The veil prevents them from eating quickly because they need to sneak one bite under the veil while ensuring that no one (e.g. a waiter or a passer-by) is looking at them.

122. Swimming: On beaches, some women swim while being veiled and wearing the cloak.

123. Disrespecting: Some men complain that being veiled encourages some women to be louder so as to replace the lack of facial expressions or to stress their presence behind the veil.

Imaging and Self-Representing

124. The following visual means have been culturally perceived in different ways:

125. Statues: There are hardly any statues in the shape of humans anywhere, partly because statues are seen as an attempt to simulate God's creation. There is a concern that people may end up praying to/through statues instead of praying directly to God. Historically speaking, there used to be statues on the land of Saudi Arabia, but they were destroyed for faith-related reasons. The prevention of statues applies to wax figures. When visiting museums outside the country, the first impression that some have about wax figures is that these figures are scary, imagining that they are real. Many do not like visiting museums, because it is 'boring', 'is a waste of time', or 'lies outside their interest'. Some of them do not have the mood for museums. For some, visiting museums is not a touristic activity. Some do not see it as romantic to visit museums with their partners. Museums lack funding for acquiring more contemporary and interesting exhibits, partly because museums tend to be socially not appreciated. The national museum pushes cultural boundaries in various ways. First, there is a video of the Big Bang theory, despite its inconsistency with the national ideology. That said, there is no oral or written comment on this video, so as to make it vague. <u>Second</u>, the museum talks about dinosaurs. The existence of dinosaurs is a controversial issue, with some people doubting their existence. At times, dinosaurs are called 'giant reptiles'. <u>Third</u>, the national museum, at times, displays the scientific timeframes for natural development (e.g. the development of the Earth, oceans and deserts and the formation of rocks and oil), despite being a culturally sensitive issue.

126. Mannequins: In shops, there are normally no *full* mannequins, which are seen by some as an attempt to simulate God's creation. To avoid making mannequins look like God's creatures, their heads are cut off.

127. Cameras: Although cameras have been currently widely used, they were off-limits for a long time, for two reasons. <u>First</u>, many individuals have seen the innovation of cameras to represent risks to many norms and values of the culture. <u>Second</u>, the use of cameras to take pictures of the human form was seen as sinful, simulating God's creatures.

128. Dolls: A few decades ago, there was an attempt by tradition authorities to ban dolls because they simulate God's creatures.

129. Snapchat: The innovation of Snapchat filters is a controversial issue, as a few believe that these filters change God's creatures.

130. Remark: The national 'no-depictions-of-mankind' concept has been reportedly a partial hindrance to science, technology, business, medicine, art, museums and many aspects of civilisation.

131. There have been applied certain restrictions and strategies so as to limit the influence of cameras on events and places:

132. Changing Rooms: There are, at most times, no female changing rooms in shops, because many citizens show concern over hidden cameras in changing rooms. Some believe that any woman who agrees to try on clothes in changing rooms is a bad woman. Some western women do not like to do shopping for clothing in Saudi Arabia because of the non-existence of fitting rooms.

133. Studios: There are female-only photo studios, which women visit to have their pictures taken for visas and other purposes. These studios must maintain an excellent public reputation demonstrating their ability to keep the taken pictures of women strictly confidential. A few decades ago, such studios did not exist, as they (and the concept of photographing women in general) were socially resisted.

134. Schools: In formal online education, women do not teach at all, because it involves broadcasting the image of the teacher.

135. Salons: Some beauty salons need individuals to model for them, so that they can show their customers examples of their work. However, hardly any female Saudi agrees to act as models for beauty salons. So, these salons may have to ask foreigners to do the modelling. Some of these foreigners charge salons around US$400.

136. Weddings: Smartphones are, at times, not allowed in female-only places (e.g. wedding venues) wherein women take off the veil; to prevent people from taking photos of unveiled women. There can be a metal detector to ensure female attendees do not carry cameras when entering female-only places.

137. Universities: Some universities either do not allow female students to bring along their mobile phone with them to the university, or these universities may examine their mobile phones to check if there is any non-marital relationship with men.

138. Conferences: At international conferences outside the country, although some Saudi female participants reveal their face, some of them sit in a corner during these conferences and ask photographers not to include their corner in the pictures. Some of them do not take part in the conference group picture taken at the end of conferences. Some unveiled women, at times, do not mind being part of a group picture, as long as when the picture is posted online, their face is filtered out (e.g. by putting an icon or flower on their face and therefore hiding their face).

139. There have been applied certain restrictions and strategies so as to limit the influence of cameras on individuals:

140. Female Relatives: Although some female members of the new generation take pictures of themselves, they do not share these pictures even with their siblings. It is normal that one has no pictures of their sisters, mothers or grandmothers.

141. Wives: Some men do not have any pictures of their wife on their own devices because of their concerns about hackers. They may instead save them on an external hard drive.

142. Foreigners: Some Saudi women want to take pictures with a western woman using their own cameras, and yet they do not allow a western woman to take a picture with them using her camera.

143. There have been applied certain restrictions and strategies so as to limit the influence of cameras on tools:

144. CCTV: There are normally no CCTV cameras in female-only areas where women are unveiled. This leaves women with some space for misbehaviour and petty crimes.

145. Profiles: Many female users of social networks do not use photos of their face for their profile pictures. They, instead, use pictures of animals, babies, cartoon characters or celebrities. Likewise, many female users of photo-sharing websites do not upload pictures of themselves. They upload only parts of their body that do not reveal their identity (e.g. their hands) or pictures of their male relatives or of objects. Many romantic pictures in online national forums are not pictures of Saudis, but rather pictures of other Arabs, Turkish people or celebrities. Many such pictures are taken from the American movie Twilight or the Turkish series Silver. In general, there is no picture culture for the Saudi female face and body. Indeed, some women *do* take pictures of themselves, but their face is covered. They cannot, therefore, be identified in these pictures.

146. Satellites: The attempt to have satellites taking HD pictures of the whole world is seen by some as a risk to female privacy.

147. Advertisements: First, having Saudi female faces on walls and advertisements is not part of the culture.

<u>Second</u>, most websites of departments and agencies offer news about their female section but without photos of its female members.

148. Social Media: Many citizens nowadays take pictures of almost everything and are active users of Instagram and Snapchat. Moreover, professional photography has become a common habit among Saudis of different ages and genders. There are three main things that Saudi photographers take pictures of three things: sports, food and lifestyles. <u>First</u>, sports activity is one of the few things that these photographers take pictures of. This is because football is exceptionally common among citizens (whether to watch or play). <u>Second</u>, food is one of the few things that these photographers take pictures of. This is because food has a special value in the Saudi context, given that going out for food is, almost, the most popular outdoor 'activity'. <u>Third</u>, these photographers <u>do</u> take pictures of female lifestyles, but only those of female children (*not* female adults).

149. TVs: <u>First</u>, there were social campaigns against the idea of introducing the culture to the TV innovation. When TV satellites came to the country, some 'liberal' citizens used to buy them secretly, bring them home in a black bag at night when others were asleep, sneakily take them up to the rooftop and locate them in the rooftop in a place where people on the street could not see. TV satellites used to be 'smuggled' into houses. That said, they are now an integral part of the culture. <u>Second</u>, it is common to watch (for many hours) Arab and non-Arab (e.g. Turkish and western) movies (with subtitles or dubbed), TV shows and dancing clips. Some watch such TV shows as Triumph of Love (Spanish but dubbed into Arabic). Other (Turkish dubbed into Arabic) TV shows are '*Kuzey Güney*', '*What Is Fatmagül's Fault?*' and '*As Time Goes By*'. Some do not like to watch Arab TV shows, seeing them as 'pathetic'. Anime movies and TV shows (i.e. Japanese hand-drawn or computer animation) are well-known and followed by many. Third, many know western movie stars and other celebrities. Western movies are legal in the country, although certain aspects of these movies are filtered out. That is, there are various types of film censorship. One type involves deleting the culturally inappropriate parts of a film. Another type involves rewording culturally inappropriate terms and sentences in soundtracks when dubbing films. An additional type involves rewording culturally inappropriate terms and sentences in the captions when the film is subtitled.

150. There are certain norms and values related to cinemas:

151. Law: There had been no cinemas until 2018 owing to the social campaign against the idea of establishing cinemas. Now, there are a few cinemas in main cities.

152. Banking: The credit cards of some banks do not work when one wants to buy cinema tickets, considering that cinemas are seen by the owners of these banks to be sinful and therefore to be prevented.

153. Prayer Times: Cinemas may close during prayer times. No movies are in operation during these times. Movies are timed to start and finish after or before these times. Of course, no popcorn and drinks are served during these times.

154. Leaving Early: People tend to leave events just before they are finished. For example, people in the cinema may leave the movie one minute before the movie is finished. They have the necessary skill to sense when an event or a movie is approaching the end.

155. Headwear: At cinema halls, some foreigners do not want to sit behind a Saudi man, because the nature of his headwear (which is wide and big) may cover part of the stage view.

156. Traditional norms (e.g. gender-based separation) tend to be reinforced not necessarily by tradition authorities but also by many ordinary members of the society. Society is under constant surveillance not only by tradition authorities but also by average Saudis, who are always ready with their cameras to capture any traditionally inappropriate conduct——especially any suspicious connection between the genders. They distribute the captured pictures on Instagram or Twitter. Advertising such pictures on social networks scare people, for three reasons:

157. Wide-Reaching: Many Saudis are active users of social networks and enjoy *forwarding* messages. So, any picture showing traditionally inappropriate behaviour spreads ravenously.

158. Exaggerating: Many put the captured picture online and create drama out of it. They like to stir up trouble when traditional issues are criticised.

159. Surveillance: Tradition authorities patrol social networks, laying in wait for any picture of inappropriate behaviour. They will then start the investigation when it reaches growing media attention.

Hairdressing

160. There are certain norms and restrictions regarding the hair:

161. Prioritising: It seems that, in Saudi Arabia, wearing the female *cloak* is culturally more important than covering the female *hair*, since female expats are allowed to reveal their hair in public but are obligated to wear the female cloak. In comparison with other countries, non-Saudi Muslims may cover their hair but may not wear the cloak, implying that covering the *hair* is in these countries more important than wearing the *cloak*. Many non-Saudi Muslims do not, moreover, have the concept of wearing a cloak.

162. Attracting: The culture is structured around the belief that men get attracted to the female face and hair, unlike women who do not get attracted by the male face and hair. Hence, when being exposed to the other gender, women are the ones who cover their face and hair, whereas men do not cover their face and hair.

163. Hairdressing: Some female citizens work as hairdressers. At times, they work for employers, but at other times, they work for themselves at their own house wherein they convert one room of their house into a beauty salon and then welcome customers. Male citizens, however, do not, normally, work as hair-cutters, and this hair-related job is left to foreigners. Moreover, hardly any male citizen works as a waiter or cleaner. Men do only certain types of jobs that fit with their pride and dignity. That said, a few nationals have recently started to work as waiters.

164. Advising: Although foreigners are allowed to reveal their hair in public, some passers-by may advise them to cover their hair. Some foreigners choose to simply ignore these advisors.

165. Hair-Styling: <u>First</u>, for men, cutting some parts of the hair short while leaving other parts long is seen by some to go against the culture. <u>Second</u>, for men, haircut styling is rejected by some for cultural consideration, to the extent that a man can be told off by a stranger on streets for their haircut style. <u>Third</u>, wearing wigs is a controversial issue, with some thinking that this is against the culture.

166. There are certain values and norms concerning the length of head hair:

167. Female Hair: Some mothers do not allow their daughters to cut and/or dye their hair before getting married, because of the following reasons. <u>First</u>, unmarried women with long hair are more likely to be proposed to, as men are believed to prefer women with long hair. <u>Second</u>, some believe that, if a woman gets her hair cut or dyed (or does anything interesting) <u>only</u> after marriage, she is more likely to appreciate marriage, to be motivated to get married and to appreciate the shift between single and married lives. <u>Third</u>, it is believed that, to not cut one's hair is to appreciate it. <u>Fourth</u>, for some, longer hair is prettier and can be formed in different styles and ways. <u>Fifth</u>, it is, traditionally, not preferable for women to have short hair, partly because women are not supposed to act like men.

168. Male Hair: It is not acceptable for men to have long head hair, because men are not supposed to act like women. Tradition authorities may stop a man having long hair and advise him to get it cut. Because of the negative social attitude towards male long hair, some men hide their long hair under the headwear. If a man has long hair, he can be seen as feminine or being a bad person.

169. People have certain values regarding different forms of hair:

170. Straight Hair: The typical Saudi has naturally black curly hair, even though the curl of Saudi hair is not as much as that of African hair. Straight hair is considered by many prettier than curly hair; hence, some men explicitly ask their mother to find them a wife who has straight hair. Because of the positive social attitude towards straight hair, some women and men straighten their hair, either by using a straightener or chemically.

171. Pointy Hair: Some women make the top of their head 'pointy', by tying their hair up and then covering it with the veil. Some men find this style to be pretty.

172. Blonde Hair: <u>First</u>, some black-haired women dye their hair particularly blonde, either for a change or seeing it as a sign of beauty. <u>Second</u>, many dolls are imported from the west and therefore are blonde and white. Hence, some think of real blonde white children as if they are unreal. They, moreover, think that any blonde woman is American.

173. Grey Hair: <u>First</u>, it is common that a person (whether a man or a woman) dyes his/her hair to cover their grey hair. It is acceptable for one to dye one's hair in any colour but black. Hence, many individuals bypass this traditional norm by dyeing their hair *almost* black, e.g. a *very, very* dark purple. <u>Second</u>, there is a belief/concern that, *'if one's hair is exposed consistently to perfume, this will turn it into white hair'*. That is, some men put traditional perfume on their beard hair. <u>Third</u>, there is a saying that, *'having white hair gives one dignity and makes one worthy of honour and respect'*. <u>Fourth</u>, a belief is that, *'having white hair at an earlier age is a sign of reaching maturity at an earlier age'*.

174. Lost Hair: By covering their hair with the headwear, men cover hair-related weaknesses, such as having lost hair (or grey hair).

175. Back Hair: Some women (and men) have hair on their back (and moreover face), which they remove either by waxing or plastic surgery.

176. Braiding Hair: Some women are, in the past, used to have a simple form of dreadlocks. Now, it is not as common as it used to be.

Interval

20 married female nationals were asked: *'What would be your reaction if you came to know that your husband was in an intimate relationship before he married you, and this relationship completely ended before he agreed to marry you?'*

For one, it is 'OK, as long as he has checked for diseases'. For another, it is also 'OK——everyone has a history'. One sees it as 'OK, as long as he does well with me in the current and future times'. For another, 'it is the past which is over'. One 'will be very understanding and will try to please him more so that he does not think of his previous relationship'. One replied: 'If one gives up a sin, God will forgive him, so do I then. Anyone who gives up a sin is like the one who has never done this sin. I will try to satisfy all his needs, so that he does not go back to her'.

One said that, 'whatever happened before marriage does not matter to me'. One 'will be careful with him'. One answered: 'suspicion and lack of trust'. One 'will be sad so much'. One will be 'angry so much'. One 'will be annoyed, and we may get a divorce'. One does not 'know how my reaction will be, but my relationship with him will, more likely, end'. One 'will never accept him as my husband'. Another 'will decide to leave him as quickly as possible'.

Eyes, Skin and Brain

Seeing

177. There are certain cultural practices concerning the eyes:

178. Eye-Contacting: <u>First</u>, when men speak to a woman, many of them avoid eye-contact with her. That is, they do not look at her eyes, face or even body. Rather, they look down towards the ground or towards the horizon when speaking to her. When talking to the other gender, some do not look the person they are speaking to in the eye. This could be misunderstood by outsiders as a sign of impoliteness or disinterest. <u>Second</u>, when a woman has to be alone in the car with an unrelated driver, she, at times, sits in the back seat, particularly in the left seat behind the driver so as to make it difficult for him to see her and make eye contact through the rear mirror. <u>Third</u>, when a man accompanies a female relative and runs into a friend, they may not talk to each other or have eye contact, owing to the presence of a female relative.

179. Finding: When a man loses a face-covered female relative in crowded places where there are many other face-covered women, he can then identify her through her eyes or handbags, for example.

180. Judging: Many men think that they have gained the skill of judging the beauty of a woman through her eyes, considering that eyes are the only things that are seen in many women.

181. Gazing: Many men (be they single or married, young or old) stare at women, even if these women are fully covered. They may, moreover, stare at a woman in the presence of their wife, which is a source of constant annoyance (and complaint) for their wife. They try hard to avoid any eye-movement that gives a signal to their accompanied wife that they might have stared at a female passer-by. They eye-scan female passers-by whether inside or outside the country.

182. Eye Types: Many men give special value to the female eye, differentiating between three types of eyes: normal eyes; strongly-crossed eyes; and slightly-crossed eyes. Slightly-crossed eyes are considered by many to be the most beautiful.

183. Wrapping: New things (laptops, cars, furniture and equipment) are bought while still being wrapped in plastic. When buying these new things, many like to keep these things in their plastic wrap.

184. There are certain social issues related to colours:

185. Clothing: During hot weather, men wear a traditional cloak that is *thin* and *white*. During cold weather, men wear a traditional cloak that is *thick* and *colourful*, as they believe that colourful cloaks, unlike white cloaks, are warmer. The colours of these cloaks are normally dark (not light).

186. Street: Many streets and roads are very brightening, with shiny (orange) streetlights and so much colourful light, to the extent that they may not be eye-friendly.

187. Car: White used to be the most popular colour for cars. However, since women started driving, more colourful cars have emerged.

188. Trucks: Trucks tend to have colourful paints and lights, looking as if they are from the circuit and as if they permanently have Christmas decorations on them.

189. The white colour has a positive social value, which can be seen in the following examples:

190. Blessing: If one wants to pray for someone, one may say: *'May God make your face white'*.

191. Attractiveness: Many women whiten and lighten their skin. It is difficult to find products (e.g. face cream, make-up, removing cream and sun cream) in pharmacies that do not have a side aim of whitening and lightening the skin.

192. Marriageability: Some men, from dark-skinned families, request to marry lighter-skinned women, in the hope that this will help lighten the skin colour of coming generations.

193. White Clothing: Some wear white underwear, white cloak, white headwear and white socks, showing 'the angel look' featured by whiteness.

194. The black colour has a negative social value, which can be seen in the following examples:

195. Cursing: If one wants to curse someone, one may say: *'May God make your face black'*.

196. Evilness: A negative attitude towards the black colour can be seen in the following cultural rumour: *'Black cats are inhabited by ghosts'*.

197. Unattractiveness: Black-skinned people are normally considered by some not to be good-looking.

Hence, when they see a black-skinned man with a white-skinned woman, they feel that he is exceptionally lucky, and that life is 'unfair'.

198. Sadness: On a particular day every year, some men, from a particular ideological group, wear in black (i.e. a black cloak) in sympathy of a sad historical event that took place on that particular day in the past. They wear black cloaks for days during social life and, moreover, in workplaces and schools.

199. The country consists of five main (social) regions: east, middle, west, north and south:

200. Eastern Region: It is wealthy with oil. It is sandy, with many deserts. Its sand is normally yellow. Its landscape tends to be flat. It is by the water; hence it gets humid. There are various beaches. The ocean, reportedly, does not smell like an ocean, and one cannot smell the salt of the ocean. Non-salty water used to come naturally out of the ground, but now machines (e.g. in farms) are used to get the water out to water plants. Modernity, globalisation, global food culture and global shopping cultures, international food or shopping chains can be seen in this region (particularly, the city of Khobar and other cities around this city). In this city, it is normal to notice wealth and to come across neighbourhoods with fancy houses and villas. In this city, the influence of the west and some aspects of liberalism can be noticed. For example, a man can see be seen in western outfit. Women wear the cloak in colours and with elaborated patterns. Some people go for a walk, a run or cycling. Other people, likewise, drive fancy cars and ride fancy two-wheel motorbikes. Hence, this city attracts many foreigners. Here are other reasons why this city attracts foreigners. First, it is, relatively, liberal. Second, people in this city are used to foreigners. Third, it is close to

Bahrain (a country where social norms are more relaxed). Fifth, there are beaches. That said, there are no houses by the beach, even though the beach is very long. In other words, there are no settlements by the beach, partly because settlers in the past feared invasion by sailors. Beach culture is not common. Indeed, people do go to the beach, but only for picnics and BBQs. There are no water-based activities, such as sailing, kayaking and surfing.

201. Middle Region: It is where the capital is. It is sandy, with many deserts. Its sand is normally red. Its landscape tends to be flat. Modernity, globalisation, global food culture and global shopping cultures, international food or shopping chains can be seen in this region (particularly, the Capital). In this city, it is normal to notice wealth and to come across neighbourhoods with fancy houses and villas. In this city, the influence of the west and some aspects of liberalism can be noticed. For example, a man can see be seen in western outfit. Women wear the cloak in colours and with elaborated patterns. People go for a walk, a run or cycling.

202. Western Region: It is where the two holy mosques are located. It is mostly mountainous; hence houses are built on mountains. Modernity, globalisation, global food culture and global shopping cultures, international food or shopping chains can be seen in this region (particularly, the city of Jeddah). In this city, it is normal to notice wealth and to come across neighbourhoods with fancy houses and villas. In this city, the influence of the west and some aspects of liberalism can be noticed. For example, a man can see be seen in western outfit. Women wear the cloak in colours and with elaborated patterns. People go for a walk, a run or cycling.

203. Southern Region: It is mostly mountainous. It is difficult to see a flat landscape; hence people build their houses on mountains. The weather is never too hot because the land is mountainous and high; hence, many habitants of this region do not have air-conditioning. In this region, things look rural, and poverty is common. Besides, entertainment is even more limited. Many people of this region have moved to western, middle or eastern regions for employment and to improve their standard of living. In this region, there are a couple of historical signs, which some tourists like to see.

204. Northern Region: Some of its areas are sandy and flat whereas other areas are mountainous. Houses are normally built on its flat areas – not its mountainous areas. Non-salty water comes out naturally from the ground and runs freely among mountains. Some small villages are protective of their lands and therefore do not like others (be they non-Saudi or even Saudi) on their lands, feeling worried that these outsiders may, for example, hunt their animals and know the places for hunting. It is also because the locals are conservative and concerned that tourists may know the places for finding the assumed undiscovered gold. In this region, things look rural, and poverty is common. Besides, entertainment is even more limited. Many people of this region have moved to western, middle or eastern regions for employment and to improve their standard of living. Many tourists have reported particularly enjoying visiting this region, given its landscape and historical signs.

205. There are certain features of Saudi nature and landscape:

206. Desert and Mountains: First, the landscape is desert, mountainy or both. So, although the country is seen by many outsiders as a desert land, the desert is located mostly in the eastern and middle areas of the country. The rest of the country, however, has natural green fields and mountains. <u>Second</u>, the sand in the desert is soft, but with rain, the sand becomes thicker and almost solid, making it easy even for non-4*4 cars to drive through the desert without getting stuck in the sand. After the rain, the desert becomes full of people who have picnics there. <u>Third</u>, 4x4 cars are common, because people use them to drive in the desert. Many people drive in the desert merely for fun. Highways go through the desert. <u>Fourth</u>, at times, on these highways, it is very 'foggy'. This fogginess, at times, is *not* because of cloudy air but because of sandy air coming from the desert. Normally, fog has a colour between white and light blue, but the colour of 'fog' in this country is orange. Fog can be thick, to the extent that it is difficult for a driver to see the car in front of his car. Despite this thick fog, people still drive, and some even drive fast. <u>Fifth</u>, to prevent the sandy wind from destroying the shininess of the front part of the car, some drivers cover this front part with either soap (or transparent film that is put on professionally). <u>Sixth</u>, one of the desert-based activities is riding four-wheel motorbikes. That is, there are shops in the desert where one can rent a four-wheel motorbike that is designed to be ridden in the desert. Renting one motorbike costs around US$30 per hour. There are small motorbikes for children and large ones for adults. Women drive these motorbikes while wearing their traditional outfit. Since the outfit is loose and long, it, at times, gets caught by the wheels. <u>Seventh</u>, in cities, sandstorms happen only during the day and stop at night, perhaps because of the increase in humidity at night.

207. Monkeys: Particularly in the southern region, there are many wild monkeys, which are aggressive when dealing with humans. These monkeys chill on highways and close to parks.

208. Camels: <u>First</u>, some call a camel '*the Ship of the Desert*', given its ability to survive the harsh nature of the desert. <u>Second</u>, a camel costs between US$800 and US$1,300. People eat camels and drink their milk. <u>Third</u>, there is a particular way of transferring camels from one place to another. The legs of camels get folded and tied together. A pickup truck (which has a technological 'hand') takes camels up and carries them from the ground and places them in the cargo area of the truck. <u>Fourth</u>, there are no wild, free-spirit, owner-free camels. Although some camels seem 'wild', they belong to someone. There is an Asian or African employed by the owner to supervise his 'wild' camels from a distance. Each 'wild' camel has a big mark on its skin, with this mark telling who the owner is. At times, if a car accidentally hits a camel, and the driver is consequently dying, the owner of this camel comes quickly, removes the mark on the camel and then runs away so as to get away with murder. That is, it is common that drivers on highways between cities crash into a wild camel. There are signs on highways with an illustrated picture of a camel, warning drivers of possibilities of camels crossing. Hitting a camel has caused death to many drivers. <u>Fifth</u>, it is believed by some that '*putting camel's urine on one's hair makes one's hair straight*'. <u>Sixth</u>, many individuals make fun of their fellow citizens, saying that '*they drive as if they ride a camel*'. That is, driving a car is subject to traffic rules, whereas riding a camel is not. <u>Seventh</u>, on the right and left sides of highways, there are barriers that prevent camels from crossing. There are, however, gates, which can be opened by 'camel-carers' to let camels cross from one side to another. Car drivers are, therefore, asked to stop and wait until camels cross. <u>Eighth</u>, 'camels' and 'beauty' have exactly the same word in Arabic, with merely a different pronunciation ('jimal' and 'jamal').

209. Lizards: Lizards tend to be large (around 20 centimetres long). They dig a hole in the desert and stay in this hole. Some have lizard barbecues. Eating lizards and drinking their blood are believed by some to be a treatment for some ailments (including asthma). Lizards are usually eaten cooked (as a stew that is served with plain rice). Some get lizards out of their hole in various ways. Way 1 is by filling the hole with water. Way 2 is by connecting the hole with cars' exhaust pipes using a hose, so as to force lizards to get out because of cars' polluted smoking. Way 3 is by chasing lizards in the desert (using 4*4 cars) until lizards get tired of running and then submit.

210. Sheep: First, there is a place called '*the Sheep Market*' where sheep are bought alive. The sheep market is popular, as there are many occasions for which people slaughter sheep. Second, around 3 million sheep are killed a year for daily consumption. Moreover, on a particular day and for an ideological reason, individuals kill 3 million sheep. People usually have large weddings, inviting hundreds for their weddings and serving fresh meat, rice, salad and soft drinks. For weddings, people kill an average of around 20 sheep and serve them to guests. It is shameful and a sign of being cheap if one serves chicken for weddings. Serving sheep meat shows more generosity than serving chicken. Serving *camel* meat shows even more generosity than serving sheep meat. If a father has a male baby, he kills two sheep. Third, if the baby is female, only one sheep is killed. The father either gives the meat to poor people or holds a dinner party for friends where the whole sheep is served. Fourth, it is normal to see sheep (or camels) in the bed of a pick-up truck.

211. Pigs: First, there are no pigs in the country, nor do people eat pork. There are no pig toys, pig cartoons, pig t-shirts or pig comics. There are no video clips or bedtime-story books featuring pigs. Second, despite the illegality and social unacceptability of pigs, guinea pigs are legal and sold as pets, even though they are uncommon. Third, when going outside the country, Saudis, normally, not only do not eat pork, but, moreover, do not touch pork-based products. Some do not even eat any product (e.g. chocolate) that includes pig-based gelatine.

212. Cats: First, wild and homeless cats are common, especially by the Cornish. They are normally skinny. They beg for food from those eating or having BBQ by the Cornish. Second, normally, people do not have cats as pets.

213. Deer: Deer is associated with beauty, and monkeys with ugliness. A common saying is that '*the monkey is a deer in his mother's eye*'. This saying implies that, if a child is bad-looking and unsuccessful, a mother is more likely to talk to others about this child as if this child is good-looking and successful. Parents tend to exaggerate the achievements of their children. Here are some examples. First, if one's child received short training at Harvard University, one's parent would introduce their child as a Harvard graduate. Second, if one's child is merely a technician a company, one's parent would introduce him as an engineer. Third, if a child knew very little English, the father would say that the child is fluent in English.

214. Dogs: First, there are homeless dogs. Dogs can be seen in the wild, especially in abandoned areas. They are skinny. Second, people do not (and are not supposed to) have dogs as pets. They, moreover, tend to be very scared of dogs (even pet dogs), to the extent that some avoid even just passing by a dog. Third, it is believed that dogs are the dirtiest animals, to the extent that, if one touches a dog, one must wash one's hands seven times (six times using water and once using soil). It is believed that dogs are dirtier than pigs. <u>Fourth</u>, many dating tips exchanged online are irrelevant in the Saudi context. For example, the advice '*men should go for a walk with the dog as it is more likely to meet women through dogs*' is irrelevant in Saudi Arabia as people do not have dogs as pets.

215. Birds: Many Saudi men are into birds and have between 10 and 20 birds as pets in their living room. European turtle doves are popular as wild animals. Nationals love birds as much as people in other cultures love dogs. There are sayings that are associated with birds. <u>First</u>, '*a bird in the hand is worth ten in the bush*'. <u>Second</u>, '*birds of the same kind flock together*'. <u>Third</u>, '*kill two birds with one stone*'. <u>Fourth</u>, '*a bird that goes up considerably will come down considerably*'. This saying means that, if one is increasing or rising noticeably (particularly with regard to power), one will eventually decrease or fall noticeably.

216. Mosquitoes: <u>First</u>, there are, at most times and most places, no mosquitoes inside cities. <u>Second</u>, at the beginning of a mosquito season, a car (with a giant spray machine attached to it) goes through neighbourhoods and sprays white chemicals in a large quantity to kill mosquitoes. The sprayed quantity is very large to the extent that there is a 'cloud' of white chemicals generated beyond the car. Some children run beyond the car as a form of having fun by being in this cloud.

217. Plants: <u>First</u>, despite the lack of water in the desert, there are still small plants. There are more than 50 kinds of plants in the Saudi desert. <u>Second</u>, on highways, there are plants between the two ways of streets. There are water-trucks that feed these plants, and these trucks drive slowly in the left lane so as to be able to feed these plants. Because the left lane is the highest speed lane, and because there are hardly any obvious signs warning drivers of these trucks, some drivers crash into them and die. Third, Conocarpus Lancifolius (a kind of trees) is intensively used for streetscapes. It is robust, surviving throughout the year with very limited water. It grows fast, is too green and can be easily shaped for decoration purposes. The second most popular trees are date palm trees.

218. There are certain social issues related to the sun and heat:

219. Curtains: People close curtains, as they are not particularly keen on sunshine coming through windows into buildings.

220. Sunglasses: Although it is sunny, many do not wear sunglasses or at least do not care so much about wearing sunglasses. Even if they use sunglasses, they may use them just to look 'cool'. Some teenagers wear them indoor (e.g. inside buildings).

221. Perfume: Some men wear perfume as a strategy to cover up the sweat caused by the hot weather in summer.

222. Skin: Given the hot weather during the summer, some people take a shower more than once a day, and yet this intensive showering does not affect their skin. The Saudi skin has the ability to live in the desert in 50-degree weather without sun cream lotion.

223. Wheels: At times, one cannot touch the wheel of one's car because it is too hot because of the sun.

224. Socialising: Social events and occasions take place at night given the nature of the weather. Because of the heat, shops close in the afternoon and are open until 12:00 am (and even beyond). So, nightlife is active.

225. Air-Conditioning: <u>First</u>, on the train and in many buildings, air-conditioning is at times centralised, with no thermostat and no switch per room for personal modification. <u>Second</u>, there is a belief that one is not supposed to turn on the AC of the car if one drives above 60km/h. <u>Third</u>, some car passengers prefer to sit at the front seat especially in the summer as it is closer to the AC at the front seat and, therefore, cooler. <u>Fourth</u>, some individuals avoid travelling from one city to another by car in the afternoon given the effect of the heat on tyres and given that the AC cannot function perfectly with the high heat. <u>Fifth</u>, although it is very hot, it is over-air-conditioned inside buildings (i.e. extremely cold). It is extremely cool perhaps because women need more coolness given that they are fully covered and veiled and therefore easily feel hot and warm. <u>Sixth</u>, people do not say *'turn off the AC'*. They, instead, say *'close the AC'*. They translate it literally from Arabic.

226. Fainting: The female veil prevents the wearer from having enough oxygen. Despite the natural heat (which is generated by the hot weather) and the additional heat (which is generated by the nature of the traditional outfit), it is, however, *not* common that women faint.

227. Shops: Because of the heat in the summer, shop signs look burned.

228. Cats: During the summer, and because of the heat, cats park right below doors so as to get some cool air from below doors, or they park under parked cars so as to seek shadow.

229. Tyres: There do not exist winter and summer tyres. People use the same tyres for the whole year, since there is no snow that requires special tyres. Normally, tyres break quickly and do not last for a long period of time, for two reasons. The <u>first</u> is the heat caused by the high temperature. The <u>second</u> is the bad quality of streets and roads——there are so many harsh bumps, cracks and potholes even on highways.

230. Make-up: At female-only wedding venues, it is very cold, because women are worried that their (so much) make-up will melt because of any heat.

231. Melted Cards: In some areas, during the summer, if one leaves one's ID card in the car for a few hours, it will 'melt' because of the heat.

232. Vitamins: <u>First</u>, men and women receive limited Vitamin D owing to the lack of sun exposure caused by the nature of the traditional outfit. Vitamin D deficiency is common among men and women. <u>Second</u>, many women reportedly experience mental depression, partly because of the limited mobility and the limited exposure to the outside world and/or because of the lack of Vitamin D.

233. Water: Because it is very hot in the summer in some regions, some women carry around with them a bottle of frozen water and drink it while the ice is *slowly* melting. This means that they can drink cold water throughout the day.

234. Holidays: Sun is not associated with summer, holiday, tan and Vitamin D, but rather with being hot, sweaty, smelly and in a bad mood and having to take showers constantly.

235. Many women and men spend a lot of time and money investing in their appearance. Here are some examples:

236. Fancy Shoes: Some wear formal shoes daily despite the hot weather.

237. Fancy Watches: Many men wear big watches.

238. Fancy Pens: Many men use heavy, thick and well-patterned pens. Some have pens only for signature.

239. Fancy Handbags: Many women carry fancy-looking handbags.

240. Remarks: <u>First</u>, although people have watches, handbags and pens that appear to be expensive, they are cheap as they are fake-branded. Fake brands of bags, watches and pens are common and are sold explicitly in shops. People call fake-branded items 'first-class', making it sound classy. <u>Second</u>, although the act of using lip balms, body lotions and creams is not a common practice, at least among men.

Studying and Thinking

241. There are certain norms and practices regarding education:

242. Members: <u>First</u>, in public education, all teachers are nationals. All foreign teachers, who constituted the vast majority around four decades ago, were fired. <u>Second</u>, many universities provide only foreign academics (*not* national academics) with allowances for housing, furniture, flying tickets to go home for a visit or for good, etc.

243. Buildings: Surrounding spaces with long walls is a cultural norm, to the extent that there are long borders and gates around universities and farms. There are security and checkpoints at the gates of universities.

244. Pedagogy: At many university departments, course contents are out-of-date.

245. Job Descriptions: At many organisations (including universities), there is no such thing as 'job description'. Likewise, there is a lack of instructions on how to implement a new policy or decision, causing chaos and variance in how it is implemented. Essential instructions and significant information are, at most times, available only through 'personal connections' or by casually asking others and passers-by if they have known of these instructions and this information.

246. Finance: First, at public universities, students are given monthly allowances. The monthly allowance given to students of arts and humanities is lower than that given to students of science. Second, in many universities, if one becomes a dean of a college, one is given a car worth of US$25,000, with unlimited petrol. Third, as a 'student job', some students take care of sheep or camels in the desert or sell in a shop for fruit and vegetables.

247. Regulations: First, at some universities, female students are not allowed to leave their (female-only) campus between 09:00 am and 02:00 pm. At 02:00 pm, female students are allowed to leave *only* with their guardian or anyone authorised by their guardian to pick them up. This is done partly because these universities are concerned that these students may leave the campus with their lovers. Second, in many public and private universities, a faculty member is not allowed to bring any guest speaker to talk in a seminar without permission from the high management of the university. Third, at many organisations (e.g. universities), announcement boards are full of threats, warnings and alerts.

248. Student Night Life: First, many families do not allow their female family members to go to university or to work at night. Hence, all classes for women, at many universities, take place in the morning and early afternoon. Second, there is no nightlife for female students (or even male students). Actually, the culture of 'nightlife' does not exist among students.

249. Study Duration: Normally, doing a master's takes up to 4 or 5 years, and doing a PhD takes up to 7 or 8 years. This is because of too much bureaucracy and because processes and administrative procedures are complicated. For example, proposals have to go to a committee, whom it will take a long time to look at this proposal. This committee may ask for corrections. Besides, any change in the title must go to the committee for approval. Also, many postgraduate students (and supervisors) do not take their studies seriously and are occupied with social life.

250. Discourse: Some rumours are associated with the head, brain and cognition. Here are four examples. First, *'Indomie results in brain damage'*. Second, *'a higher level of forgetting is a sign of having a higher level of intelligence'*. Third, *'chewing gum helps enhance academic performances'*.

251. Cafeterias: First, it is not part of the culture that children take home-made meals to school. If one brings a home-made meal to school, other children may make fun of one and see one as having poor or cheap parents. Second, at the beginning of a semester, students buy shares in their school cafeteria. They sell their shares at the end of the semester. The profit is normally around US$50 per student.

252. There is social sensitivity towards certain forms of education:

253. Male Education: For men, being a student was seen as sinful. Up until the 1930s, there had been no formal state education system for men. The idea of establishing such a system was resisted socially, for certain reasons. <u>Reason 1</u>, this system was criticised for involving painting, drawing and photographing humans and animals in textbooks, which was seen by some individuals as culturally unacceptable, since painted, drawn and photographed humans and animals simulate God's creatures. <u>Reason 2</u>, this system was perceived as a secular and western innovation. Despite the social resistance, the system was introduced anyway, as powerful reformists saw it as a necessity for civilisation. Yet, despite the top-down introduction of this system, this system was, however, fundamentally adjusted so as to make it fit within the culture, for example, by de-secularising the system, incorporating a large number of faith-based courses and excluding music courses and dancing courses given that music and dancing are culturally sensitive matters. At first, merely primary schools were established, followed by high schools and then higher education. The diffusion of education and higher education across the country has been a challenge, with the land being widely spread through the desert and the population being scattered according to geographical and living conditions. When Saudi Aramco (i.e. the world's largest oil and gas company by revenue) started in the 1930s (i.e. the decade when the male education system was founded too), literacy was very limited in the country, and therefore Saudi Aramco had to recruit adult nationals who were illiterate. These illiterate nationals were taught how to write *not* in Arabic but rather in English. The outcome is that these illiterate Saudi Arabian employees have become literate in English and yet has remained illiterate in Arabic (i.e. illiterate in their mother tongue).

254. Female Education: For women, being a student was seen as sinful. Up until the 1950s, women had been confined to the home with no formal state education system, for various reasons. <u>Reason 1</u>, some individuals perceived female education as making women lose interest in their traditional home-based role and as undermining the foundations of their morality and family life. <u>Reason 2</u>, some individuals saw the idea of women going out (here, for education) as being strange and putting them in danger. <u>Reason 3</u>, for some individuals, the education of women could make them more sophisticated, thus challenging the male-female hierarchical structure. <u>Reason 4</u>, some disapproved of female education in the fear of perceived ill social effects that would be caused by coeducation or because of the indecency associated with it in many other countries. There was a violent rejection to the idea of female education for women, which was mediated either by military forces and/or by the announcement that this education was intended only for those willing to join and therefore was not compulsory. At first, only primary education was established for women, because if women were educated beyond the elementary level, they might have access to men's professions or become associated with them. Besides, some men did not want to marry a highly educated girl, preferring their wife to be 'half-educated', as female university graduates would be conceited. Initially, female education was managed by tradition authorities whereas male education was managed by education authorities. One reason why tradition authorities were assigned to female education, because female education is culturally very sensitive, and hence only tradition authorities would know how to shape and direct female education in a way that would be in line with the culture. Although the idea of educating women was socially resisted firmly a few decades ago, nowadays, parents and spouses do their best, use their connections and 'die' to get their women into universities. That said, there is still a concern among some mothers that university social life affects daughters and their loyalty, attitudes and commitment to traditional norms.

255. S*x Education: <u>First</u>, there is no 's*x education'. Moreover, the Saudi media and literature tend to intentionally avoid the use of the term 's*x'. <u>Second</u>, in the national newspapers, the word 'sex' is normally replaced with 'relationship between men and women'. <u>Third</u>, 's*x education' is normally replaced with 'family education'. <u>Fourth</u>, actually, the English word 's*x' is used literally as it is by nationals.

256. Art Education: Although there is 'art education', many schools do not teach students about artists. This kind of education is not taken seriously by many schools, teachers and students.

257. Philosophy Education: <u>First</u>, at school, students do not really study philosophy. This is partly because the culture is not comfortable with the 'why' question, i.e. with critical thinking. <u>Second</u>, critical thinking is seen as a form of rebellion, which is culturally seen negatively. <u>Third</u>, it is a 'norm' or even 'value' that individuals do not admit the negatives and weaknesses of their society, nor do many of them even have critical thinking skills. In other words, a widely common belief is that *'it is okay to make a sin, as long as you neither admit it nor talk about it'*.

258. Biology Education: Students are educated to undermine *'Darwin's Theory of Evolution'*. Some perceive this theory as a foreign value that must be prevented from entering national education. Some do not even know this theory. Some hold the belief that this theory undermines humanity, seeing humans as being, originally, 'monkeys'. Some see this theory as a myth. Many believe in a theory that is the opposite of Darwin's. That is, their belief is that monkeys were originally humans who were punished and therefore turned into monkeys.

259. Home Economics Education: Only women study (and specialise in) 'home economics', which teaches them how to be, culturally, effective members of the domestic domain. Men neither study nor specialise in home economics.

260. Sports Education: <u>First</u>, there had been no 'sports education' for women until 2017. Hence, when a woman decided to do any form of work-out at home or anywhere, they used to do it without the background knowledge about healthy work-out which one would have normally received through formal education. This meant that women's work-out was normally done based on ignorance, resulting in consequences that might harm their bodies and fitness. <u>Second,</u> in educational institutions, many 'dirty' tasks (e.g. organising exam timetables or teaching practical matters) are left to non-Saudi Arabs. At times, if a national is a professor of sports education, he teaches only theoretical courses, leaving practical courses (i.e. 'dirty' work) to foreigners, because he does not want to get his hands dirty. Many professors of sports education never come to work in sport outfit (but rather the traditional outfit), seeing sport outfit to undermine them. This is why they want to teach only theoretical courses that do not require any form of engagement with sports.

261. Music Education: Whereas one may think of music as an art that all societies appreciate and promote, it is, however, a controversial issue. There is no music or dancing education. Some individuals do not listen to music at all. Others do not listen to music during three months of the year, either because these months are holy or remind them of sad historical times when outstanding figures died naturally or were killed. There are limited publications on music as an art form and academic discipline. Indeed, there have been a large number of 'political' writings against music. Moreover, there have been virtual and real-life campaigns against music.

262. Environmental Education: Many individuals lack environmental awareness since there is no environmental education. This has resulted in a number of anti-environmental practices. Here are some of them. <u>First</u>, some do not care about the environment as much as they care about their own houses and private domains (e.g. their own cars). They clean their car by throwing the rubbish on the street. <u>Second</u>, some individuals clean their car by throwing the rubbish out of the car window on the street. <u>Third</u>, the desert (and parks, be they natural or artificial) are full of rubbish. Many people drive through the desert, stop by, have a picnic and/or fire and then leave the rubbish behind. Also, if some people have large pieces of rubbish (e.g. broken tyres and soil), they drive to the desert and throw them there. <u>Fourth</u>, after occasions (e.g. weddings), so much leftover food (especially rice) is thrown away in bins. That said, there has been a well-promoted campaign whereby people are encouraged to reduce the amount of food served in occasions or to give leftover food to poor Asians or animals.

263. There are certain characteristics of some national professors:

264. Cruelty: Some professors are mean to students. Here are some examples. <u>First</u>, some professors look down at their students, make fun of them and mock their way of walking, their accent, their weight, their height and their clothes. Second, some professors do not allow their students to eat, drink (except for water), yawn, stretch, go to restrooms, cross their legs, hold their phone, fix their outfit and interrupt professors' lectures, since such behaviour is seen by professors to undermine the educational 'ritual' and formality and to humiliate professors. Third, some Arab professors reportedly use bad and insulting wording when calling students, such as dog, monkey, duck, bull or shoe. Fourth, many supervisees suffer from a bad treatment from their supervisors.

265. Formality: First, many professors have formal relationships with students. The culture tends to maintain and enforce certain societal standards of formal, disciplined behaviour. To illustrate, students have to use formal titles to address their professors. They have to ask for permission to enter or leave the classroom. They have to sit in a way that shows great respect to professors. They are expected to show (through their gesture, their body language and the way they speak) a sense of acquiescence and subordination when talking to professors. Second, social research is expected and supposed to show only positive results. If one wants to conduct research that seeks to improve the society, one may put into question and be interrogated so as to really ensure that this research does not cause any trouble or show negative results, to the extent that the researcher may feel as if s/he is a 'criminal' and is about to do something bad. If this research causes trouble or brings negative attention, the researcher's boss may lose his or her managerial position. This is why the boss works hard to make sure that the researcher 'behaves' and does not report negative findings. Third, if one conducts a 'good' project, one's manager will constantly question the project to ensure that it does not attract negative social attention, to the extent that the manager focuses on potential negativity while ignoring the good nature of the project. In this case, the manager makes one feel as if one is a bad person, instead of supporting one and making one feel good for doing good.

266. Inconsistency: Some professors engage in double-standard practices. Here are some examples. Example 1, some students complain that professors see it as fine if professors come late to the class, but when students come late to the class, it is problematic. Example 2, some academics teach students the concept of copyright from a book that is illegally photocopied, validating the law of copyright. Example 3, some professors teach about effective, modern teaching methods, and yet their own teaching methods are conventional. Example 4, normally, there are, officially, hardly any female preachers and 'issuers' of cultural rulings; hence men issue rulings about female concerns (for example, their menstrual cycles) and teach women rulings on female-specific cases. Example 5, most conference presenters and writers about women are men.

267. Power: First, many national professors love managerial positions and power. By law, only nationals can be managers in public universities. This is challenging given that the number of national academics is limited. Hence, national academics tend to occupy more than one managerial position at their universities. Second, many national academics are desperate and have a strong desire to get a managerial position, even if they do not have the ability to meet the requirements for this position. Third, some national managers at universities do not do their work themselves and instead use their power to exploit foreign academics to do their work for them. Many such foreign academics put up with this exploitation because these national managers are the ones who renew their contract every year and therefore have power over them. <u>Fourth</u>, when becoming in charge, some make the lives of their 'subordinates' difficult and try to make processes and procedures complicated. <u>Fifth</u>, many compliment their superiors although they dislike them and although this compliment is untrue. This is done in line with the saying that '*if what you need is granted by a dog, say Sir to the dog*'. <u>Sixth</u>, in public universities (where only Saudis can be managers), a non-Saudi academic writes an article and puts as a second author the name of his Saudi department head or college dean so as to make the head or dean like him. In other words, there are many publications with a non-Saudi being the first author, and a Saudi manager being the second author. In short, for many Saudis, being a manager helps get publications under their names, thus getting eventually academically promoted to Associate Professor and Full Professor. <u>Seventh</u>, when some employees become managers, they prefer to keep quiet, to keep things low-key and not to make any (even needed) change. This is because if one becomes noticed or make a mistake, one may lose the position and moreover be placed on 'the blacklist'.

268. Hierarchy: Academia sustains a hierarchical structure. Here are some examples. <u>First</u>, PhD holders are called (by their students, by their colleagues, by the public and, at times, by their relatives) using the form '*Dr + First Name*'. PhD holders normally get offended if their academic title is not used. <u>Second</u>, in universities, when professors are asked to list their names on a document and then sign it, those who first write their names sometimes choose to write their names at the bottom of the list to show 'modesty' and 'respect' to the other professors. In other words, when writing a list of names, the names of the most important people are located first on the list. The name of the most important person comes first, then the less important until the least important.

269. Money: Many professors are money-oriented. Here are some examples. Example 1, many professors are business-people and have their own businesses, even though they work for a university in the public sector and therefore are not supposed to work in the private sector as well. Because academic jobs for nationals are normally permanent, and it is difficult for a national academic to be fired, many national academics have published hardly any articles since they got their PhD. They, instead, have used their academic time to open and run their own businesses. These businesses have nothing to do with their own expertise or even with academia. These businesses include engaging in real estates and opening restaurants and coffee shops. Because of their involvement with business (and because of other non-academic reasons), many national academics are not available at their office during their office hours. Example 2, at public universities, national professors used to be given allowances for attending meetings and for using computers during their teaching practices. After a national financial challenge, many such allowances were stopped, and consequently, many national professors have been discouraged from (or even have stopped) using computers and attending meetings.

270. Prestige: Being a professor is prestigious. Here are some examples. Example 1, being PhD holders (or medical doctors, engineers or judges) makes men excellent candidates in the marriage market. Having a doctorate is held in high esteem. Yet, it may, negatively, affect the chance of women to marry. Example 2, university life has been promoted as a prestigious space, to the extent that it has been made 'exclusive' in the sense that not anyone can get a place at Saudi universities. For instance, if one's grade average at high school is low, getting accepted at a university to study a bachelor's degree is impossible. Likewise, if one's grade average for a bachelor's degree is below B, it is, by law, not possible to do a master's degree.

271. Social Status: Some professors want to sustain a certain social status everywhere. Here are some examples. Example 1, many professors do not want to be seen anywhere (even outside the university and outside academic life) wearing anything but formal clothing; full traditional outfit. Example 2, some professors do not go to any place (for example, students' restaurants) that undermines their academic, social status. Example 3, professors normally receive special treatments not only by society, but moreover, by their relatives, who want to exploit these professors to gain certain benefits (for example, to get their children into university considering that getting accepted at a university in the public sector is difficult).

272. Bias: Professorship is biased towards the west. Here are some examples to illustrate the point. Example 1, any Arab that has graduated from the west can get a better salary. Example 2, earning a degree from a western university is highly prestigious.

273. There are certain characteristics of students:

274. Social Behaviour: First, some students are emos. Some education authorities and tradition authorities have tried to combat the emergence of 'emo' aesthetics in female-only venues. That is, some female students wear dark clothes and tight trousers and make 'bangs' (long hair at the front of the face) that cover their face. Some Saudi emos cannot admit that they are emos because they are scared of their families. They are seen as emotionally and psychologically unwell and are criticised for stepping outside their own gender. It is believed by some critics that emos worship the devil and that the emo fashion is a sin. Second, there has been recently a subculture known as 'female boys' (similar to 'tomboys'), whereby some young female students cut their hair short, use male body language, wear male clothes and put their hands on other women's shoulders. Some female boys are part of an online union through Twitter, which is called '*The Gulf Female Boys Group*'. Education authorities and tradition authorities have attempted to prevent the phenomenon of female-boys from proliferating inside schools. Some see female boys as a shameful and/or western phenomenon, which is to be prevented. For some individuals, women act as female boys because of their bad upbringing.

275. Professional Behaviour: Some students do not know how to maintain professional relationships with their professors. Here are some examples. Example 1, some students call their professors on their own mobile phone in the morning, in the afternoon and even late at night. Students have their own way of getting professors' numbers, even if professors try hard to hide their numbers from students. Example 2, some students (and some Saudis in general) beg so much for things that they do not deserve. A student may beg for a grade that s/he does not deserve. People beg, in governmental agents, to get a service they are not eligible for. Individuals are known for using their connections to get things done. These things include getting a quick renewal of a passport, waiving of traffic fines, getting employed for a job and, indeed, getting a place at a university.

276. Academic Behaviour: First, students' performance varies based on ideology and gender. As for ideology, a certain ideological minority tend to perform better academically. As for gender, women constantly outperform men in educational tracks. That said, female students tend to postpone their higher education studies because of family matters, such as their husband moving to another town. Because of this, university managers and teachers show in this respect more tolerance towards female students than towards male students. Second, collaboration tends to be weak among male students. Some students do not want to work with anyone not from their tribe, family, region or even ideology, even if s/he is clever. Third, there are no officially recognised, face-to-face students', teachers' or academics' unions, whether at the local or national level. That said, web-based forums are popular in universities and in wider society. Fourth, in some universities, there are no (or, at least, limited) student clubs (for example, archery club, go-carting club and music club) or societies (for example, Italian Society or French Society).

277. There are certain cultural practices regarding reading and literary:

278. Reading: First, reading books is not part of the culture. The society maintains an oral culture, in that many individuals do not read and yet prefer to listen. They do not read books, to the extent that if one reads a book in the presence of one's siblings, they may, in all likelihood, mock one and make fun of one. Second, because the culture tends to be audio-based (and video-based), one, instead of reading books, listens to (and watches) lectures. Recorded lectures are widespread, whether in cassettes or lately digital forms. Third, parents normally do not read to their children, whether during bedtime or anytime. Fourth, local public libraries (and, moreover, university libraries) are normally empty of visitors, being dusty and deserted. Fifth, on trains, planes or anywhere, it is not normal to see one holding a book. Sixth, individuals avoid reading in public because some of them are worried that someone may hit them with 'the evil eye', which is a look that has the psychological 'power' to make them lose interest in reading and moreover make them lose their reading skill. The evil eye is given when someone, deep inside him/her, feels jealous of someone else who has a certain good feature in the hope that this other person loses this feature.

279. Contents: <u>First</u>, faith-based books are very popular and well sold. Most books in libraries, bookshops, book fairs are faith-oriented, spiritual and emotion-driven books, with a limited number of academic, scholarly and non-emotion-driven publications. Faith-based books sell well and have a large market. Books that promote critical thinking do not sell and are rare. <u>Second</u>, the norm is that a household has no 'mini-library' and, moreover, no single book. That said, many strong believers have their own (relatively large) mini-library at home. Normally, they, however, may not read any or most of the books that they buy. They may buy books merely to increase the size of their own mini-libraries. <u>Third</u>, many faith-oriented books are hard-bound, and the text on the cover is written in gold. Many faith-oriented publications exist as a series of many books. At times, a series consists of dozens of books. <u>Fourth</u>, many faith-oriented publications show many detailed rulings on what humans should or should not, must or must not, do in their public and private lives. <u>Fifth</u>, at times, faith-based books get sponsored and therefore distributed for free.

280. Events: In the past, it used to be mostly religious people who were interested in (or at least known for being interested in) 'serious' matters such as reading. Hence, book fairs are populated by religious people (and religious books). A widely common belief is that, once one stops being religious, one more likely stops being interested in serious matters such as reading. Nowadays, it has become a 'cool' thing if one appears to be interested in reading books (mainly, novels). Many young people buy popular books, take selfies with them, take some pictures randomly from different pages in these books and share these pictures on social networks. This is done only to show off and look 'cool', although they have not actually read these books.

281. Reading is used for treatment and remedy. Here are some examples.

282. Illness Remedy: When someone gets ill suddenly, many individuals seek treatment from a traditional figure who reads them certain texts for a while, spits in a cup of water and then asks the patient to drink the water.

283. Ghost Remedy: Reading certain texts is seen as a powerful tool to get ghosts out of human bodies. A common belief is that a ghost may colonise a human (or an animal). When this human dances excitingly, the ghost may become hyperactive, make the human jump up and down and moreover lie on the floor shaking as if the human is having an epilepsy attack. When ghosts colonise one's body, they may hurt one and/or take over one's consciousness. Ghosts can even colonise one's voice. If the colonising ghost is female, and the colonised body is male, the voice will become feminine. If the colonised body speaks only Arabic, but the colonising ghost speaks only German, the language will be German. One way of getting the colonising ghost out of the colonised body is to take this person to a traditional figure who will read certain texts that force the ghost to leave the body.

284. Evil Remedy: First, reading prevents the 'evil eye'. The typical Saudi believes in the 'evil eye', i.e. a look that is able to cause injury or bad luck towards a person. The evil eye is directed at anyone for reasons of envy or dislike. One gives others the evil eye because they are better than oneself in certain aspects of life. They might consequently lose their ability to be good at these aspects. If a woman shows others that she is happily married, the evil eye might be directed at her. She might, therefore, start to have problems in her marriage. The evil eye might be placed on two sisters that have a joint wedding, as this shows that the female members of this family are in demand for marriage and can easily find husbands. Second, the evil eye is given based on jealousy. For example, one gives others the evil eye because one is jealous of their food. Hence, some mothers ask their teenagers not to post pictures of their lunch or dinner on Instagram or Snapchat, because they are scared of the evil eye and therefore will develop stomach-ache, for example. Third, when some male nationals travel and take pictures during their travel, they share these pictures without them being in the pictures, because they are scared to be hit by the evil eye for having money and for having fun. When one travels on more than one trip for one summer, one may mention to others only one trip because of the concern that s/he may be hit by the evil eye for travelling too much. Fourth, one could protect oneself from the evil eye by reading certain texts in the morning and evening. Sixth, if one can guess who has hit one with the evil eye, one can do two things may help eliminate the evil eye that has hit one. The first thing is to drink from the same cup that the 'hitter' of the evil eye has drunk from. This is why the 'victim' of the evil eye may invite the hitter for tea. Once the hitter leaves after drinking tea, the victim will drink from the same cup that the hitter has used to drink tea. The second thing is to secretly collect some sand from the area of the entrance to the hitter's house (i.e. to collect the sand that the hitter has stepped on), put the collected sand in a container, heat up the sand (without water), ask the victim to stand above the heated dry sand, spill water on the heated dry sand and let the steam go up through the victim's body.

285. Physiognomy: Some individuals are interested in physiognomy (i.e. the assessment of character/personality from one's outer appearance).

Working

286. There are certain features of some Saudi employers, which some Saudi and non-Saudi employees do not like:

287. Self-Centeredness: Some employers are interested in accumulating wealth with no regards to employees, work conditions, etc. They do not like that some employers do not do the following. First is ensuring safety issues and safe work environments. Second is offering employees enough continuing professional development training opportunities. Third is ensuring that Saudi employees gain their legal rights, which has made these employees busy perusing legal advice and action.

288. Interest in Cheap Workers: Some employers seek merely cheap workers. They are criticised for employing workers who are cheap labour, poorly qualified and inefficient. In workplaces where English is the formal language, Arabs, who are fluent in English, tend to be the ones who are employed, as some of them are 'cheaper' and less demanding, compared with 'westerners', for example.

289. Being Emotional: Some employers are emotional. Many nationals tend to appreciate the human, emotional connection. Hence, an outsider business-person, who would like to achieve a successful business with Saudis, may need to act and play 'emotional' with them, for example, using emotional phrases with them, accepting their invitation to meals, saying how generous Saudis are and complimenting Saudi culture. It is easy to trick some Saudi business people by playing with their emotions. Nationals tend to focus on the technical aspects of spiritual matters, instead of concentrating on their spiritual aspects. Nationals tend to focus on the technical aspects of spirituality, without understanding or realising the spiritual aims that lie beyond this technicality.

290. Lack of Business Skills: <u>First</u>, some employers do not care about their own continuing professional development, being unorganised and showing no interest in reading, for example, about how to manage one's business effectively and how to manage employees effectively. <u>Second</u>, some individuals have businesses just because everyone else is having businesses these days. <u>Third</u>, business is a dominant discourse in Saudi daily life. Besides talking about women, sports and faith, many men extensively talk about business and how to get involved with (and therefore profit from) this sector. <u>Fourth</u>, it has become a 'fashion' that everyone wants to (or at least, should) be involved with business (for example, real states), even if he has a proper job and even if he works in the public sector (even though one is not supposed to get involved with business if one works in the public sector). <u>Fifth</u>, many people get loans to get involved with the business sector. There are so many failures because of lack of professional knowledge, for example.

291. Being Conventional: Some employers are conventional, lack creativity and want to make easy money through ready-made, franchise-based business projects, or through a series of sub-contracting. <u>First</u>, Franchise has become a 'fashion', with many ordinary Saudis (who may not even speak English) seeking a license to allow them to have access to foreign business-people's proprietary knowledge, processes and trademarks to sell a product or provide a service under these business people's name. Franchise licenses seem to be involved mainly with restaurants, cosmetics, perfumes and handicrafts. Second, contractors and sub-contractors are common and get fired and replaced constantly, thus delaying projects. When one signs a contract with a company for a certain price, this company signs the same contract for a less price with a sub-contractor. This sub-contractor then signs the same contract for a lesser price with a sub-sub-contractor. This sub-sub-contractor then signs the same contract for an even more lesser price with a sub-sub-sub-contractor. Such a chain of sub-contracting is common.

292. There have been attempts to encourage the employment of nationals. However, some Saudi owners of small businesses would not like to employ some of their fellow Saudi men, for certain reasons:

293. Arrogance: Some male Saudi employees are not good with accepting orders and are choosy. For some business-owners, some Saudis do not want to get dirty hands and take menial jobs even if their skills and qualifications are limited. Some nationals are, as some employers say, worried that they will not be accepted by a potential wife if they do certain kinds of jobs, making them refuse to do these jobs. So, these young men, as remarked some business-owners, see '*becoming a groom*' as more important than make-a-living and growing in life.

294. Disloyalty: Some male Saudi employees lack loyalty. That is, companies invest heavily in training employees only to have them leave for a better offer as soon as it is made. This implies that loyalty is something that some employees do not have. Moreover, some employers complain that some employees do not have a sense of belonging to their organisation.

295. Jealousy: Some Saudi employers are annoyed that some of their male Saudi employees feel jealous of them. That is, when some Saudi owners of small businesses employ their fellow Saudi men, some of these employees deal with their employers as 'peers' and 'fellows' since all of them (employees and employers) are, eventually, Saudis. This makes these employees feel jealous of their employers given that these employers have been 'successful' and therefore have their own business whereas these employees have not been successful and therefore have not managed to have their own business.

296. Lack of Work Ethics: Some employers believe that some male Saudi employees have limited work ethics and yet expect high salaries. Some business-owners complain that some Saudis are not competitive, want easy money, want to be coddled and are too 'lazy' to work. Some employers claim that, although some Saudis are supposed to work for eight hours, they actually work a few hours a day. They also claim that some Saudis are undisciplined. That is although, as claimed by some employers, many Saudis' salary expectation is high. Many employees do their best and various strategies so as to be the least at work. They cover the absence of one another and do tricks to make the absence of their colleagues go unnoticed. When visiting a company, one will notice that there can be five reception desks, and yet only one receptionist is working and the rest are not there. Moreover, many employees lack the ability to pay attention to details.

297. Lack of Ambition: Some employers believe that some male Saudi employees are not ambitious and are distracted. For these employers, some Saudis' concern about continuing professional and personal development is limited. Besides, some Saudis, as added by these employers, cannot stay focused during work, playing with their phone, chit-chatting via social apps, checking sports news and having coffee and/or tea with their colleagues. Moreover, some Saudis' involvement with their social and family dramas is seen by some employers as 'just too much', influencing their professional life and making them less focused. It is normal that an employee (or a student) does not come to work (or classes) because his wife is at the hospital——it is not because he is visiting or accompanying her at the hospital, but just because of the general fact that she is hospitalised. Besides, some nationals, as believed by some business-owners, lack the ability to simplify matters and tend to complicate issues.

298. Lack of Professionalism: Some employers complain that some Saudi employees do not know how to act at a professional level. Here are some examples to illustrate the point. Example 1, many Saudis lack the ability to communicate professionally and the skill to keep a professional distance with their clients. Example 2, when writing emails in professional settings, many over-use emotional terms, phrases and sentences. When sending an email or letter, many do not go straight to the point but rather 'circle' until they hit the point. They think that this is a polite way of saying something. When sending a thank-you email, they thank lengthily, to the extent that it sounds over the top. Example 3, a common problem with many Saudi employees is that they give away false information. When visiting a health insurance company, for example, the Saudi receptionist may give away information, even though this information is false, or s/he is not supposed to the one giving away this information.

299. Chained to Cultural Constraints: Some employers complain that some Saudi employees cannot do certain tasks because of cultural and social considerations. To illustrate, some women do not allow their husband to teach women, even though this teaching is, completely, done only via technology, and even though male teachers are not supposed to ever meet female students in person or even know how these women look. In this case, some male employees cannot perform certain tasks (here, teaching women) because of social and cultural reasons.

300. Some Saudi owners of small businesses would not like to employ some Saudi women, for the following reasons:

301. Unfriendliness: Some business-owners complain that some female employees are too strict, too inflexible and harsh on their male colleagues. Some sale-women stand next to each other and chat all the time. When a customer asks them for something, they give a short, swift answer and then get back to chatting with the other sale-women.

302. Softness: Some business-owners are worried that being veiled makes some women speak quietly to reflect the expected decency, which is not good for their business. Some employers are unpleased that some national women act too 'cute'. The owners of some supermarkets say that some of their female cashiers act too cute, to the extent that they have tissues that they use to hold 'dirty' products (for example, salmon projects) to scan them, although these salmon products are actually clean since they are already wrapped in plastic bags. Other employers, likewise, complain that some female employees do not want to do any (even little) physical efforts because they are concerned about their make-up and the smoothness of their hand skin.

303. Immobility: Some employers are concerned that some national women are physically immobile and unfit. Some business-owners believe that the nature of the Saudi female outfit limits the physical mobility of their female employees. Besides, some Saudi women are, as reported by some employers, unfit and overweight, because of their culturally-driven limited mobility and because there is no 'gym culture' among women, meaning that many female employees cannot perform tasks that require physical efforts even if these tasks require only little physical efforts. Some employers are concerned that some national women can do only certain kinds of tasks and jobs. For these employers, some aspects of Saudi culture allow women to do only certain kinds of tasks and jobs that go along with their culturally perceived female nature, meaning that employers are culturally restricted in terms of the kind of tasks and jobs that they assign to many female employees. Other business-owners add that they normally think a lot before they assign any task to a woman, because they need to carefully think about all cultural ramifications and implications of this assignment.

304. Lack of Cross-Gender Communication Skills: Some employers are concerned that some Saudi women feel uncomfortable dealing with men. Some business-owners report that, in public, if oral communication across gender lines has to happen, it is kept to a minimum. Besides, many women do not like it when a man is close to them or even passes closely by them. They may ask him to move and make a *lot* of space for them to pass through, even if the space normally seems enough for one to easily pass through. In public, if a man lets a female stranger go first through the door, she may not thank him for that courtesy, as this can be perceived as communication across gender lines. All this gender-based sensitivity is seen by some employers to risk disturbing the professional atmosphere of their businesses.

305. There seem to be certain characteristics of expats:

306. Hypocritical: Some expats are believed to 'suck up' to those nationals in a position of authority in order to get some kind of reward or perks. They are seen by some nationals as the biggest problem of workforces in the country. They are assumed to be in Saudi Arabia simply for money and to do whatever they can to stay in the country. Their strategies are agitation and false glorification. They do not express constructive critics because they think they would be fired. They glorify whatever a Saudi manager does, even if it small and simple. They, moreover, fool Saudi managers and give them a false sense of success. In meetings, they dedicate a lot of time to the glorification of Saudi managers. In general, if one wants to make many nationals happy, one simply needs to 'over-compliment' them (and their roots and family or tribe). Some expats pretend not to understand the norms, so they can take advantage.

307. Superior: <u>First</u>, some expats (especially white people) are thought to be in Saudi Arabia just because of the special treatment received from nationals. Many nationals grant white people a considerable level of respect and a *very* special treatment. For example, some western conference-speakers and consultants, who come to Saudi Arabia merely for a few days or weeks, are paid for first-class return flight tickets, are picked up from the airport, are hosted in five-star hotels and are given a generous amount of money for every day during their visit. <u>Second</u>, many nationals grant 'white people' a considerable level of respect and a very special treatment. If one has white people as guests or visitors, one will use them to show off. The use of white people as a means of showing off annoys some white people, but, on the other hand, other white people like this attention. At times, if a university signs with a western institution a contract of consultancy, it is an implicit agreement that consultants are to be white; yet if there is any black westerner in the consultancy team, this may result in disappointment on the part of the Saudi university.

308. Uninterested: Some expats do not like to be in Saudi Arabia, but they are staying anyway for eight reasons. <u>Reason 1</u>, it is the only place where they could have a good-paid job or even have a job at all. Some expats are, it is believed, not 'good', as otherwise they would not leave their home. <u>Reason 2</u>, expats' partner works in Saudi Arabia, or because their partner is Saudi. <u>Reason 3</u>, job expectation and workload are low in Saudi Arabia. <u>Reason 4</u>, they can easily make money and can get so much money through so much over-time. <u>Reason 5</u>, they (especially some Americans) need money to pay their student loan. <u>Reason 6</u>, they (especially some UK citizens) need money so that they afford to buy a house, or because they already have a house but need to pay its mortgage loan. <u>Reason 7</u>, some Muslim expats want to be close to the holiest sites in Saudi Arabia and therefore to be able to easily visit these sites on a regular basis. <u>Reason 8</u>, their research (for example, their master's or PhD research) is based on Saudi Arabia. Because some expats do not like to be in Saudi Arabia, they live in Bahrain and commute between Bahrain and Saudi Arabia. Or, they spend almost every weekend in Bahrain. Some expats feel more comfortable in Bahrain because the culture is somewhat more liberal, especially for those who are accompanied by a wife or girlfriend. That is to say that one cannot bring one's partner to Saudi Arabia unless the two are married, meaning that one cannot bring one's boyfriend or girlfriend.

309. Optimistic: Some expats are hope-oriented and sympathetic towards nationals. They argue that, to shine, Saudis, like any other humans, only need good training. They have the expectation that many young Saudis have the capacity to transform the Saudi industry to an unexpected stage if they become more confident with change. They argue that many Saudis have proven themselves in many industries. They think that, if Saudis are given the opportunity (training, support, and fair benefits), many of them will perform well. This sympathy with Saudis is perhaps because some of these expats have established emotional connections with Saudis, whom they have found to be 'the friendliest people one can ever meet', to be willing to help one when in need and to be always willing to offer one food and things to make one feel welcome.

310. Defenders: Some expats are defensive of some nationals. They think that some of their fellow expats are afraid of nationals who can take their job, and hence these expats start claiming that Saudis are irresponsible, do not come on time, etc. They think that some Saudis, unlike some other non-Saudis, do not like to be 'informers' or 'ass-kissers' for managers or high-position figures, choose to work with sincerity and dedication, are not just for money and do not accept manipulation, corruption or 'money under the table'. Some expats defend Saudi employees, arguing that the problem is not with the Saudi young workforce but with the small business owners who lake business knowledge and etiquette as they want to hire an inexperienced Saudi and expect him/her to do 'wonders' to their businesses without setting a clear job description or a training plan to their employees.

311. Admirers: Some expats are 'complementors'. They think that many Saudis are hardworking, responsible, good at doing their jobs, fearless, very competent, very good decision-makers, humble and understanding. They think that many Saudis are on time, respect time, respect people older than themselves, and tell the truth no matter what. They believe that many Saudis are probably among 'the most loyal co-workers one can ever have' and among 'the most dedicated and hardworking employees'. They believe that Saudi Arabia's youth has some of the best educated people, who are eager to work, take on challenges, have the drive to progress and advance, have great work ethics, are very professional, are very intelligent and are career-focused.

312. Feminists: Some expats are gender-sensitive. They stress the fact that social and cultural prejudices are the culprits and the ones behind the constant struggle of women to get the suitable job, to be productive and to contribute economically. They believe that gender issues have affected negatively the way in which recruiters see women. They have 'never seen professionalism as much as that in Saudi women': they are basically organised, clever and get the job done. They complement women on working very hard, being educated, being very good at their job, enjoying the work and showing passion. Some Saudis are annoyed that some non-Saudis do not respect those Saudi norms and values concerning women.

313. Self-Interested: Some expats are self-centred. Some Saudis think that western human resources managers and non-Saudi recruiters are biased towards non-Saudi employees. For these Saudis, most human resources managers in the private sector are foreigners who look for lowest payments; payments that many Saudis cannot put up with. Some Saudis argue that there is normally an environment that is controlled by non-Saudis who do not like to transfer knowledge fearing from losing their jobs. Some Saudis think of their fellow Saudis as being not less qualified, not less smart and not having less loyalty than foreigners, and yet non-Saudi recruiters hire more and more of their (non-Saudi) people. Hence, some Saudis complain that unqualified foreign people get hired in jobs that are way above their level of education and understanding.

314. Disappointed: Some expats are disappointed at many nationals. They criticise them for not coming on time, not coming regularly to work, being unable to hold responsibilities and not completing the job on time and with least mistakes. On the other hand, some Saudis are disappointed at some non-Saudis. They are annoyed that some non-Saudis do not want to learn about Saudi culture. They argue that expats should remember that they have signed job contracts to work in Saudi Arabia, and one clause stipulates to respect Saudi customs and cultural values. Some expat managers complain that their power is limited by their Saudi superiors to merely signing papers.

315. Supporters: Some expats believe in the importance of support through training, good leaderships and positive work environments. They make the argument that, if given an opportunity (for example, proper training and development programmes), Saudi men and women can prove themselves. They think that, when the right leadership is in place, Saudis have shown enthusiasm, dedication and interests in productivity prevail. Some believe that, when hard work and effort are rewarded, and training is provided, Saudis perform just as well as non-Saudis. Some think that, if non-Saudis mentor Saudis well and give them the fair salary and the right environment to grow, one will be amazed how much loyal and eager to learn to grow and serve Saudis can be.

316. Missionary: Some expats are 'missionary'. They see themselves as those whose mission is to help change and improve the country. They seek to develop their Saudi colleagues and subordinates. They believe that, since there are simply not enough qualified Saudi personnel to fill every position, these expats report working diligently to share their experience and to 'get Saudis there'. Many of those westerners who are associated with the country and write about Saudi culture either have never been to the country, or they have been for short visits and for short periods of time.

317. Reflective: Some expats like to compare Saudis with others. At times, Saudis are compared with westerners. Some expats believe that some Saudi women are efficient, courteous and thoroughly professional, compared to their counterparts in the USA. They think that many Saudis (and Saudi culture) are a lot easier going and friendly than those in the USA. At other times, Saudis are compared with Asians. For example, some expats believe that many Saudis are better educated, competent, loyal and more exposed to the world than Asians. Others, however, think that Saudis are equally competent with Asians. Some believe that Saudi employees are just like any others in the world, who are educated, are dedicated, are ambitious and need to be well managed and mentored.

318. Aged: Many western expats are believed to be old. It is believed that westerners in the country are normally old, as young people are believed not to be willing in their youth to cope with the lifestyle of the country. When many young westerners come to the country for work, they are said to quickly escape within the first few years or even months. Particularly German expats are believed to be the ones who are least able to tolerate Saudi culture, critically and reflectively repeating '*this doesn't make sense*'.

319. Adventurers: Some expats are adventurous. They are into exploring the world and want to see Saudi culture for themselves——away from the media-cultivated dramas. They have noticed that Saudi culture is uniquely different from the rest of the world cultures and hence has been on their list of countries-to-visit. Yet, getting a touristic visa is difficult. But, getting a work visa is easy as long as one is offered a job in the country; hence, some foreigners come to the country on a work visa and do not mind any job offer as long as they come to the country and explore its culture.

320. Uncultured: Some expats (especially Asian expats) are, reportedly, not interested in doing reading books (including books about the culture). They are believed by some nationals to be interested in simply collecting as much money as they can. To collect as much money as possible, they do any kind of jobs and work all day and night.

321. Partying: Some expats (and some nationals) are so into embassy parties, seeing 'embassy crawl' as the Saudi version of 'pub crawl'. Others produce their own home-made drinks, or they, like some nationals, go to neighbouring countries (e.g. Bahrain) for drinking.

322. Exaggerators: Some expats share only negative stories with Saudi culture and exaggerate bad experiences with Saudis. They stress the negative aspects of the culture while leaving positive components in the shadow. They never complement anything related to the culture and show a high level of negativity. They tell newcomers that *'whatever you do, you will be punished'*. They exaggerate the consequences of any culturally inappropriate behaviour, such as cutting off one's heads or arms.

323. Academics: Some western academics, reportedly, do not want to come to the country, for various reasons. <u>First</u>, funding is limited, and there is limited academic competition. <u>Second</u>, there are mainly undergraduate degrees. <u>Third</u> is the lack of focus on research. <u>Fourth</u>, focus goes to teaching and administrative matters. Many bureaucratic complications weigh down Saudi academic and social lives, discouraging some western academics from having a job in the country. <u>Fifth</u>, the job opportunities for westerners are limited, considering, for example, that there are only a few universities and colleges where English is the formal language. <u>Sixth</u>, working and social conditions (such as many restrictions in daily life, limited public outdoor activities and poor housing systems) are poor. <u>Seventh</u>, working in Saudi Arabia for a long time is, at times, not good for professional reputations and does not represent one in a good way in one's CV, especially for academics.

324. There are certain issues regarding professional life:

325. Offices: <u>First</u>, normally, men do not have, at their office, pictures of their family members (whether male or female members). <u>Second</u>, people have their own small fridge (around 40cm*40cm) at their office.

326. Finance: Interest (charged on loans) is religiously illegal. However, some banks have their own roundabout strategies to make 'interest' sound as if it is not interest, thus getting away with it.

327. Rewards: Giving personalised 'thank-you trophies' is a common practice. Trophies are made of wood or glass.

328. Direction: <u>First</u>, people write from right to left. Computers accordingly work from right to left. <u>Second</u>, the *Start* menu on the desktop is located at the right of the window.

329. Choice: A common argument is whether every human in his/her lifetime is forcing into going through one specific path that is already set for him/her, *or* they have the choice to choose from different paths. This is why, if asked to choose from options, one may choose 'randomly' because of a belief that humans have no choice in their life or that so-called 'randomness' is a natural response to the good will of God. This represents a challenge to social research that aims to measure human behaviour and generate a pattern for societal behaviour.

330. Standing Customers: Office-based workers normally do not like it when a customer is standing while waiting to be served. They found it annoying and would say: '*don't stand on my head*'.

331. Many services and projects (e.g. construction projects) take a long time to be done. Here are some related issues:

332. Lack of Qualification: Many employers hire poor foreign workers who are poorly qualified and inefficient, partly because the salaries offered are low. Many nationals are poorly qualified, do not care about continuing professional and personal development and do not work hard.

333. Slowness: People tend to be slow when completing tasks. This is not to mention that many are not good with emergency and urgency. They are not good at putting themselves in others' shoes.

334. Incompleteness: Many new businesses and projects (e.g. hotels or centres) start operating even though half of the facilities are not ready and are not functioning yet. It may take a long time for these dysfunctional facilities to be ready.

335. Imperfection: Outages (e.g. water outages, electricity outages, telecommunications outages and outages in gas stations) are common. Although some outages are crucial, they are not talked about by the media. Media coverage is limited. A whole train industry may shut down for a whole week, and yet there is hardly any media coverage. Despite the widespread of cashpoints, it is normal that one struggles to get money from a cashpoint, as one cashpoint is broken, one cashpoint has run out of money, one cashpoint is not in operation, etc. *'Sorry, the system is down'* is a common sentence said by an employee to a customer. At times, the system is actually down, but at other times, it is not down, and such a claim is just a lie that is used as an excuse for not doing the job.

336. Unproductivity: During the working day, many Saudis are distracted by social responsibilities such as driving their female family members. For many Saudis, there is almost always a reason (or excuse) why they do not do their job. This reason or excuse can be related to daily social responsibilities, such as dropping and picking up their female family members and handing so much bureaucracy. Many nationals (alongside their formal job) run their own business; a business that is given more value than their formal job and distracts them from doing their formal job. Some pretend that they are busy although they are not. Some do not do what they are supposed to do at work and use their family matters as an excuse. A manager is socially expected (and moreover supposed) to accept any excuse from their subordinates if these subordinates state that this excuse is 'family-related'. The phrase 'family circumstances' is widely used as an excuse by employees and is widely accepted by managers. Some employees do not elaborate on what these family circumstances are, whereas others mention such excuses as 'my wife is at the hospital', 'my aunt has just died' and 'I need to pick up my kids from school'. Many employees use their lunch break to pick up their children from school.

337. Lack of Preparation: Many queues (and services) are slow and long, because many families are large, have many children and therefore is difficult to serve. Many customers reach the end of queues (i.e. cashiers) without having thought (or at least without having decided) about what to order. Besides, some argue (loudly) with cashiers about a problem associated with the service.

338. Inefficiency: Completing many application forms is time-consuming, for various reasons. <u>First</u>, there is so much information that has to be provided more than once in one single application, with no clear justification of this repetition. <u>Second</u>, so much information is requested at the application, although this information is not needed or even not relevant to the purpose of the application. <u>Third</u>, the applicant needs to get one application signed by many people, even though only *one* signature is essential, and the rest of the signatures serve no reason except complication and bureaucracy. Chasing these people to get their signature on the application is exhausting, as these people are hardly at their office— even though they are supposed to be at their office all the time. <u>Fourth</u>, in CVs, it is normal that one writes one's religion, marital status, age and how many children one has. Likewise, in job applications, one may be asked for these pieces of information.

339. Absence of Employees: At a company, it is normal to see, say, five offices of customer services representatives, but most of these offices are empty of any representative.

340. Deficiency of Communication: Many employers employ many workers (e.g. cleaners) who do not speak Arabic. Because of the popularity of foreign workers, it is easy for one to live in the country without being able to speak Arabic. It is becoming more and more difficult for Saudis and Arabs to live in the country without being able to speak English, given that many foreign workers hardly speak Arabic. Normally, information on products and street signs is written in Arabic and English.

341. Inconsistency: Administrative inconsistency is a common problem. That is, today, there could be new policies and regulations, but tomorrow, there could be policies and regulations that are different from yesterday's policies and regulations. This is why, if current policies and regulations are offering certain benefits, one should quickly take advantage of them, as they can be soon changed to policies and regulations that prevent these benefits.

342. Lateness: First, everything is normally arranged at short notice. Second, being too late is normal. When someone or train is late, one may say the widely common belief: *'Perhaps, we are meant to be late because of good reasons beyond human awareness'*. Third, in many organisations, it is not good for one to be on time and to meet deadlines as this can be interpreted as if one is 'easy'. Fourth, at many times, others hate one for working hard and make one feel guilty for working hard. In short, others may not appreciate it if one works hard (and is not corrupted).

Interval

'*Would you marry an American man?*' This question was directed to 13 female citizens. Some would marry an American man, but only if he agreed to move to their country and only if they shared the same religion or he agreed to convert. Others, however, would not marry an American man, because of the language, cultural, social and ideological differences. For some, the American man 'are narcissists and self-centred, with almost ignoring others'. He 'lacks jealousy and must have already touched other women'. He 'is not from my religion, and therefore it is a sin to marry him'. He is 'confident with women and is used to the norm of freedom, and I can also expect him to cheat on me'. He 'checks out women'. He 'would not fill my eye'. One 'hates foreigners'. For another, 'the men of my nation gain priority'. Besides, 'the domination of a non-Arab is not acceptable'.

'*Would you marry an American woman?*' was a question asked to 27 male citizens. Some would not. For them, the American woman 'is very open'. She 'would not have the emotion I would require'. Others would, but under certain conditions. She must 'convert and at least commit to Saudi culture'. She has to 'assimilate the image of the Saudi woman'. She must 'be moral', 'be pretty' and 'be noble'. She has to 'become based in Saudi Arabia'. She must 'no longer have friendship with men and go to bad places (e.g. nightclubs)'. She has to wear a headwear or wear modestly. One 'would convince her of the religion, clothing and cultural behaviour'. Another would 'not force her' into such conditions. One would 'impose nothing on her'. Marrying an American would be 'good for practising English, teaching her the religion and getting the citizenship, not to mention that Americans are pretty'.

Mouth, Ears and Nose

Talking

343. There are certain cultural norms and practices regarding speaking, socialising, communicating and expressing oneself and one's feelings:

344. Male Chatting: <u>First</u>, Saudi men tend to be chatty (more than the average human being) and exceptionally social. Hence, some men talk to one another while the movie is on, making some foreigners angry and distracted from focusing on the movie. <u>Second</u>, men in a lecture hall tend to talk while the speaker is talking, making foreign speakers uncomfortable, unable to concentrate and think that the audience are not interested in their talk. <u>Third</u>, if a man sits next to another male stranger on the train or plane, they are more likely to start talking to one another for the whole journey and may exchange numbers by the end of the trip.

345. Cross-Gender Chatting: <u>First</u>, because of the norm of gender separation, some men (be they married or single) are not 'grown-up' in their dealings with women. They lack confidence when it comes to women. They are scared to be left alone with 'females' and avoid any kind of communication with them. They, just like 'teenagers', do not know how to deal with women. <u>Second</u>, because men are used to talking to only men, and likewise women are used to talking to only women, when it happens that a man talks to a woman, it is likely that he mistakenly addresses her as a man, for example, referring to her using male pronouns. Similarly, when it happens that a woman talks to a man, she may mistakenly address him as a woman using female pronouns.

346. Friendliness: First, in public life, a man, normally, greets any man he comes across, whether he knows him or not. Not greeting passers-by is seen by many individuals as being rude and stuck-up. For greeting, people say: '*peace be upon you*'. Second, commonly exchanged gifts are watches, pens and perfume.

347. Apologising: If one does to others something that seems impolite, and then s/he apologises, they may respond by putting the palm of their right hand on the left side of their chest (i.e. above their heart) so as to show that it is fine.

348. Discussing: First, when discussing matters, many individuals give others no chance to entirely express their thoughts. They see themselves as right, speak loudly and even yell. It is difficult to have a calm and objective discussion with them. They react sensitively and defensively and address others in an authoritarian way. Second, when asked if they like to take risks, people's spontaneous reaction would be '*Risk? Of course not*'. However, they, in reality, tend to take risks all the time, for example, driving recklessly and leaving their children unsupervised and unattended.

349. Whistling: Whistling is a controversial issue. Some men think that whistling is culturally inappropriate and religiously forbidden. Others think that, when one whistles, one undermines those around one. For them, if a man whistles, he sounds feminine, which is culturally inappropriate.

350. Deviating: When talking formally or casually, people have the tendency to constantly deviate from the main topic.

351. Teasing: In some towns and tribes, some avoid anything that makes others laugh at them. They are exceptionally sensitive about being laughed at. This is partly why humour-based events (e.g. stand-up comedies) are not part of the culture. In other towns and families, mocking and teasing one another in a very harsh and rude way has become a 'fashion' in Saudi society. Some make fun of almost everything (i.e. of tweets, newspaper articles); yet conveying no constructive criticisms. They mock just for the sake of laughing and having fun, with no genuine interest in initiating fundamental changes and reforms. Many individuals, aggressively, tease each other extensively, which discourages people from making anything outside the norm. That said, at times, one, aggressively, teases others to get oneself out of embarrassing situations.

352. Sitting: <u>First</u>, normally, in gatherings, Saudis do not like to stand, nor are they used to standing for a long time. This is why, in gatherings or events, Saudis tend to sit down. Many Saudis get tired quickly when standing, as their body is not used to it. The norm is that Saudis like to sit and chat, instead of standing and chatting. The sitting-down position is seen as superior to the standing position; hence, to show respect to others, one may ask them to have a seat. Older and respected people are seated. <u>Second</u>, in gatherings, guests sit in one single large square on sofas located against the four walls of a room. Every time a guest joins a gathering, s/he goes in a circular motion greeting people who stand up, shake hands, kiss cheeks or foreheads and say traditional and religious sentences. Although one shakes hands with everyone when *joining* gatherings, no hand-shaking is done when *leaving* gatherings.

353. Repeating: It is common that people say words and phrases more than once. For example, *'turn right, right, right'*, *'look, look'* and *'tomorrow, tomorrow'*.

354. Pronouncing: There are different accents based on the region. In one region, people speak slowly. So, as a joke, they are called '110 volts'——as if the 'power' coming to their mouth to speak is too weak (i.e. like 110 volts compared to 220 volts).

355. Responding: Responding by saying 'HA' to show that one has not heard what is said is considered to be rude.

356. Gaming: <u>First</u>, a known game is 'Telephone', in which one person whispers a message to the next person's ear through a line of people until the last player announces the message to the entire group, to see how much the original message has been changed. <u>Second</u>, playing cards, carrom boards, monopoly boards and computer games is common among friends and among family members. <u>Third</u>, any game that involves the use of dice is seen by some individuals as against the culture. <u>Fourth</u>, playing chess is forbidden and therefore not part of the culture.

357. Researching: It is difficult for researchers to make their participants achieve self-reporting, as participants normally provide vague indirect responses. For example, if one is asked if one is happy, one may say: *'God's will'*. If one is asked to share what one thinks the reason for poverty is, one may respond: *'God's will'*.

358. There are certain norms and practices regarding male swearing and anger:

359. Local Phrases: Many swear, using such phrases as: *'you, dog's son', 'you, dog's daughter', 'God damn you', 'God damn your mother', 'God damn your sister', 'Damn your parents', 'I will f*ck your parents' parents', 'you, sh*t'* and *'you, on my pen*s'*. Other swearing phrases are *'your mother's vag*na'* and *'your sister's vag*na'*. Swearing phrases tend to be used mainly by men. Besides, mothers' and sisters' vag*na is used here instead of fathers' and brothers' pen*s, because swearing related to female family members is more insulting than swearing related to male family members, given that women are associated with morality and family honour.

360. International Phrases: The English phrases *'f*ck you'* and *'son of a b*tch'* are well-known and used by some nationals.

361. Mocking: Some call black-skinned individuals 'slaves'——normally, as a joke or as a way of showing anger at them.

362. Loudness: The Saudi dialogue and accent (and some certain Arabic letters) make people sound as they are angry at each other when they chit-chat to one another. Some are loud when speaking. Given that the number of members per family is large, when they gather, many members speak loud so as to be heard by all gatherers and to dominate the conversation.

363. Threatening: Some men use their cord (which they wear on their headwear) as a 'sword' when getting into fights with others. Some refer to their cord when threatening others, saying something like this: *'I swear that I will hit you with the cord if you do not do that'*. So, the cord is used as a threatening tool. An additional threatening tool is a flip-flop. Some fathers hit their children with a flip-flop if they misbehave or do not listen to them.

364. Conditioning: Some individuals use the following phase ('*I swear I will divorce my wife if you do not do so*') to encourage others (who are not their wife) to do certain things. For example, a man may say to his guests: '*I swear I will divorce my wife if you* [i.e. his guests] *do not come over to my house for dinner tonight*'.

365. Stressing: People intensively use traditional and religious words and phrases for swearing and to stress certain matters. The name of God is, always, used to stress the accuracy of statements, or to affirm one's commitment to one's promise.

366. There are certain norms and practices regarding female swearing and anger:

367. Cursing: As a way of expressing anger at children, some women shout at them wishing them to be cursed. People around may tell mothers off for wishing their children to be cursed.

368. Annoyance: A female teenager may call a good friend of hers '*the sh*t*', '*O the sh*t*' or '*O animal*' if she gets slightly annoyed by this friend, or if she wants to tell off this friend.

369. Cuteness: If a female teenager wants to call a good friend of hers in a cute way or if she is slightly upset at this friend, she may call this friend '*the chubby*' or '*O the chubby*'——even though this friend is slim.

370. Controlling: Some husbands refer to their wife as '*The Minister of Internal Affairs*', showing a sense of authoritarianism and control exercised by their wife over them. A man would say to his male friends that *'I need to consult the minister of internal affairs'*, meaning his wife.

371. Harshness: Some employers believe that some veiled sales-women or female cashiers can appear rude because they fail to deliver to customers their emotions via the veil; when people smile at a veiled woman, they find it hard to know if she has smiled back. The owners of some supermarkets say that some male customers complain that, when these customers say Hi to female cashiers while checking out, these cashiers do not say Hi back and moreover think that these men are flirting with them. Some business-owners complain that being veiled encourages some women to be rude (or ruder) because these women know that no one really knows who they are. If a woman is veiled, this means that her identity is hidden, discouraging her from taking responsibility for her behaviour. When some women take off the veil, some of them suddenly feel they have to take responsibility for their facial expression, for being disciplined and for their behaviour, since their identity is now known, in the open and under the social radar. If a woman is veiled for all her life and suddenly is unveiled, she realises that people expect her to smile at them, for example.

372. Stop Talking: When one wants to tell others to stop talking or tell them off, one may say the phrase *'eat sh*t'*.

373. There are certain nicknames that are commonly used. Here are some of them:

374. Friendliness: <u>First</u>, in some areas, the phrase 'the father is the youth' is used as 'mate', 'pal' or 'dude'. <u>Second</u>, some use the term 'Father' with everyone, in the same way the term 'Sir' is used.

375. Intercourse: 'Sheep' is a term used by some young people. It is a nickname for anyone who promises people intercourse if s/he, for example, gets her/his phone topped-up. But, when the phone is topped-up, s/he breaks her/his promise.

376. Parents: Some call their mothers 'the female birth-giver' and fathers 'the male birth-giver', instead of calling them mum and dad.

377. Wives: In one's contact list, one, at times, name one's wife or one's mother using an expressive nickname, such as *'The Smile of My Life'*. One may, moreover, add a picture of a nice thing (e.g. a flower) as the profile picture of her contact——one, normally, does not put a real photo of her.

378. Nursing: Some call Asian nurses 'sisters' (literally, without any translation). The use of 'sister' is *not* done out of respect. Rather, this term is used only as a nickname when one wants to call these workers but does not know their names. There have been campaigns warning citizens not to call foreign workers 'sisters' if they are not Muslims.

379. Students: In some schools, every class has a 'general' (i.e. a student) assigned as a 'military-like figure' to ensure that his fellow students behave in the absence of the teacher.

380. Parents: One is to call one's parents *'mom and dad'*. In other words, one cannot call one's parents using their names. Calling one's parents with their names is culturally seen as showing no respect, no appreciation or acknowledgement for the effort and time that parents have put into raising one. It is seen by many as absolutely rude to call parents (and grandparents) using their real names.

381. Things: <u>First</u>, naming things is a social norm. At times, governmental services are named. The e-service for civil affairs is called '*Under Your Service*'. The radar service is called '*Watchful*'. <u>Second</u>, the names of things tend to be metaphorical (and not reflect the reality). For example, the word '*Riyadh*' (which is the name of the Capital) means '*gorgeous gardens*'. <u>Third</u>, many men call marshmallows '*girls' cheeks*', because of the soft texture.

382. Citing sayings in daily conversations is widely common. Examples of these sayings are offered below.

383. Judging: <u>First</u>, '*how one sees others is a reflection of how one is*'. So, if one sees others as bad, this is because s/he is bad. <u>Second</u>, '*if people have only one taste, only one product will dominate, and the rest of the products will not be sold*'. This saying promotes the belief that a diversity of opinions is the norm of humanity. <u>Third</u>, '*you appreciate me only if you try someone else*'.

384. Helping: '*I sought help from someone who, I realised, receives help from someone else*'. This is used when someone resorts to someone else who turns out to be helpless.

385. Hope: <u>First</u>, '*something bad may turn into something good*'. <u>Second</u>, '*patience is the key to relief*'. This means that it will pass whatever it is.

386. Seeking Alternatives: '*I have been advised to divorce her and marry her sister, but the two sisters are awful*'. This is used to show that the alternative is as bad as the original.

387. Abilities: <u>First</u>, '*the eye can see, but the hand cannot reach*'. This is used by those who would like to get something, but they do not have the means to get it. <u>Second</u>, '*stretch your legs as far as your blanket goes*', meaning that one should not do anything that lies outside one's league and capability. <u>Third</u>, '*if you can achieve this task, I will shave my moustache*'. This is used to stress how difficult the task is. This saying shows the social value attributed to the moustache. <u>Fourth</u>, '*a cat has nine lives*'. So, if one has survived many difficult situations, one may be described as a 'cat'. <u>Fifth</u>, '*treat your cow nicely, it gives you more milk*'. Likewise, if one treats one's body well, one's body will allow one to be more productive and effective.

388. Cruelty: <u>First</u>, a common saying that a woman may say to her husband: '*When you deal with me, you act like a lion, and when you deal with wars, you act like an ostrich*'. This means that some men are cruel in their domestic life and yet cowed in their public life. Second, a saying that is popular nowadays is: '*kind people died*', showing how kind the previous generations were and how unkind the members of the new generation are.

389. Talking: <u>First</u>, '*say something useful, or be silent*'. <u>Second</u>, '*silence gives consent*', meaning that if one asks for permission and yet does not respond, this means that permission is granted. <u>Third</u>, '*talk to people according to how much their mind weight*' is the same as '*address people in the language they can understand*'.

390. Projecting: '*One projects one's own faults or proclivities onto others*'.

391. Balancing: '*One person's loss is another person's gain*'. Another translation can be: '*the misfortunes of some people are advantages to others*'. A further translation could be: '*Good news for one person can be bad news for another*'.

392. Carelessness: <u>First</u>, '*he sh*t in the fuel tank*' is almost the equivalent of the English saying that '*he does not give a sh*t*'. <u>Second</u>, '*he has turned off the reverse lights*' refers to one who is reckless and does not think of the implications of one's actions.

393. Experience: <u>First</u>, '[one] *is not taken twice in the same snare*'. <u>Second</u>, people say '*one ate sand/air*' to show that one encountered a difficult situation.

394. Friendship: <u>First</u>, '*a friend in need is a friend indeed*'. <u>Second</u>, '*tell me whom your friends are, I tell you whom you are*'. <u>Third</u>, '*when your son is grown-up, become his friend*'. <u>Fourth</u>, one would said '*you have expanded my chest*' to someone who has done something that has brought happiness to one. <u>Fifth</u>, '*the absent has his reason to be absent*'. This saying is used when one did not show up, as a way of being nice to others.

395. Family: One saying is that '*every daughter is proud of her father*'.

396. Misbehaviour: <u>First</u>, '*if you have no shame, then do (or say) as you wish*'. <u>Second</u>, '*when the cat is away, the mice play*'. <u>Third</u>, '*everyone claims association with Lily* [an attractive historical character], *but Lily does not acknowledge that*'. This is said when one lies about one's association with something good. <u>Fourth</u>, '*to add water to the mud*' has a meaning similar to '*add fuel to the fire*'.

397. Habits: '*The same you are raised up, the same you will be when you are old*'. This is similar to '*always has been, always will be*'.

398. Improving: When one wants to improve something, others may discourage one by saying: '*Don't move anything still*'.

399. International Relations: <u>First</u>, '*O foreigner, be respective* [of the host culture]'. <u>Second</u>, '*if one socialises with a foreign community for 40 days, one becomes one of them*'.

400. Options: Some have changed the saying '*all roads lead to Rome*' to '*all roads lead to Makkah*'.

401. Success: '*Waking up all night is a precondition for being successful*', which is inconsistent with the concept of 'early bird'.

402. Law: <u>First</u>, '*what is forbidden is desirable*'. <u>Second</u>, '*it is the end that counts*'. <u>Third</u>, '*the end justifies the means*'. Some, however, question this saying, believing that the end does not justify the means. <u>Fourth</u>, '*every son of Adam is to make mistakes*'.

403. Money: '*one should not serve stingy people*'. This means that one should not serve others if no profit is expected in return.

404. Management: <u>First</u>, '*one should strike while the iron is hot*'; a saying that encourages one to take advantage of opportunities. <u>Second</u>, managers normally assign any task to a committee, even though there is a saying that, '*if you want to kill a task, assign it to a committee*'. <u>Third</u>, '*giving or doing little but continuously is better than doing or doing a lot but non-continuously*'.

405. Request: When one asks another to do something but this other person apologises for being unable to do it due to his/her busy schedule, one would say '*don't occupy the occupied*', meaning that one totally understands and that apology is accepted.

406. Revenge: '*On me and on my enemy*'. One says this to show that one does not mind losing as long as one's enemies lose too. One does not mind doing something that will result in a lose-lose situation for both one and one's enemy.

407. Efficiency: *'Where's your ear, Joha?'* This proverb is said to be a person who wants to take a long way, even though there is an easier way to reach the same goal. S/he is like Joha who asked to point at his left ear, and he used his *right* hand to point at his *left* ear, even though it would have been easier if he used his left hand to refer to his left ear.

408. Taking Advantage: <u>First</u>, *'one shall make use of one's free time before one is busy. One shall make use of one's health before one is ill. One shall make use of one's youth before one is old'*. <u>Second</u>, people say *'this thing is good for life and afterlife'* when they do something that is useful for themselves and for others (e.g. their employers). To illustrate the point, if there is a conference in Paris, to which one is sent by one's employer, one may say that this conference is good for life (for fun, i.e. tourism) and afterlife (for work, i.e. conferencing).

409. Ignorance: *'I always win when I argue with a scholar; yet, I always lose when I argue with an ignorant person'*.

410. Certainty: It is normal that one says: *'I am 1,000,000% certain that this is the case'*, so as to show confidence and certainty.

411. Complementing: *'You have exhausted the one who comes after you'*. This saying is said as a complement to a manager who has done well. That is, it means that this manager has set the standard so high, to the extent that the manager that comes after him/her will find it difficult to match this previously set standard.

412. Spoiling: *'Don't burn the movie on me'* means *'don't reveal a critical part of the plot and spoil my enjoyment of the movie'*.

413. Socialising in a 'farm' is part of the culture. The word 'farm' is used mostly to refer to a land surrounded by long, concrete walls, with trees (e.g. palm trees), fake or real grass and a swimming pool. There are normally no animals. Here are some issues related to farms:

414. Family Gathering: Some families (whether immediate, extended or moreover *'very* extended' families) gather together in a farm that they rent (or own). When gathering in a rented place, each adult family member may contribute to the renting cost, dining and any other expenses. Farms are normally rented for a half day, for example, between 6:00 pm and 6:00 am. In gatherings, people speak at the same time.

415. There are certain social practices and issues related to technologies and devices:

416. Censorship: Public access to the Internet was delayed until almost the start of the 21st century, by which time an elaborate national system had been established to filter out any inappropriate and unwanted content. The delay of public access to the Internet reflected concern about the influence of the Internet on the national culture, through destabilising its internal homogeneity and causing 'cultural pollution'. Not only erotic pictures, videos and games but also erotic texts can be blocked. This blocking system moreover filters out not only digital contents (e.g. websites) but moreover physical content (e.g. books). Despite this filtering, 'sexting' (i.e. sending, receiving or forwarding erotic texts, images and videos, primarily among mobile phones) is common among many of all different ages. Besides, some use TV receiver cards, phone applications, browsers and services (e.g. VPNs, Hotspot, UC and Puffin) to get around this blocking.

417. Adult Materials: Some men have on their smartphones pictures of their lovers and 'adult materials'. To hide these pictures and materials from their wives and their parents, some men have an app that its icon looks *exactly* like the icon of the normal calculator. In this app, these pictures and materials are stored. If one presses this app, a calculator will be shown, and one has to run a certain 'calculation' (e.g. 165+34)——this 'calculation' is the password for accessing the storage (i.e. their lovers' pictures and the adult materials).

418. Plate Letters: Plates consist of three letters. Those plates that display the work 's*x', 'a*s', 'bad' or 'bar' is filtered out.

419. Privacy: Some are very careful when it comes to female privacy, to the extent that some men cover their phone-screen with special film that enables only the one facing the phone-screen to see what is on the screen, therefore preventing those sitting on one's right and left sides from seeing what is on the screen (which can be pictures of mothers, sisters and wives and/or 'adult materials').

420. Picking up Phones: When picking up the phone, nationals say 'hello' in the same way French people say it. That is, they sound French when saying 'hello'.

421. Attention: In their communication with their lovers via. WhatsApp, some women send just a dot and then delete it immediately just to draw the attention of their lovers. Lovers will then see the following message: *'This message was deleted'*.

422. Landlines: Some shops stopped putting a landline as their shop number. Instead, they put their mobile phone. This is why shops can be reachable even outside working hours. Having a landline is disappointing, replaced with mobile phones.

423. Traffic Lights: The traffic light is the spot where drivers catch up with their phone. This is why when the traffic light becomes green, no car, at times, moves since all drivers are distracted with their phone. Hence, horning is normally used to tell other drivers that the traffic light is green and that all are ready to go. If one horns, this is actually appreciated by other drivers, who see this horning as doing them a favour, so they can focus on their phone without having to constantly check the traffic light.

424. Horn: People normally do not use their horn (even when it is needed). They, however, use it (extensively) _only_ to notify other drivers that the traffic light has become green. Most drivers (when stopping at the traffic light) do not pay attention to when it turns green, because they get busy with their phone or their children.

425. Some care about how they smell because many forms of Saudi greeting require close contact. Here are some of these forms.

426. Chest-to-Chest: Hugging each other is a traditional norm and value, whether among men or women.

427. Nose-to-Nose: A common greeting among men is similar to the 'Eskimo kiss', where the noses touch.

428. Cheek-to-Cheek: In gatherings, one way of same-gender greeting is cheek-to-cheek touch, where one's cheek touches another's cheek. Some people get very excited when greeting others, to the extent that they greet others by making their cheek not *touch* but rather *hit hard* others' cheek, which hurts.

429. Lip-to-Forehead: To show respect, some kiss their parents, older siblings, aunts, uncles and the elderly on the forehead and/or on the back of their hand. Yet, this means leaving a lip mark on the forehead if women are wearing a lipstick. To prevent this from happening, some women (just before kissing the forehead) place a tissue on the forehead, kiss the forehead *through* the tissue and then remove the tissue.

430. There are certain practices and norms regarding the Saudi Bedouin lifestyle:

431. Bedouin Types: There are three types of nationals. First are Bedouins, who live in the desert or among mountains. Second are civil Saudis, who live in cities. Third are civilised Bedouins, who have moved to and settled in cities. Civil Saudis call themselves (and are called by Bedouins) 'the civil'. Civilised Bedouins call themselves (and are called by civil Saudis) 'the civilised'.

432. Bedouin Heritage: Although civilised Bedouins have moved to cities, some of them still set up a tent in the desert or among mountains and have camels and sheep around the tent. They, however, do not live in the tent, nor do they themselves take care of the animals. Instead, these Bedouins employ a foreigner (e.g. an Asian or African) to take care of almost everything, and these owners come to the tent from time to time just for fun.

433. Bedouin Influence: Many civil Saudis have got influenced by some aspects of the Bedouin lifestyle, thus going into the desert for drifting and spending a few hours or days in the desert (with or without a tent) where they make a fire, barbecue and hunt animals. There are areas in the desert where there are already-set tents (that can fit up to 20 people). These tents are for rental and cost around US$80 per day. Some tents are surrounded by long fences as they are for female family members, given that the perceived privacy of women. Many of these areas are dirty, since many guests throw rubbish everywhere——yet, neither the owner nor the guests clear and collect their rubbish. These tents are rented not only by civilised Bedouins but moreover by civil people, showing another way of how the Bedouin lifestyle has influenced civil people.

434. Bedouin Hair: If a man has long hair, this could suggest that he is a Bedouin.

435. Bedouin Cars: Bedouins are known for having (normally brown) pick-up Toyota Land Cruiser 4*4 cars.

436. Bedouin Skills: There are certain Bedouin figures who are believed to have the skill for understanding the meanings and implications of a footprint in the sand, be it the footprint of a human or an animal (e.g. a camel or a horse). These figures claim that they can distinguish between the footprint of men and women, virgin and non-virgin women, pregnant and non-pregnant women, old and young people, blind and non-blind people and one-eyed and two-eyed people. These figures are said to have the ability to distinguish the footprint of their close and distant family members, friends and, moreover, enemies.

437. Bedouin Tribes: Bedouins (whether civilised or non-civilised) belong to certain tribes. Each tribe has a certain name——all the members of a tribe use the tribe name as their surname. These members can be spread throughout the country. They gather in one place only if there is a major issue to discuss. Main tribes in the country are Al-Otaibi (around 50,000 members), Al-Anzi (approximately 45,000 members), Al-Ghamdi (roughly 45,000 members), Al-Qahtani (nearly 45,000 members), Al-Zahrani (40,000 members), Al-Mutairi (35,000 members), Al-Shammari (35,000 members), Al-Shahri (30,000 members), Al-Dosari (25,000 members), Al-Harbi (25,000 members), Al Shahrani (20,000 members), Al-Subaii (15,000 members), Al-Qarni (15,000 members), Al-Harthy (15,000 members), Al-Jahani (10,000 members) and Al-Maleki (10,000 members).

438. Bedouin Hierarchy: Each tribe has a certain hierarchical structure, with there being a general leader. There are sub-tribes (namely, 'thighs'), each of which has a sub-leader. Leaders and sub-leaders have certain tasks, such as ensuring the harmony, unity and stability among members, looking after members, making sure that members are fine, intervening to handle any conflict among members, seeking to improve and develop the tribe and managing the tribe's fund. If the leader or sub-leader dies, the succession passes either to a close relative or to someone that is known for bravery, religion, generosity, honesty, wisdom, experience, awareness, crisis management and the like. Being a tribal is seen by some as a sign of being generous and having deep roots. Some non-tribal families have tried to associate themselves with certain major tribes, so as to enjoy the tribal benefit of having deep roots, for example.

439. There are certain cultural values and practices regarding naming and calling things and people:

440. Male Names: Some are conservative when it comes to the first names that they give to their male babies. That is, they use old and conventional names. It is very common to find many male students in one class having the same first and/or second names. Male names that are mostly common include Abdullah, Muhammed, Ahmad, Abdulrahman, Abdulaziz, Ibrahim, Ali, Hassan, Omar, Saleh, Saad and Khaled. A common male name structure consists of two parts. The first part is 'Abdul', which means a 'servant of'. The second part is one of God's 99 names, such as Rahman. So, Abdul + Rahman = Abdulrahman (i.e. a servant of Rahman who is God).

441. Female Names: Some are relatively liberal with the first names that they give to their female babies, using new and unconventional names. Female names that are most common include Fatemah, Maryam, Nura, Layla, Ayasha and Sarah.

442. First Names: There is a 'cute', causal form of any first name. Saudi adults normally do not like it when they are called using the cute form of their first names, since cute forms of first names undermine them and are used with children.

443. Fathers' Names: When individuals write their names in applications, presentations and the like, some of them intentionally include their father's name so as to show appreciation and to show that they are proud of their father.

444. Children's Names: Many individuals give to their firstly born child the same name as their parents. This is done as a way of showing respect to one's parents. Parents are known for loving most of their grandchild who has the same name as theirs. It is common that a father has five sons, each of whom gives to his firstly born son the same name as his father. Then, the father has five grandchildren who have the same name as himself. It is reportedly confusing to have six family members having the same name.

445. Last Names: Normally, 'Al' (which is an article meaning 'the') is added to nouns. For example, 'communication' is said and written 'the communication'. Many last names start with 'Al'. 'Al Lily' means 'The Night', with 'Al' meaning 'The', and 'Lily' meaning 'Night'. It is common that last (and first) names have meanings. Examples are 'Al Sadah' (i.e. the elite), 'Al Laab' (i.e. the player), 'Al Faraj' (i.e. the relief), 'Al Jomaah' (i.e. the Friday) and 'Al Mandeel' (i.e. the tissue). Further examples of last names are 'Al Salem' (i.e. the safe), 'Al Aseel' (i.e. the original), 'Al Khareeb' (i.e. the stranger), 'Al Saqer' (i.e. the falcon), 'Al Saleh' (i.e. the Godly) and 'Al Shams' (i.e. the sun).

446. Maiden Names: Nationals do not (nor are they allowed to) take their spouse's last name. That said, foreigners can take their Saudi spouse's last name. If westerners get married to a Saudi, take his/her name and apply for a job in the west, western employers may treat the application as an application of a non-westerner. Likewise, if this foreigner applies for a job in Saudi Arabia, employers may think of the application as an application of an Arab.

447. Full Names: When writing their full name, many individuals sometimes add the word 'bin' between their name and their father's name. For example, 'Abdul Essa Al Lily' will be written like this 'Abdul *bin* Essa Al Lily'. The term 'bin' means 'is a son of'. So, 'Abdul *bin* Essa Al Lily' translates into 'Abdul *is a son of* Essa Al Lily'.

448. There are certain norms and practices related to ID cards:

449. Family ID: A 'Family ID' is issued for a married man, on which it is written the name of his wives and children. Family IDs are slightly bigger than business cards. Family IDs are issued for men only. When booking a hotel room for a couple, a Saudi is asked to show his Family ID. Likewise, in checkpoints on streets, roads and highways, a man may be asked by policemen for his Family ID when policemen are suspicious of the relationship between the driver and the female passenger. Men are supposed to carry their Family ID all the time for verification. That said, since women cover their face, married men may use their Family ID to claim that their 'lover' is their wife, since hotel receptionists or policemen do not (dare) check the female face. This means that it is easier for married men to go out with their lover, since she is covered and moreover since Family ID does not show a photo of one's wife.

450. National ID Cards: First, if a photocopy of ID cards is required, some women cover their photo with tape when providing a photocopy. Second, when one's national ID card expires, all one's bank accounts will be frozen until one renews it.

451. Residency Cards (a.k.a. Iqama): First, once one lands in the country, one's photo will be taken and used for one's residency card and for everything. Some expats complain that they look terrible in this photo as it is taken after a long flight and yet used for everything for the rest of their stay in the country. Second, when one's residency ID card expires, all one's bank accounts will be frozen until one renews it.

452. Names on Cards: On the street, if one shouts Abdullah and Muhammed, many people will think that their name has been called. Because of this similarity of names, it is stated in the national ID one's first, second, third and last name. In the passport, however, it is stated one's first and second names, the initial of one's third name and the last name. It is normal to see, in a class, two students with the same first, second and family names.

453. National Passports: <u>First</u>, it is compulsory that male citizens wear the traditional cloak (and the headwear) in official photos, such as passport photos. <u>Second</u>, one is supported to go through passports from right to left. Passport pages are numbered from right to left. One's photo and passport information are located on the first page from the right, making the officers of foreign customs confused. <u>Third</u>, many tend to incorrectly spell their names in English. They may spell their name differently from how it is spelled in their passports. They may not know their birthday in English, since they have their own calendar.

454. International Passport: <u>First</u>, discrimination based on nationality is common to the extent that Arabs with American passports, for example, can be treated differently from those without. At times, any Arab member of Saudi universities who holds the American passport is given certain privileges, including better treatments and higher salaries. In some jobs (for example, academic jobs), merely being American can make one eligible for an increase in one's salary. <u>Second</u>, at some universities, non-Saudis, unlike Saudis, must give away their passports to their employers on arrival, preventing them from running away or travelling without permission.

455. Many do not like to be 'direct'. Here are some examples.

456. When Referring to a Restroom: Instead of saying '*I will go to pee*', one would say '*I will go to throw away the drink*'.

457. When Initiating a Conversation: one habit is the custom of beginning oral or written communication with another person with the phrase *'I hope that you are well'*. Starting an email without such a sentence is direct and, therefore, can be seen as impolite or even disrespectful.

458. When Calling Others: Many do not like it when they are called using their first names. In other words, using first names is direct and, therefore, impolite. Hence, people call each other indirectly by using the form *'Abu + Name of Oldest Son'*. *'Abu'* means *'The Father of'*. So, 'Abu Essa' means *'The father of Essa'*. If one has no child, one will be called *'Abu + Name of Father'*, assuming that one will eventually name his oldest son after his father. Rarely, the name of the oldest daughter is used *only* if the daughter is the oldest child and therefore older than the oldest son. It is normal that, when meeting others for the first time, one will be asked about the name of the oldest child, and consequently others will start calling one accordingly *'Abu + Name of Oldest Son'*. Women are called by their first names until they get their first child, and then they will be called according to this child. That is, they will be called using the format *'Aum + Name of Oldest Child'*. *'Aum'* means *'the mother of'*. So, children are used as a tool to define parents. The value of people is seen in their ability to 'produce' children.

459. When Informing Patients: Some doctors do not tell the patient the result of diagnosis and, rather, outsource this task to his/her families, who then tell him/her the result. This is the case especially when the problem is severe.

460. The Saudi dialect uses metaphors extensively. It incorporates phrases and expressions, many of which may not make sense even to Saudis themselves.

These expressions can sound emotional and/or metaphorical. Below are some examples.

461. When Thanking Others: If one has entertained others, they would thank one by saying, metaphorically, '*thank you for expanding our chest*'.

462. When Greeting Others: Instead of saying '*good morning*', some men say to each other '*flowery morning*', despite the fact that their region lacks (naturally and wildly grown) flowers.

463. When Referring to Individuals: <u>First</u>, if an employee has nothing to do, one would comment: '*This employee is counting flies*'. <u>Second</u>, some would say '*You are empty*' to someone wanting to do unimportant things while important things need to be done. <u>Third</u>, some would say '*You do not have a story*' or '*Just stand up, just stand up*' to someone talking nonsense. <u>Fourth</u>, one would say '*It has come over you and over your face*' to someone who is complimenting himself or herself for something that s/he does not deserve.

464. When Expressing Frustration: Some write (as their status or in their profile picture) an extremely emotional and metaphorical sentence that shows a sense of love or emotional frustration——e.g. '*I wish there were some drugs I could take that would make me forget about you*'. The pronoun 'you' here can refer to a 'cruel lover' or a 'recently dead friend'. Non-Saudis may take such a sentence at a face value and see this person as 'creepy' or a 'freak'.

465. When Undermining Others: <u>First</u>, to undermine the strength that someone is claiming, people would say '*Find your friends*' or '*You do not have what my grandmother has*'.

<u>Second</u>, some would say '*Your mother has no invitation/cause*' to someone who has done something inappropriate.

466. When Showing Sympathy: <u>First</u>, some would say '*You broke my mind/mood*' to tell someone that s/he has made them sympathetic towards what s/he is saying. <u>Second</u>, to show sympathy to a sick person, some say: '*in me, not in you*', meaning that I wish I was the one who was sick, not you. <u>Third</u>, when Saudis refer to one as '*having a thin heart*', they mean that one easily cries and is emotional when one is exposed to an emotional happening. This is normally said as a compliment, not a criticism.

467. When Showing Dissatisfaction: <u>First</u>, some would say '*I took a situation/attitude from you*' to tell someone that they are being disappointed at what they are doing. <u>Second</u>, some say '*Oh man, walk your condition*' to advise one not to be picky or advise one to let things go.

468. When Making Predictions: If one predicts that something bad may happen to one's friend, the friend would say '*I wish for God's prediction, not for your prediction*', believing that God's prediction is always positive, and therefore the thing that may happen to the friend will not be bad.

469. When Stressing Embarrassment: <u>First</u>, some say '*just pick up your face*' to someone who is getting embarrassed. <u>Second</u>, some say '*turn your face*' to ask someone annoying to go away.

470. It is difficult to deal with many citizens since they manoeuvre so much, and their manoeuvrability is active. They have unique ways of covering up their dishonesty and insincerity. Below are some examples.

471. Dishonest Employers: Some employers are not honest enough. Here are some examples to illustrate the point. <u>Example 1</u>, some employees do not like that some employers are not committed to timely payments. <u>Example 2</u>, some companies over-exaggerate and lie to shine their public image, making it look over the top, even if this image is totally different from reality. Some employers may employ a westerner *not* because of his/her expertise but rather to show off that their company is associated with the west. Some western employees complain that they end up having no tasks at work, given that the aim of employing them is merely to make the public image of the company look prettier. Some employers do not want their western employees to develop the company and therefore to destabilise their company and the wider social culture. Moreover, some westerners are not qualified or specialised and yet are employed anyway because they make Saudi companies look good. <u>Example 3</u>, employment can be biased towards certain families or tribes. Certain families can occupy most managerial and administrative positions. 'Vitamin W' or 'Mediation' are phrases that some use to refer to the practice that one exploits personal contacts (for example, relatives, colleagues or friends) to help one go 'above' regulations, to speed up formal procedures or to gain advantages. This practice is widely common. It is, at times, a must, as one's matter cannot be handled unless one resorts to 'Vitamin W'.

472. Dishonest Employees: Many employees are not honest enough. They, constantly, make excuses why they need to take breaks during working hours——not to mention that they even sleep during work time. They postpone what they should or even are supposed to do. A postponing phrase that people commonly say when being asked to do a particular thing: *'tomorrow, tomorrow'* (that is, repeating twice the word 'tomorrow'), thereby removing out of their immediate awareness what they are supposed to do. It is normal that nationals promise to do something quickly but without any intention of quickening themselves. Many nationals make promises beyond their ability and beyond what they can do. They are people of words, not actions. They are good at making promises and convincing others that they would surely honour their promises, and yet they eventually do not honour their promises. Some employers believe that some male Saudi employees are unable to meet deadlines and honour promises. Some nationals add the phrase *'God willing'* or *'if God wills'* after any sentence where they promise someone to do something, whether in the near or distant future. For example, *'I promise to send you the email tomorrow; if God wills'*. Some nationals misuse the phrase *'if God wills'*, to the extent that its practical meaning has become *'forget about it'*. Put simply, if some nationals condition their statement with *'if God wills'*, this is not promising, as this means that they will more likely not do it.

473. Dishonest Female Employees: For some, many female employees are dishonest. Women are, as pointed out by some business-owners, culturally believed to naturally have a great ability in craftiness. Some Saudi female citizens are taught that 'females' are the best in terms of craftiness. Hence, some of them have tried to apply this craftiness to go around rules in workplaces, schools and universities. Some Saudi women are manipulative, using the 'cry-on-demand' strategy to get what they want; they cry at work (or home) to seek sympathy from their managers (or parents).

474. Dishonest Professors: Some professors show dishonest practices. Here are some examples. Example 1, some professors are sympathetic towards those students who are the children of their colleagues, department heads or deans. Example 2, some individuals call themselves doctors even though they do not hold a PhD. Example 3, there have been PhD holders with fake doctorates, to the extent that there has emerged a Saudi Twitter trend intended to expose the names of fake PhD holders. Example 4, some professors write a book and make it a compulsory textbook for their students, therefore forcing students into buying their own book and therefore benefiting themselves financially. Example 4, some professors fake research findings and make references to non-existent or irrelevant publications. Example 5, when doing survey-based research, some researchers complete all the survey sheets themselves and claim that these survey sheets have been completed by real participants. Example 6, some universities get their academics a licence for plagiarism software, making one wonder why an academic needs to check if s/he has plagiarised. This suggests that plagiarism is a normal practice and that a non-confident academic needs such software to check if s/he can possibly get caught.

475. Dishonest Students: Some students are into well-crafted trickery. Here are some examples to support this claim. Example 1, when students are questioned about missing a class, they claim that they could not attend class because a close relative of theirs just died. This is a common excuse, and if such an excuse is always true, the Saudi population is expected to be extinct within a decade. Example 2, a common excuse among female students for missing classes and exams is that '*my driver had a car accident*'. Many students miss the class because they take a relative to the airport. Example 3, many individuals (be they students or professionals) fake a sick certificate to excuse their nonattendance at school or work. Some doctors issue fake sick certificates when requested by students or professionals. Hence, some universities accept sick certificates only from certain trustworthy hospitals. Example 4, many students 'act' more religious during exams, for example, by growing their beard and sending religious texts via social networks. They do that in the hope that they will be blessed and helped in return and therefore perform better in exams. Example 5, some female students are manipulative, using the 'cry-on-demand' strategy to get what they want. They cry at school to seek sympathy from their teachers. Example 6, some female students take exams in full traditional outfit, not because they are committed to the culture but because having so much material around them helps them cheat in exams and hide information within these materials. Example 7, in overseas classes containing many national students, some female teachers reportedly cover up more than usual (via longer skirts, higher necklines and no sleeveless blouses), because some such students do an eye-scan of their female teachers' bodies yet behind sunglasses. Example 8, many postgraduates ask shops or individuals to do their dissertations or theses *for* them – whether in part or whole.

476. Pregnant Women: After 40 days of pregnancy, women are believed to start to dramatically hate or love certain things (for example, ice-cream) and even certain people (for example, her brother). They begin to respond differently to certain smells (for example, the smell of her husband), and her ability to smell increases noticeably. If a female student during her pregnancy starts hating the smell of perfume, she may not attend classes since many women (that is, her peers) wear strong perfume, using this as an excuse for missing classes. It is believed that, if a woman loves something (for example, strawberry) during her pregnancy but this is not made available for her, the shape of this thing will appear on the skin of her baby as a 'tattoo'.

477. Personal Fabrication: First, even if the achievement of their children is so little, many parents hold big celebrations. This is not necessarily because they want to motivate and support their children. Rather, this is done because they want to show off and show the public false qualities of their children. Second, some citizens' act is derived not from whether this act would fulfil a certain level of quality and efficiency or address certain requirements. Rather, it is based on whether one would be embarrassed when others hear about this act. Others' response to one's behaviour is crucial and determines the ways in which one acts socially and the kind of offers one accepts or declines. The first criterion according to which individuals' behaviour is judged is whether this behaviour is religiously allowed. Because of the strong social pressure over individuals to do what is socially seen as 'the right thing to do', such acts of laying, fabricating and making one's behaviour fit within social norms are common among many. Many do not hesitate to lie to get what they want or to prevent social criticism or embarrassment.

478. Organisational Fabrication: First, a university put so much effort and time into publicising itself to the public as '*Leader of Excellence in Research*', although it is a teaching-oriented university and does not, in reality, care about research. Second, a university may put so much effort and time into publicising itself to the public as a '*Leader of Excellence in Teaching*', although it has no basic pedagogical equipment for their classrooms and labs, and moreover, its course contents are outdated. Third, 'quality assurance' at many universities is a matter of so much paperwork, administration, bureaucracy and fabrication.

479. Inaccurate Public Image: First, when an important person visits a university to give a talk, faculty members and students are sometimes forced into attending so as that the public image of the university looks good. Second, the presentation of self is important to many citizens. Maintaining one's social image is essential, even if this image is not genuine. Many citizens show a false representation of themselves in public life. When organising events, many care about 'the periphery' (i.e. presentation such as decoration), yet they pay limited attention to the content (i.e. 'the essence'). When there is a large-scale event, there is a lack of crowd-management and crowd-control. Organisers of such an event are more likely to show a lack of the skills necessary to manage crowds. Besides, there are limited safety procedures and considerations (e.g. fire exists and capacities).

480. Corruption: Many schemes have been initiated to fight corruption, to the extent that banners have been placed in agents, departments and roads, which stress how corruption can delay the progress and development of Saudi society. Yet, one cannot be expected to be honest if one's own father and family push one so much to be corrupted and irresponsible. Below are examples to support this claim. First, if sons or daughters are in a position of power and do not use this power to help their father to get advantages, he may show considerable dissatisfaction and disappointment in them, instead of being proud of them for being not corrupted. At times, one is encouraged by one's father (and one's family in general) to be corrupted. At times, corruption is seen as a 'value', perceiving the 'misuse' of power to help one's father *not* as a corrupted action but rather as a good, noble action to help one's family. Second, anyone having a job in the public sector cannot open a private business. To circumvent this rule, some men open their own business under the name of their unemployed wife or mother. Despite this, these men advise their children to be moral and ethical. Some employers do not like that some employees are distracted by dual, two jobs——a job in the private sector and another job in the public sector. Third, driving irresponsibly is the norm. Irresponsible drivers are of different ages; not only teenagers. Many fathers drive irresponsibly even in the presence of their children. So, these children cannot be expected to end up being raised by their father to be responsible drivers and moreover responsible citizens if these fathers themselves are not responsible. <u>Fourth</u>, when the school day is over, the way in which students get out of the school gate is messy. Students squeeze themselves and fight to get out of the gate. Besides, the way in which drivers (e.g. parents who pick up their children from school) park outside school is messy as well. They double-park and even triple-park. They park in the middle of the street. They park sidewise. They park on sidewalks. To handle this messiness, a traffic guard is employed to handle traffic, but normally this person fails to handle traffic because this messiness can hardly be subject to organisation. In this case, no one can expect students to end up being organised individuals if their school and parents are not and do not show them otherwise. <u>Fifth</u>, some want to work with neither those who are *too* corrupted nor with those who are not corrupted *at all*. Rather, they want to work with those who are medium corrupted (i.e. a little bit corrupted) and, therefore, cannot be easily noticed and therefore caught.

481. Acceptable Lying: There are situations in which the culture allows one to 'lie' (to be precise, to narrate words in a twisted form). <u>First</u> is to trick enemies during battles. <u>Second</u> is to bring reconciliation among people (e.g. couples).

482. 'Good' People: Some users of WhatsApp, Facebook, Twitter, Instagram and other social networks use, as their profile photos, pictures displaying texts reminding others of traditional norms and values. That said, these users' act of displaying traditional texts may not be genuine, in the sense that this act is seen by some of them as a way of helping them gain the trust of the other gender during the course of flirtation. That is, people supporting traditional values are trusted and seen as 'good people'. Bad boys' and bad girls' act of displaying traditional texts help them trick their parents and friends to believe that they are good people who are into traditional values and therefore do not flirt with the other gender.

483. Current Lovers: When a man wants to talk about his lover to his friends but is worried that someone may overhear him, he talks about her as a man, using the pronouns 'he, him and his' instead of 'she or her'.

484. Previous Lovers: <u>First</u>, when some men decide to get married, the first thing they do is to change their email addresses, phone numbers and Facebook accounts. This is done to escape from their previous 'immoral' relationships. <u>Second</u>, normally, a man does not marry the woman he secretly talks with. This is because he thinks of her as a 'bad girl' who breaks the law. Since she has broken the law by talking with him, she is more likely to break the marriage law by cheating on her husband. It is said: '*the Saudi does not marry the one whom he loves. He marries the one whom he does not love*'. Some men promise their dates and lovers marriage and moreover claim to be single. Yet, once these men satisfy themselves, they just leave, leaving these women in pain. They are into the philosophy of '*love 'em and leave 'em*'. They are good at promising women whatever these women want to hear without any intention of eventually honouring their promises. Many non-Saudi women fall 'victim' to such a game of some Saudi men. Some Saudi men abroad believe that they could have any woman they want off the street with a little bit of Arab charisma, generosity and/or romance. Many foreign women get swept up in the "gentleman" act. Instead of thinking that '*he is really charming*', some think that '*he must really love me very much to do/say all of this*'. When being abroad, some Saudi men claim that they are single, even though they are engaged or even married back home.

485. Misbehaviour: <u>First</u>, to avoid traffic, some (especially taxi drivers) go through neighbourhoods. <u>Second</u>, there is a saying that, '*if you do not act like a wolf, you will be eaten by wolves*'. That is, if one does not act as bad, one will be the target for bad people. <u>Third</u>, there is a saying that '*an adulteress would like all other women to experience the hell she endures*'. This means that, if one is experiencing a bad thing, one wants everyone to be experiencing the same too. <u>Fourth</u>, it is believed that, '*if one knows that he will not be caught or punished, one will misbehave*'. <u>Fifth</u>, in some neighbourhoods, some men kill time by making fun of (and/or orally or physically harassing) their disabled neighbours. <u>Sixth</u>, when there are more than one queue, a family may ask its members to stand in all the queues, and whoever member first reaches the cashier, the rest of the members will join the queue of this member.

486. Fake Companies: If one holds an important position at a university, one does not steal money directly. Rather, one forms a fake company and uses the power of his position to sign a contract with this company at a high price. One may ask different companies to make offers to his university, and then one makes one's company win.

487. Saudi Arabia is a collective society. This has various implications:

488. Social Responsibilities: Many individuals are preoccupied with their cultural, social and family responsibilities and expectations (e.g. the social obligation to attend any invitation to a wedding or gathering that one receives). Being preoccupied with cultural, social and family responsibilities has kept many individuals away from personal and professional development and from contributing to the progress of society. Continuing professional and personal development is not an integral part of the culture.

489. Siblinghood-in-Ideology: Because Saudi Arabia tends to be a 'parental' and collective society, many citizens feel in charge of each other, advising, influencing and directing one another's not only public but moreover private lives, beliefs, emotions and actions. Many feel a sense of what they call 'siblinghood-in-ideology', acting responsibly towards their 'siblings-in-ideology'. The parental nature of the culture has influenced what individuals exchange via social networks, seeking to 'parent' their fellow citizens in such networks. Social networks are areas where a citizen normally directs other citizens, attempting to spread social and cultural beliefs and values with the political aim of influencing others and pushing them towards the culture. Many national users of social networks send extensive messages and entries that either warn fellow citizens against certain culturally inappropriate practices or remind them of social norms. The interest of some in controlling their fellow citizens is a reason why social networks are popular in the Saudi context. Social networks in the country have turned into intensively persuasive and political milieus.

490. Representativeness: Many individuals act and speak as representatives of the culture, expressing their views in a way that is compatible with the social fabric. Many people ensure that they express themselves in a way that reflects and does not upset the social sense of 'collectivity'.

491. Social Exclusion: At most times, Saudi society makes any citizen who is critical of cultural norms feel unwelcomed, marginalised and excluded. In this society, there is a generic 'mask' that everyone wears. Conformity is deeply implemented, with individuals constantly making changes in their beliefs and practices to fit into society and to fit their beliefs and practices into the culture. 'Fitting-in' is a force that drives the whole society. Many individuals find it difficult to act differently from the rest of their society, as any departure from the norm can ruin one's reputation and/or results in punishment or ostracism. Compliance is common, with many individuals publicly accepting social views while rejecting them privately or outside the country. Individuals feel obligated to act in line with social norms, considering that social control and order are gained through inculcating feelings of guilt and shame for culturally inappropriate practices. Honour-shame culture is well-enriched, in that practices are based on pride and honour, and that such things as appearance and presentation are what count.

492. Cultural Loyalty: <u>First</u>, within organisations, if an employee wants to take revenge against other employees, the best and common strategy is to question their loyalty to tradition. If employees' loyalty to tradition is questioned, they may consequently become excluded within their organisations. Also, managerial positions may not be given to them, and their requests may be rejected. If employees' loyalty to tradition is questioned, their professional life may become so difficult due to the assumed disloyalty to tradition. This happens even within organisations that have nothing to do with tradition. <u>Second</u>, if an individual chooses not to follow social norms, some of his/her fellow Saudis will look him/her down, fight against him/her, do not want to be friends with him/her, make his/her life difficult and think that s/he is 'crazy' and not normal. S/he would not get a managerial position. Some of his/her friends will avoid being seen with him/her in public so as not to let society know that they are associated with someone who does not follow social norms and values. Because of the social pressure against those individuals who wish to choose not to follow social norms, one will pretend to follow social norms and values, and yet when going outside the country, one acts otherwise according to what one sincerely believes. Many of these Saudis abroad, still, pretend to follow Saudi norms and values *but only* when going to *certain* places (e.g. London), as there are many Saudi tourists in London.

493. Gossip: <u>First</u>, many people avoid anything that may make them subject to gossip; especially that the society is collective and therefore 'gossipy'. <u>Second</u>, those who are so much into gossip are labelled a 'news-reporter'.

494. Advice: <u>First</u>, Saudi Arabia is an 'advice society'. In daily life, it is normal that one receives many pieces of advice, because the society is a collective society where people feel that they must be responsible for one another and, therefore, must advise each other. <u>Second</u>, during house visits, unsolicited advice is given to hosts or hostesses on how to dress, how to decorate their home and how to raise their children. <u>Third</u>, people may give advice although they do not know what they talk about. They may advise one to do things that they themselves do not do. <u>Fourth</u>, normally, people tend to talk a lot (mostly 'nonsense') and act as 'advisors'; not listeners. They may intervene in one another's life so as to guide (or misguide) each other. <u>Fifth</u>, there is a belief that one is not supposed to do a bad deed or even to let others do a bad deed. <u>Sixth</u>, it is normal and socially acceptable to see young religious leaders (e.g. 18 years old or even less) advising and directing others and telling their communities what (and what not) to do.

Listening

495. There are five types of music:

496. Very Conservative: There is traditional Arabic 'acapella' (singing with no instruments). It is music without instruments. Men and women listen to this kind of music. It is very common and traditionally very acceptable.

497. Medium Conservative: There is traditional Arabic music that uses *frame-drums*. Men and women listen to this kind of music. It is common and traditionally medium acceptable.

498. A Bit Liberal: There is traditional Arabic music that uses '*lutes*' (similar to guitars)——at times with singing but at other times without singing. Men listen to this kind of music. It is common and traditionally medium unacceptable.

499. Liberal: There is *modern* Arabic music that uses modern instruments——at times with singing but at other times without singing. Men and women listen to this kind of music. It is common and traditionally unacceptable.

500. Very Liberal: There is modern *non-Arabic* music that uses modern instruments——at times with singing but at other times without singing. Men and women listen to this kind of music. It is medium common and traditionally very unacceptable.

501. There are certain norms and practices regarding singing:

502. Context: <u>First</u>, music is believed to contradict spirituality and prevent one from real happiness. The lyrics and rhythms are so memorable that it distracts people from their focus on spiritual matters. Acapella is popular, and this popularity is because acapella is used as an alternative to music that uses instruments (either with or without vocals), which is a traditionally sensitive issue. <u>Second</u>, despite the traditional sensitivity to music, people still listen to it, although many feel the traditional guilt of listening to such music. Besides, YouTube, Spotify and the like are available, unless videos show women with revealing clothes. Such videos are, at times, blocked. <u>Third</u>, some parents do not allow their children to listen to music. Some children circumvent such restrictions by using headsets to hide this behaviour from their parents. It is difficult to know the kind of music that young individuals listen to during their social life, since the use of headsets is common among young people.

503. Content: Acapella is normally about ethics, morality and spirituality, whereas music is mostly about love and romance.

504. Conditions: Some believe that only modern and western music is against the culture, whereas traditional frame-drum music is fine.

505. Female Singers: <u>First</u>, acapella video clips do not show women, whereas music video clips show unveiled women (at times, with revealing clothing). Acapella videos show girls who are not adult. <u>Second</u>, throughout Saudi history, there have been 13 female instrumental singers, whether they are fully or partially Saudi. <u>Third</u>, there are professional groups of female instrumental singers, who can be hired for private female-only occasions (e.g. weddings). <u>Fourth</u>, while singing on the TV, some female singers reveal their face and moreover hair and do not wear the female cloak.

506. Male Singers: <u>First</u>, throughout Saudi history, there have been around 80 male instrumental singers, whether they are fully or partially Saudi. <u>Second</u>, throughout Saudi history, there have been around 30 male composers and hardly any female ones. <u>Third</u>, the number of male singers who sing accompanied by instruments is much smaller than the number of male acapella singers. There are no female acapella singers. <u>Fourth</u>, some Saudi male singers wear western clothes while being on stage or on TV.

507. Singers: <u>First</u>, Saudi instrumental singers produce video clips and hold concerts, mostly outside the country. <u>Second</u>, it is normal to hear that an instrumental singer has become a strong believer and therefore given up singing. <u>Third</u>, some nationals know the names of western singers, even if they do not listen to western music. <u>Fourth</u>, karaoke does not exist.

508. Events: Conventionally, the tradition does not promote (legal and publicly announced) musical concerts, ballets, nightclubs, musical schools or musical associations. Yet, there are officially permitted and publicly announced acapella concerts. That being said, there have been lately a few musical concerts, but such concerts are very complicated to gain permission for. Only the authorities can be the sponsor of such concerts. Besides, such concerts are held only at the macro level. Also, only high-profile performers are hosted. In other words, it is difficult to get permission for micro-level and low-key concerts and to host unknown and decent performers. Moreover, small shops or decent event-organisers cannot get permission to hold an instrumental-musical concert. There are no theatre companies that run instrumental-musical concerts. All this is because the idea of such concerts is still not totally socially accepted, and many people still do not feel fully comfortable with this idea.

509. Channels: <u>First</u>, there were social campaigns and resistance against the idea of introducing the culture to the radio innovation. When the radio innovation came to the country, people thought that there was, inside radio devices, ghosts who make the talks. <u>Second</u>, there are radio stations and TV channels dedicated only to acapella. <u>Third</u>, there are radio stations and TV channels wherein only modern and western music are played. Saudi Aramco offers a radio station (where such music is played) to the public. Many Saudis listen to the radio station of their neighbour (Bahrain) where such music is also played.

510. Shops: Music shops are separate from acapella shops. Men with long beards (who are supposed to be loyal to the culture and believe that music is a sin) do not visit music shops given that music is traditionally sensitive.

511. Production: For the production of acapella, software is used to make rhythms out of human voices.

512. There are certain norms and practices regarding dancing:

513. Female Dancing: <u>First</u>, women do many different styles of dancing, including Gulf dancing, 'Samri' dancing, 'Samba' dancing, Egyptian dancing and Iraqi dancing. Women are known for dancing extensively in gatherings. <u>Second</u>, women do only solo dancing. <u>Third</u>, although some female users of video-sharing websites upload videos of themselves dancing, these videos do not reveal their face and thus their identity.

514. Male Dancing: <u>First</u>, men do two types of dancing: solo dancing and group dancing. As for group dancing, in traditional dancing, stand next to each other, moving up and down with a long sword (and, at times, having a gun or small sword in their pocket). <u>Second</u>, there are professional groups of male frame-drum dancers, who can be hired for social public occasions and events. <u>Third</u>, black-skinned nationals are known for enjoying dancing. If professional groups of male dancers have black-skinned members, this is seen as an indicator of good quality. <u>Fourth</u>, some forms of modern male dancing are seen by some foreigners to be 'feminine', even though men are not supposed to act in a feminine way.

515. Cross-Gender Dancing: Normally, people do not do swing or ballroom dancing, given that men do not dance with women. In some families, people of one gender do not dance with those of the other, even if they are related. For some men, dancing with women is considered to undermine masculinity. Moreover, some couples do not dance together. Some do not even feel comfortable hugging their siblings of the other gender, seeing this as inappropriate.

516. Below are some singers and short descriptions of their musical activities:

517. Tawha: She is a singer and songwriter from the 40s-50s generation. She is added to the list of '*the Singers of the Golden Age*' in Arab regions. She sang from the 40s until the 80s. She sang around 400 songs. The instrument that she is known for playing is 'oud' (similar to modern lutes). A song of hers is: '*He waved at me with the tissue... Ah... He said he was going away... His dress is long blue... Yahooh... In the path, he is going away... Please slow down... O the master of the whole neighbourhood, how pretty the wink of your eye is... Ah... It very well irons my heart... Make me understand why you*

*are going away... O my master... What is the reason? Tell me...
My mind is going after you...O my soul... Please tell me... This is
not you... O my master... Make me understand what you mean...
O my eye... You are going away without asking about me... How
cute anger is when it comes from you... when you are displeased...
Being too hard to get is your art... You are the impresser of passers-
by'.*

518. Ibtisam Lutfi: She is a blind singer and songwriter
from the 60s-70s generation. She is added to the list of
'the Singers of the Golden Age' in Arab regions. She sang
from the 60s until the 80s. She described as *'the Planet of
the Island'* and as *'the Literature Lover'*. The instrument that
she is known for playing is oud. A song of hers is: *'He is
in our neighbourhood, but he does not come over... His sweet voice
sings songs that please us...It keeps us up at night... It wakes up
early in the morning... With his sweet oud, he sings... With pretty
melodies, he entertains us... Hours have passed, while me trying to
be patient... I say he may come over... He should try to be nice
and kind by reaching to our house and coming over... He should
give up by at least saying one word... From him, the word stratifies
us... Please do not be stuck up by not cheering us up... He should
write to us two lines to rejoice and please us'.*

519. Etab: She is a singer (and actress) from the 60s
generation. She is added to the list of *'the Singers of the
Golden Age'* in Arab regions. The instrument that she is
known for playing is oud. An 80s song of hers is: *'The
brown-skinned is now coming back to me... He is just now
remembering my time... After he forgot me, he is now coming back
to me... He is now coming back to me with regret for the
separation... He is coming back to remind me of the nostalgia,
which I have forgot for years... He is coming back to hand in his
apology... He is thinking that I will forget what has happened...
What does he think my heart is... Does he think of my heart as a
game for him... I am seeing in his eye a tear, which is telling me not
to be harsh on him... Fancy cannot be trusted... He is my lover*

whatever has happened… I and my heart is becoming in conflict… between desire and abstention… I do not know what to do… Should I come back to his lover or not?'.

520. Mohammed Abdu: He is a singer, composer and vocalist from the 60s generation. He has been active since the 60s until present. He is described as *'the Artist of Arabs'*. The instruments that he is known for playing are oud and vocal music. A 60s song of his is: *'I have disputed my eyes for years… Because of all the whining, I have now mercy on my heart … I have continued thinking… Of whom?… I have asked my eyes why you are crying… On whom?… My confusion is wandering freely because of suspicions… Insomnia is playing with eyelids… In my imagination, there is an image… But, of whom?… I have asked my suspicions to tell who he is… Who is he?… The love has taken place for a long time… Its fire has become smoke… And the secret is my heart… It is buried in my heart… All people said that that would be impossible to answer the question… Please help me by telling who he is… Who is he?'.*

521. Talal Maddah: He is a singer and composer from the 60s generation. He is described as *'the Earth's Voice'*, as *'the Philosopher of the Original Melody'* and as *'the Golden Throat'*. He recorded around 100 albums and composed around 1000 songs. The instruments that he is known for playing are oud, guitar, violin and piano. An 80s song of his is: *'There is something in my mind… I wish I could say it… When will my circumstances permit me to say it… I wish I could say the most elegant words… I wish for a moment of warm-heartedness with you… I have had enough with wandering off in dreams… I am devastated because of abandonment… We are awash with illusions… We cannot reach it… Come over, the days have been wasted… I want a reality that I can get hold of'.*

522. Abadi Al-Johar: He is a singer and composer from the 70s generation. He is described as *'the Octopus of Oud'* and as *'the Ambassador of Grief'*. He recorded around 50 albums. The instruments that he is known for playing are oud and violin. A song of his in the 2010s is *'Forgive me… Or, have you forgot that I am your lover? Love my weakness, and I will gain strength… Embrace my coldness; I want the shudder of your flame… and I put my faith in you; do not let me down… I have come to you like a sin that is seeking your forgiveness… I have come to you in shame that is overriding my pride… I have come as a sunrise that does not want to glimpse your sunset… I have come to you as an excuse that is racing my mistake… I have come as a night that breathes nothing but your kindness… I have come to you by force, but with my own will… and if I ask you, my life, 'who is your lover?', do not answer… Just do not look away and be in silence'*.

523. Mazal Farhan: He is a singer and composer from the 80s generation. The instrument that he is known for playing is oud. He is described as *'the Musician of Sadness'* and as the *'Artist of Elegies'*. A 90s song of his is: *'My life, do not cry… She smiled at me… After you left, I am a body without a soul…I die for the days I had, during which I did not know despair, anxiety and weeping… Today, there are many things I have come to realise… Long distance has made the tears drop like waterfalls… If you would enjoy your life if you killed me, kill me, and my body will be thrown in the of sand… The black years after you have long narrated for me… during which time, I could see blindly, and my heart was wounded… After you, my tears have cried for me… I have no nation, I have no sky, where can I go?'*.

524. Rabeh Saqer: He is a singer and composer from the 80s generation. He has been active since the 80s until present. He is described as *'the Musician of the Gulf'*. A song of his in the 2000s is: *'I have put up with you long enough… I do not think I can put up with you again… That you do not do enough for me has exhausted me… It is a shame, I did not expect that you were selfish… I was clear with you from the beginning… I thought that things were going my way… The wounds you caused for me have come to me from behind… The luck that raised me up* *to you has thrown me down… I am aware that everything has an end… You and I are humans, and life comes to an end… Since you do not want my closeness and interest, it would be pathetic to waste my tenderness through trying to be close to you… I just want to know what my mistake and fault were… I want to know why you would let me suffer… Tomorrow, you will come begging for pleasing me… But, I can never accept the one who once did not accept me'.*

525. Rashed Al-Majed: He is a songwriter, singer, composer and vocalist from the 80s-90s generation. He has been active since the 80s until present. He has recorded almost 40 albums. A 90s song of his is: *'Do not wave at the traveller… The traveller left… Do not call for the traveller… The traveller left… Our voice will be lost in the ocean and in the wind… We missed the train… The traveller left… O my heart, let us leave the train station as we are tired of standing… Neither spectrums nor stars remained at the night… The lights of the streets dimmed, and the lighting of the letters faded away… O my heart, let us go, the life is being narrowed on us… I do not know how this town will look like tomorrow… What will happen to the daylight, the yellow rose and twigs… This is the face of the traveller when I had eyes… Where are my eyes?… My eyes left just as he did…'.*

526. Khalid Abdulrahman: He is a songwriter, singer, composer and vocalist from the 80s-90s generation. He is described as *'the King of Art'* and *'the Night Dweller'*. He has been active since the 80s until present. The instrument that he is known for playing is oud. A song of his is: *'How can I not love you?… You are the one who has taught me how to love you… You are my obsession… My love is for your eyes… Ask me, and you will read the answer through the look of my eyes… You are my charming… Your love is a representation of the prettiest torture… My whole life is a taste of love… No matter how long I stay up… or how hard my circumstances are… or for how long I live in emotional deprivation… you will find my whole life to* *be a pleasure of love... You are the best of pure character traits... You are the whole life'.*

527. Abdul Majeed Abdullah: He is a singer, composer and vocalist from the 80s-90s generation. He has been active since the 80s until present. A 90s song of his is: *'You cannot imagine how big your love is... My heart beats with your lover...Who looks like you, angel?... You are an extraordinary human being... In you is amazing beauty... You are awesome, really awesome... You have gathered sweet charms... The beauty of the moon and the deer is nothing when compared to yours... Your love dwells in this heart... The description of it has gone beyond imagination... The moon is grey, compared to you... You are the distant and the close... You miss me in my absence, as much as the dewy misses the flowers... I miss you, my torment... In your absence and attendance... You are what I want and what I target... In you are the hope and luck...You can ask me whatever you want... I will obey to what you request...You are the happy life...You are the flower of the spring season... My wound heals when you are close'.*

528. Sarah Al Ghamdi: She is a singer from the 2000s generation. She recorded four albums. A song of hers in the 2000s is: *'Finally, he felt in love with me, after I died because of him... I will show him love that he has not seen or even heard of... He has tortured me; he has repulsed me... He knows that I love him...After I have seen the woe through him... I have managed to reach to his heart... He has defeated me; he has realised that I love him... And he has become a bit harder to reach... I have been patient and I have said that there would be a day when I make his emotions confused'.*

529. Aseel Omran: She is a singer and actress from the 2000s-2010s generation. A song of hers is: *'I will come to him; I will come to him... If he does not come to me, I will come to him... and place him in the middle of my heart... I will carry him with my eyes... I will tell those who want us apart that we are now* *back on good terms with one another... We will sing together, in our happy and sad times... He has become the owner of my heart and soul... I will not leave him... My lover... No matter how means he becomes, I remain the lover...Even if it is his fault, I will come to him... My lover deserves that I treat him well and make him feel special*.

530. There are certain norms and practices regarding poetry:

531. Socialising: First, poetry is an integral aspect of daily educational and social lives. Second, each semester, students are required to memorise a number of poems in order to pass a particular course. Third, people cite poetic lines in their daily conversations. They cite them in their speeches, for preaching and for greetings. They cite poetic lines when flirting with a woman. They cite them as proverbs. They tweet poetic lines. Fourth, even in *rational* discussions, people recite lines of poems or read religious passages, which accordingly makes many get carried away emotionally. Their emotional response to language and their cultural norms and values, normally, results in weak reasoning and thinking. Fifth, it is almost impossible to live in the country without hearing poetic citations every day. Sixth, recording poems and distributing them via social networks is a common practice.

532. Reading-Out: First, many poets read out their poems in public events. Second, there are '*poetic nights*', where poets individually or jointly read out their poems. Third, people are very proud of Arab poetry, to the extent that they invest and dedicate grants for it. There is a regional competition similar to X-Factor. But, the aim of this contest is to choose the best poet. Poets read out their poem on the stage, in front of a judgement board.

533. Gaming: One of the games that friends sometimes play among themselves is called *'Poetic Correspondence'*. One player states a poetic line from literature. The next player responds with another line. The first letter of this second line is the same as the last letter of the first line. The third player does exactly the same, responding with a line that starts with the last letter of the second line. And so on.

534. Types: There are eight recognised sorts of poems. <u>First</u> is *'Flirting Poems'*, through which one flirts with a lover. This type is the most popular one. <u>Second</u> is *'Descriptive Poems'*, which describe places and individuals. <u>Third</u> is *'Praising Poems'*, complimenting individuals for having certain qualities, such as morality, intelligence, justice and courage. <u>Fourth</u> is *'Moaning Poems'*, showing the pros of the dead, sharing their memories and showing how much they are missed. <u>Fifth</u> is *'Satirising Poems'*, which deny any virtues of a person or tribe. <u>Sixth</u> is *'Wisdom Poems'*, which stem from wisdom. <u>Seventh</u> is *'Apologising Poems'*. <u>Eighth</u> is *'Pride Poems'*, wherein one praises oneself and one's tribe. All these eights types of poems are taught in educational institutions.

535. Communicating: <u>First</u>, up until recently, women, unlike men, were not socially allowed to undertake certain hobbies (e.g. writing poems about intimacy); hence they used to write poems in newspapers and magazines using nicknames and fake profile pictures. <u>Second</u>, many men and women do not use their real name for their email account identity, but rather a line of a love poem (i.e. *'I die for you, who is worth all my life'*) or a love-oriented nickname (e.g. *'Emperor of Lust'*).

536. Below are poets and novelists, with short descriptions of their artistic activities:

537. Abdullah Al Faisal: He is a poet, businessman, minister and senior prince. Many of his poems are sung by national and international singers. His first poetic book was published in the 50s. One of his poems is: *'I am almost suspicious of myself, because I am almost suspicious of you, and you are me... People say that you have betrayed our covenant... If I assemble all my hopes, these hopes will drive me to you... My heart is saying that what people are saying about you is a lie, and yet my ear is listening to all these people... I am questioning my ear, and my eye is seeing what makes me non-suspicious of you... I am not the one who believes in any gossip about you, but I am doing badly because of my never suspicion... My spirit is being in pain because of the flame of suspicion... Answer me... Is what people are saying true that you have betrayed our covenant?'*

538. Khalid Al Faisal: He is a poet, poem-reader, painter, minister, governor and prince. He has organised galleries for his artworks. His poems have been translated into various languages. One of his poems is: *'I can prevent my tongue from saying... I can prevent my eyes from seeing... I can prevent my hand from taking... I can prevent my ear from chit-chatting... But the question is: How I can prevent my thought if it is led by my imagination? My thought wanders above my will whenever the fancy takes place or whenever his name is mentioned... You are the spring for the heart in all the seasons... The fragrance of your love flower has spread... Your spectrum has passed by me quickly, as usual...'*.

539. Ghazi Al Gosaibi: He is a poet, poem-reader, novelist, ambassador, minister and bestselling writer of fiction and non-fiction works. Two of his 13 novels are translated into English: *Seven* and *An Apartment Called Freedom*. One of his poetry books is translated into English: *Feathers and the Horizon*. One of his poems is: *'Our conversation is a waste of time... I am alive, and you are dead... Because I believe in sunrise and flowers... and the dancing of the spring in valleys... and the laughter of dreams in the gaps... And* *the pulse of joy in the human… And you are only into graves… and shouting in ruins… Because I glorify life… and write my poems about its brave individuals… and implant its paths with hope… and scatter flowers over its sadness… And you are into merely the remains… Because I care for every child… I love every trench… I love every sand… And I love mountains, plains and seas… And you live in a captive because of your hatred… and you wish you could stifle sunlight in the daytime, kill the melody in the flute and commit the infanticide of love in thoughts'.*

540. There are certain practices and norms concerning paintings:

541. Appreciating: It is not only that many do not appreciate art and do not hang paintings on walls, but moreover that they do not even *notice* if there are paintings hanged on walls, even if the hanging paintings are paintings for well-known artists.

542. Slashing: In primary school, some students slash the neck of the painted and photographic God's creatures (e.g. humans and animals) in the textbooks, believing that they have killed them by doing so.

543. Toileting: Hanging paintings or adds on walls at restrooms or houses is not part of the culture. Yet, patterned paper walls are commonly used to cover and therefore decorate house walls.

544. Outsourcing: Many nationals do not themselves paint (or re-paint) the rooms of their houses. Asians (or people of other nationalities) do the painting for them. When, however, a national does the painting himself, this is called '*American Style*'. Likewise, when nationals go to a restaurant, everyone insists on paying the whole bill. If they, however, agree to share the bill and distribute the cost among themselves, this is, again, called '*American Style*'.

545. Trimming: Some women want to trim their eyebrows; but, because the act of trimming eyebrows is traditionally unacceptable, some women go around this by dying their eyebrows in a way that makes their eyebrows look as if they are trimmed. For some women, trimming eyebrows means painting them to look bigger, thicker and therefore 'prettier'.

546. Tattooing: Hardly any woman has tattoos, and if one does, this is a sign of being open-minded. There are no tattoo shops.

Drinking, Eating and Fasting

547. There exist various technologies that are associated with food.

548. Dishwashers: Normally, families do not have dishwashers, for various reasons. First, dishes are big given the large number of family members. Second, the nature of Saudi meals and spices makes it necessary to wash dishes manually. Third, washing dishes is outsourced to maids.

549. Toasters: There is no toaster culture. Many do not have toasters at their places.

550. Food Trucks: There had been hardly any food truck until around 2015, when such trucks have started to emerge and form a new phenomenon.

551. Water-Tankers: There are mini water-tankers that go through neighbourhoods, supplying houses with water. Some houses have their own water-tank which water-tankers fill up.

552. There are various types of people that are associated with food:

553. Tippers: Tipping is not part of the culture and could moreover be interpreted as a bad thing and a form of bribery.

554. Passers-By: While eating, some invite any passer-by to join and share their food. A hungry person may decline an invite to food, so as to show a good manner, pretending that s/he is full.

555. There are various types of things that are associated with food:

556. Right Hand: One is supposed to eat with right hands. Many people take so seriously this norm——here are some examples. First, left-handed people are taught to use (actually, are forced into using) their right hand for eating. Second, one is, at times, told off even by random strangers for eating with one's left hand. That is to say that, if one does not follow even small social norms and makes socially technical mistakes, one may be told off even by strangers. Third, although one is not supposed to eat with the left hand, it is OK if one writes or plays with the left hand.

557. Main Courses: First, traditional food (meat and rice) is sold in large portions. That is, one person's portion is enough for two people. Second, there is a dish that is similar to lasagne. It is called 'marquq' or 'madazeez'.

558. Markets: <u>First</u>, in many cities, there is a *very* large, daily outdoor marketplace that is dedicated only to fruit and vegetables. Only men sell in this place, and there are hardly any female customers. <u>Second</u>, in supermarkets, it is part of the service that a worker (in addition to the cashier) packs for a customer. This worker normally packs only a few items (sometimes, only two items) per bag, with the customer ending up having *so many* bags. This worker does so, because some customers are fussy about the kinds of items packed together. These customers complain about certain items being packed together even though they belong to different 'categories'——i.e. these customers want vegetables to be packed in a bag, and milk to be packed in a different bag. So, these workers choose to go for the safest option, which is to put the least items in one bag. <u>Third</u>, many families buy supplies from supermarkets only once a month. Hence, they buy a large number of supplies and freeze them. This is why they have a *very* large fridge and freezer——at times, more than one fridge and freezer per family.

559. Restaurants: <u>First</u>, the restaurant business is popular and successful. There are many Saudi and non-Saudi restaurants. Going to the restaurant is one of the few activities that many couples do together. <u>Second</u>, the culture is good at resisting foreign cultural values, but not when it comes to food cultures (and also shopping cultures). There are a large number of large malls wherein all different kinds of international brands are available. The culture is very good at importing international products. In supermarkets (which are normally large and spread throughout cities), there are available almost all international products and supplies. <u>Third</u>, some order at restaurants collectively (i.e. to share dishes), leading to chaos over what to order and how to share served dishes. <u>Fourth</u>, many love to eat and do not think about the cost of what they order. They order too much, and there is so much leftover food.

560. BBQ: Many do only limited activities, including having picnics (and attending weddings and gatherings, shopping, going to restaurants, watching TV and playing games). When having a picnic, people tend to have a wood-burning campfire, thanks to the Bedouin lifestyle. Many individuals are good when it comes to things related to the Bedouin lifestyle, including making fire and having a BBQ. When having a BBQ, men normally take charge of handling the fire. Picnics are common outdoor activities, taking place in the desert, in (artificial) parks, by the beach, or by main roads.

561. There are certain activities that are associated with food:

562. Walking: One is not expected to eat while walking or on the street, for various reasons. First, this behaviour is seen to undermine oneself. Second, this behaviour is inconsistent with the 'high' standard of living, which is important for many. Third, people may talk and criticise one for this behaviour. Fourth, the male traditional costume is white and may easily get dirty if one eats while walking or being in the car. Fifth, it is difficult for women to eat from below the veil.

563. Sharing: First, sharing a table with strangers at coffee shops is something that is not welcomed by some individuals. Second, there is a particular term used to refer to those individuals who feel disgusted by drinking from the same cup that others (including their relatives) have drunk from. They, first, carefully wash the cup before using it.

564. Dropping: When a piece of fruit is dropped on the ground, some do not eat it because it is believed to have been 'licked by the devil'. That is, any piece of fruit that has been licked by the devil is not supposed to be eaten.

565. Articulating: One is supposed to say certain religious sentences before starting drinking and after finishing drinking.

566. There are certain values and practices regarding drinking, cooking, eating:

567. Hygiene: People wash their hands before and after eating.

568. Legality: The word 'halal' is commonly misunderstood by foreigners, who see this word to be associated *only* with food. This word is associated with things other than food. The word means 'religiously allowed', meaning that not only food but also practices, habits and ideas can be referred to as 'halal'. It is the opposite of 'haram', which means 'religiously forbidden'.

569. Eat-and-Leave: 'Eat-and-leave' is a norm among men. That is, in male gatherings, people normally leave immediately after finishing eating. In other words, when eating is over, the gathering is over. In gatherings or restaurants, people leave immediately after they have just finished eating. After the last bite, people instantly ask for the bill. In weddings (in the male wing), the minute the food was eaten, that was it. This norm has two implications. First, some non-Saudis still want to stick around and talk and think they have done something wrong when Saudis start to depart. The flip-side is when traveling——many Saudis do not understand that their hosts *do* carry on talking after dinner, and it is good manners to stay 'at the table'. Second, the problem is not the suddenness of the departure, but rather the reversal of the communal 'networking' time. That is, in many countries, the real conversation happens only after the meal has been served——that is where the deals get done. In Saudi Arabia, however, there is a reversal of the conversation. The deal happens before the meal, when drinks (coffee and then tea) and dates are served, then the meal and departure. It is a reversal of order that one has to mentally prepare for.

570. Purpose of Life: There is a saying that *'we eat to live, not live to eat'*

571. There are certain cultural beliefs and practices regarding fruit, vegetables and dairy:

572. Onion and Garlic: Many individuals care about odours, avoiding onion or garlic. Because of their smell, individuals are discouraged by the culture from eating onions and garlic before meeting others, to the extent that one is not supposed to go to worship places if one has just eaten either of these two types of food. Some couples find onion or garlic odours a disgusting turn-off during the course of kissing, foreplay and intercourse. Some eat onion because of its health value but use the following three strategies to get rid of the smell. First, some eat parsley after eating onions. Second, some think that rubbing the board on which onions are cut with lemon kills the smell. Third, some use mouth sprays, fresheners or gums to kill onion smell. Fourth, some eat only *cooked* onions because of their belief that cooking kills their smell. Fifth, some wear gloves when cutting onions so as to avoid their hands smelling onions.

573. Banana: Being tall is culturally perceived positively and seen as a sign of intelligence; hence, there is a rumour that *'eating bananas helps one become tall'*. So, when a tall person did something 'stupid', others would comment: *'his length is the length of a tree, but his mind is the mind of a cow'*.

574. Egg: <u>First</u>, there is a belief that *'eating both eggs and bananas, or eating paracetamol and soft drinks, or drinking both cough medicine and buttermilk can result in death'*. <u>Second</u>, many individuals prefer their food (e.g. eggs and burgers) to be well done.

575. Lettuce: There is a rumour that *'British people avoid eating lettuce, which causes infertility'*.

576. Date Fruit: People place dates in thick bags and then place these bags on one another. They after that place heavy concrete blocks on these bags. They leave these bags under these heavy concrete blocks for weeks until dates start producing thick, sticky liquid (i.e. syrup). Date fruit is widely common and served for guests as a sign of generosity.

577. Orange: It is believed by some that *'drinking orange juice, putting on burns raw eyes, melon, halva, flour, pure coffee, toothpaste or honey can cure burns'*.

578. Lemon: A belief is that *'putting on the scalp of the head lemon or olive oil or parsley juice can help treat the scalp of the head'*.

579. Mint: <u>First</u>, it is believed that *'covering the head with mashed mints, cucumber skin or eating aubergine can help overcome a headache'*. <u>Second</u>, mint lemon juice is commonly drunk.

580. Pineapple: 'Ananas' is a word that is used to refer to 'pineapple'.

581. Sunflower: Many people, especially in the eastern province, enjoy eating sunflower seeds.

582. Flowers: Flowers are sold at the reception in hospitals. Visitors can buy them and give them to those hospitalised, unless patients are in intensive care units.

583. Buttermilk: Buttermilk is widely sold and drunk.

584. Seafood: <u>First</u>, any type of seafood is culturally allowed. That being said, mussels are not served and eaten. <u>Second</u>, finishing is a common habit.

585. Sauces: Some avoid using many sauces (e.g. ketchup) in their food, thinking that when they eat ketchup, they will smell ketchup (which is seen by some as an 'unpleasant' strong smell). Caring about how one smells is essential in the culture.

586. Water: <u>First</u>, a rumour is that '*drinking hot water heals from diabetes*'. <u>Second</u>, a belief is that '*drinking so much water causes heart attacks*'.

587. There are normally three meals a day:

588. Breakfast: There are two types of food that people eat for breakfast. <u>First</u>, breakfast can be traditional, i.e. Egyptian, Sudanese or Afghani food (mashed beans or lentils). This kind of food is served in a ball and is eaten with wraps that are in a circle shape (width 14cm, depth 0.2cm). These wraps are freshly baked by being placed in a concrete oven that is similar to the pizza oven. <u>Second</u>, breakfast can be modern, i.e. soft sandwiches that are either in a circle shape (width 8cm, depth 2cm) or in a rectangular shape (width 12cm, length 3cm, depth 2cm). These sandwiches are filled with eggs, small pieces of livers, medium pieces of meat or minced beef. Beef burgers, eggs burgers, liver burgers, fresh juice and soft drinks are common for breakfast. Livers are widely eaten for breakfast. People are normally meat-eaters, to the extent that the act of eating meat is a key component of every meal, including breakfast.

589. Lunch: The main meal of the day is lunch. It normally consists of meat and a large quantity of rice—— as if rice is the main course and meat is the side. The rice is served in a circle tray, and the meat on the rice at the middle of the tray. People sit in a circle around the tray and eat directly from the tray using their right hand. Salad and soft drinks are placed around the tray. At times, buttermilk is served as well. In most cases, lunch is not eaten at work and rather with family, as people normally finish work in the late afternoon and then go home for lunch.

590. Dinner: There is no tradition when it comes to dinner. For dinner, people at times go out for food, eating international food. That said, if there is a formal gathering (e.g. a wedding), what is served for dinner is almost the same as what is normally served for lunch. Guests eat on the ground using their hand. They sit in a circle, surrounding a very large plate filled with rice and meat. They all eat directly from the plate. Salad and soft drinks are, at times, served and placed around the big plate. The big plate is placed on a very thin plastic sheet that is 1m × 1m. As eaters are moving their hand from the plate to their mouth, many drop some pieces of rice on the plastic sheet outside the plate. This dropping of rice is socially acceptable.

591. There are certain norms and values regarding weight:

592. Hiding Weight: <u>First</u>, the male and female outfit (the long loose cloak) hides how overweight one is. Because the outfit is loose, it does not encourage one to notice if one has gained weight. Yet, wearing trousers and belts makes one aware of one's weight. Second, some have surgery to shrink the size of their stomach, making them lose weight dramatically.

593. Gaining Weight: First, many individuals gain weight (and also become more conservative) when entering married life. Second, being overweight is interpreted by some as a sign of wealth and a consequence of a stress-free life, or because their wife is a good cook. Overweight married men are seen by some to be overweight simply because of their happy and relaxed married life.

594. Liking Weight: When one is told: *'oh you look slimmer'*, this is normally not a compliment. It rather means: *'are you sick?'* or *'is there anything that is making you sad and therefore consuming your health, weight and energy?'*.

595. Considering Overweight People: First, guests sit on the ground for food in a small circle of around five people. Sitting on the ground for eating makes it difficult for the elderly and overweight people to join; hence, there is a table dedicated to the elderly and overweight people. Second, when going for picnics, many people take with them chairs, as some are overweight and therefore cannot sit on the ground. These chairs are flexible and can be folded and therefore fit in cars.

596. There are various issues and practices regarding addiction:

597. Drugs: First, the most common drugs that some take are believed to be hashish, fenethylline (captagon), amphetamine, petrol, glue, gas in lighters, paints, nail vanish remover, alcohol, crystal meth (which s is a new happening in the country that has come from the Philippine people) and Sedatives. Second, there are believed to be various reasons why some take drugs. For example, the influence of peers is a major reason. Almost 90% of drug addicts are assumed to get influenced by their peers. This is in addition to the curiosity of the individuals to explore drugs. People say: '*I will just try it and I can give up anytime*'. Some people just want to take it during exam periods or during travels. This is not to mention boredom. Also, the reason can be a shock, such as divorce of parents, death of a family member or rape. Some just want to forget about their bad or traumatic experiences. This is as well as the addiction of one's role model. That is, sometimes, everyone around them is addicted, for example, the father, or the oldest brother. The poor economic situation has made some people take drugs. To illustrate, poverty has led some to addiction. Third, there are various issues regarding how some get drugs. For instance, the country is believed by some to have been 'targeted' by smugglers. Drugs are smuggled over the borders via land, sea and air, especially given that the country is widely spread. Drugs are smuggled during pilgrimages. Fourth, most drug addicts are assumed to be young people between 20 and 30 years old. Some are older 40, 50, 60 or 70, but most of them are young. Fifth, women are reported to hardly take drugs, but it is normally their father, husband or brother who is an addict.

598. Smoking: First, there are anti-smoking charities. Although shisha is a common practice in the Arab world, it (and cigarettes) is resisted by many individuals. Second, there are limited places where shisha can be found and smoked. Third, the act of smoking shisha and cigarettes is seen by many individuals to have bad implications (e.g. being a bad person surrounded by bad friends). Fourth, some men and women smoke shisha, although the number of women smoking shisha is limited and seen as considerably worse than men smoking shisha. Smoking cigarettes for women is culturally considered particularly bad behaviour. Many women are scared to smoke shisha and cigarettes in public. Some taxi drivers complain about some women wanting to smoke inside their cars. <u>Fifth</u>, when renting a car, some smoke inside the car, without showing any consideration of future renters who could be allergic to the smell of cigarettes. <u>Sixth</u>, indoor emergency stairs are places where people smoke. There is an accumulated smell of smoking in indoor emergency stairs.

599. Alcohol: <u>First</u>, alcohol is illegal in the country, even in products such as mouthwash. Beers exist but do not contain alcohol. Foreign airlines stop serving alcohol once their plane enters the air zone of Saudi Arabia. <u>Second</u>, accidents caused by drivers under the influence of alcohol or drugs are not an issue, since alcohol and drugs are strictly prohibited. <u>Third</u>, although alcohol and drugs are not allowed and not part of the culture, many Saudi jokes are about drunk and stoned people. <u>Fourth</u>, perhaps as an alternative to alcoholic beverages, many individuals drink soft drinks extensively, even for breakfast. <u>Fifth</u>, there is a Champagne-like drink called '*Saudi Champagne*', which is sparkling, served in a Champagne-like bottle and yet non-alcoholic. <u>Sixth</u>, there is a drink that its bottle, its colour and the way in which the text is written on the bottle are similar to those of Pimm's. Yet this drink has zero alcohol. <u>Seventh</u>, since there is no alcohol, there are no bars, no bar culture, no pub crawls, no bins full of bottles and the like. <u>Eight</u>, in hotel rooms, there are mini-bars, yet with no alcohol.

Interval

42 Saudi male undergraduates were asked if they would marry Christian women. Nine said that they would, 'because our religion allows us to do so'. One said: 'Yes, because Christian faith is similar to Islamic faith'. Another responded: 'Yes, for love and beauty, if she is not a good Christian'. Some would marry a Christian, but under certain conditions: 'if the kids follow my religion'. Another said: 'Yes, as I may manage to make her convert to Islam, but if she does not, then damn on her – I will divorce her'. Some said that they would not marry a Christian, as 'my family would look me down'. Christian people 'do not accept to marry people from other religions'. If one marries a non-Muslim, 'she will definitely cheat on him from the first day'.

'Would you consider seeing a Saudi?' asked 28 Italian undergraduates and postgraduates. Some would not, 'but in life anything can happen'. One thinks 'it could be difficult for me to consider seeing a Saudi man because in my opinion a relationship with a Saudi man could impose restrictions on my freedom'. One would like to 'meet a Saudi man and talk with him before making any choice'. One sees 'a Saudi man as a Muslim, and for this reason, I think it is difficult to have a relationship with him… I would impose conditions such as residence in Italy'. One 'would date a Saudi woman if I really loved her, but I would hide our relationship from her relatives, as they would oblige me to marry her. If possible, I would go to Saudi Arabia every few months, but I would not move there'. One said: 'Why not? I have got many Arabic friends'. One has 'never met a Saudi man. I would date one just out of curiosity, to see how he would behave with me'. For one, 'dating a woman and finding the right one is not a matter of "race" '.

Stomach, Waist and Heart

Proposing, Marrying and Divorcing

600. Below are various ways of finding a spouse:

601. Finding a Spouse through Relatives: People are not supposed to have any relationships before engagement. One's family normally chooses a woman for him to marry, and then he immediately proposes to her. At first, single men tell their female relatives what they want in a potential wife. These relatives start searching. If a man has *not* maintained a good relationship with his relatives, they warn him that they either will find him the wrong wife or will not help him find a wife at all, showing power relations between the genders. At times, parents offer their single daughter to another family as a potential match.

602. Finding a Spouse through Matchmakers: Some families rely on a 'matchmaker' to find a spouse for their child. Matchmakers are, normally, women. Whenever a matchmaker notices that a family has a child at a marriageable age, she asks this family if they want her to find a spouse. If the family give the approval, she will start looking for a person who looks for a spouse with characteristics that are available in their child. Whenever the matchmaker finds the right match, she contacts both families. At times, the matchmaker has a photo of the potential wife, showing it to the potential family of the son. If their first impression, based on the photo, is good, relatives of the son come to visit the relatives of the potential wife. The son's relatives tell him about her features. If he thinks that he might like her, his family asks her family for a 'speedy blind date'. Some families allow such a date. Others do not, and hence grooms can only see, for the first time, brides on the wedding night. On this date, he comes alone to visit the male members of her family. During this visit, she comes in unveiled for a few seconds to serve drinks. In this visit, he wears the traditional cloak and headwear. This means that she cannot figure out if he is bald. This quick visit does not allow the two to figure out other issues beyond their appearance, e.g. whether they snore. After the visit, he and she meet up with their families to inform them of their decision. Before making the decision, he may perform a particular kind of praying, which is intended to guide one on a particular issue/decision in one's life. If they decide that they are a good match, the two families start organising the engagement party within a few months, followed by a wedding party within a year. If the two connect, the matchmaker receives around US$500 from each party. The family of a son may resort to a matchmaker if his mother is not good at finding a wife for him, or if the characteristics that he desires are difficult to find. The family of a daughter seeks help from a matchmaker if no one has come to propose to her. Nowadays, some matchmakers offer their services via social networks.

603. Finding a Spouse with no Help from Others (e.g. through Crushes): Many prefer to marry cousins, for various reasons. <u>First</u>, for some, it is such an honour to marry a relative. <u>Second</u>, for some, marriage within the family results in compatibility between couples given that they come from the same family. A saying promoting marriage among relatives is: '*a piece of fabric remains beautiful only if the additional fabric attached to it is from the same kind*'. <u>Third</u>, some families (especially tribal families) may reject a marriage proposal from anyone from outside the family. <u>Fourth</u>, marrying one's first cousin is preferable, because there is no way a man can meet a woman to assess her suitability for marriage without getting into trouble. However, a man got the chance to see how his cousin looked when she was young. Once a child is born, the family may decide which relative to marry when they grow up. Some feel forced to marry their close cousin, because if they do not, they may hurt the relative, and this may cause a rift in the family. Marriage to a relative is not necessarily arranged and conservative, as some people marry a relative on whom they have had a 'crush' since childhood or teenager-hood. A man may go and talk to his parents, telling them that he has had feelings for a relative. Or, parents may sense that their child is into a particular relative. A man may have had a crush on a relative with whom he grew up with, and therefore the two are almost the same age. If the two are close in age, they end up *not* getting married. The reason is that women get married almost four years before men. Boys are advised by older relatives not to consider relatives of the same age range but rather four years younger.

604. There are certain arrangements regarding engagements, weddings and marriage:

605. First Dates: When a man proposes to a woman, they start to get to know one another for a couple of months. Getting to know each other happens in three ways. <u>First</u>, he may go out with her on dates——no intercourse indeed. <u>Second</u>, he may visit her at her house. Her family may leave a child with them to prevent them from acting inappropriately. <u>Third</u>, he may extensively call her and chat with her on the phone. Friends and families tease engaged people for being on the phone all the time. The engagement period is seen as exciting and emotionally intense since this is typically their first time to legally, freely and explicitly speak romantically across gender lines. A fiancé may try to impress his fiancée by doing some of the following things. He may show his fiancée how many men he physically beat up when he was in school. He may wear ironed clothes with cologne. He may shave well. He may have a fancy phone. He may buy his fiancée presents and perfumes. He may show his fiancée that he is charismatic. He may tell her about his past 'fake' travels and victories. He may tell her that, at work, everyone needs him. He may speak in a cool accent. He may act dominantly, even if he is 'dumb' in the absence of his fiancée.

606. Medical Screening: A pre-marital medical screening is done to examine, for example, genetic disorders between a potential couple. At times, the results of this screening show one or both to be carriers of a genetic disorder, and therefore they are advised by doctors against getting married to one another. Despite this advice, they proceed with the marriage. The most common genetic disease is sickle-cell disease.

607. Wedding Invitation: First, one cannot predict the number of wedding attendees, since confirmation is not required. Second, display of wedding invitation cards is not required for men, unlike women. For women only, there is a security person who checks invitation cards, since some people make fake invitations to gain access. Third, many people like to go to weddings, to the extent that they may complain about not being invited. They, moreover, might 'crash' weddings that are not related to them. Sometimes, people get into fights over who should be invited to the wedding of their relatives. So, an uncle might design fake invitation cards for the wedding of his niece, because his niece did not invite his contacts. Fourth, some individuals are known for crashing weddings, to the extent that there is a phrase in Arabic that could be translated into 'wedding crashers'.

608. No Children Policy: children (whether male or female) are, at times, not allowed at the female venue in weddings. That said, male children are, always, allowed at the male venue. One polite way of saying at the invitation card that children are not allowed is to write: *'We wish pleasant sleep for your children'*.

609. Wishes: To congratulate a groom, many say: *'You may provide the money, and she [the bride] may provide the children'*.

610. Hotlines: There is a formal charity that individuals call or message to seek advice on their relationship. The advice given is, normally, within traditional and religious boundaries.

611. Cuddle: Cuddle between spouses is not part of the culture.

612. At weddings, there are single-gender venues (i.e. female-only and male-only venues):

613. Female Venues: There is a stage, which can be fully set up by an independent company with laser lights and fog generators. This is along with live music from 9:00 pm till 3:00 am, with women dancing all night. Because of the performance of music at weddings, some women choose not to attend because they see such music as a sin. Some single women dance to attract the attention of mothers looking for wives for their sons. So, women dress up to attract not guys but their mothers. Mothers find weddings a good opportunity to seek a wife for their son. If a mother checks out a lady who she thinks can make a good wife for her son, the mother then seeks some extra information about the lady, for example, whether she is single or not and from which family she is. Along with buffets, there can be elegant tables and chairs, with impressive and well-assembled collections of traditional and modern desserts. How a bride shows up at her wedding is organised as if it is a drama. For example, the groom arrives at the female section, waiting for the bride to show up at the wedding. Just before the bride shows up, a poem and a song are read out with her name in it. Alongside the music, two little girls with wings may walk slowly on the bridge towards the stage. When these two girls reach the stage, they may turn around and nod to welcome the bride. The two girls may keep nodding while the bride is walking towards them and eventually towards the groom who is waiting for her on the stage. While the bride is walking, people may throw money at her. The live music players, eventually, take the money. After a while, the groom leaves the female section, so the bride's sisters and all the (female) attendees can take off their veil. After a while, the bride goes out the female section to meet the groom. They then leave the wedding together. The time that the bride spends at her wedding is only one hour. Although the wedding starts at 9:00 pm and ends at 3:00 am, the bride is there only for around an hour (e.g. from around 11:30 pm to 12:30 am). The dinner (i.e. the wedding meal) for women is served after 1:00 am (i.e. after the bride has left the wedding). The bride does not get the chance to have the wedding meal.

614. Male Venues: The wedding starts at 8:00 pm and ends at 11:00 pm. The wedding meal is served at around 10:00 pm. There are teas, dates, no stage, no special decorations, standard chairs, no tables, usually no dancing, a decent dinner and often no music——at times, there is traditional music. At times, there are no male guests whatsoever, and only women are invited to a wedding.

615. There are seen certain advantages of getting married:

616. Erotic Advantages: Many believe that men should marry as early as they can afford it, so as to find a moral way for their erotic desire.

617. Educational Advantages: If a teenager is 'wild', unsuccessful and undisciplined, his family may try to get him married. Many families believe that marriage transforms 'wild' men into 'good' men.

618. Business Advantages: One might get married to a woman not because he loves her but because he (or his father) wants to go into a business partnership with the potential wife's family. This means that getting a divorce is particularly difficult as it will affect this partnership.

619. Liberty Purposes: Some believe that, when the Saudi man gets married, his life stops, and his freedom will become limited. He accompanies his wife whenever she goes outside. He acts as her driver and guardian. She imposes restrictions on him in the name of jealousy. It is, on the other hand, believed that, when the Saudi woman gets married, her life begins. Before marriage, the Saudi man has so much freedom and can have a 'wild' time. Yet, the Saudi woman has restricted freedom before marriage and is hyper-vigilant of doing anything that might affect her marriageable status. When a woman gets married, she becomes more relaxed about her reputation. The husband takes her out of her 'sheltered' pre-marital zone and shows her the world.

620. There are certain responsibilities before and during marriage:

621. Female Responsibilities *before* Marriage: Some believe that a key responsibility before marriage for women is to maintain a high level of morality. Many women want to sustain their morality, as any criticism against it means that she can lose the chance of getting married. To many national women, marriage means 'everything', as many families prevent their daughters from doing exciting things before marriage. This prevention is done for two reasons. <u>First</u>, such exciting things might affect the reputation of their daughters. <u>Second</u>, these families want to encourage their daughters to get married.

622. Male Responsibilities *before* Marriage: Some believe that a key responsibility before marriage for men is not to travel abroad. If a man travels abroad, this is seen by some as a sign of being a 'bad boy'. If one has travelled extensively, the impression is that one has been exposed to a large number of women. In the past, a (rare) case was that some fathers would ask the one proposing to their daughter for his passport. This was to check the countries to which he had been, as some countries had bad reputations for prostitution. A woman may not mind her husband travelling to countries known for prostitution. Travelling is considered by some individuals *not* to be favourable. Some families do not allow their sons to study abroad unless they marry first. There have been campaigns to encourage Saudis to travel inside Saudi Arabia. Nationals are raised to believe that travelling abroad is a bad thing as other cultures are full of sinful things.

623. Female Responsibilities *during* Marriage: In married life, there are certain responsibilities undertaken by many women. <u>First</u> is to raise the children. <u>Second</u> is to cook. <u>Third</u> is home-keeping. <u>Fourth</u> is erotic availability.

624. Male Responsibilities *during* Marriage: Many husbands are 'over-demand' by their family. <u>First</u> is to rent a flat and eventually get a new, large house and to pay for new furniture from time to time. <u>Second</u> is to buy supplies for the house and pay the wife and children for their daily expenses even if the wife has a salary. <u>Third</u> is to fund, at least partly, children's marriages and pay a car for the children at the age of maturity. <u>Fourth</u> is to pay for all female family members when going out for meals. <u>Fifth</u> is to fund family travels and act as a tour guide for the wife and children. <u>Sixth</u> is to employ a maid and driver and fix any problem at the house.

625. There are certain norms, values and regulations regarding married life and divorce:

626. Heritage: Heritage is distributed among spouses, children, grandchildren and siblings.

627. Insurance: <u>First</u>, although *Saudi* singles are not eligible for health insurance, *non*-Saudi singles are eligible. <u>Second</u>, in some Saudi companies, salaries vary based on whether one is married or not. Married employees get higher salaries than singles.

628. Permission: Some wives do not leave the house without seeking oral permission from their husband, even if the one with whom they are leaving the house is their brother or father. They call their husband (if he is not in the house) and ask him via phone if it is OK if they leave the house. Husbands may then ask where they are going and with whom.

629. Conditioning Wives: Some men prevent their wives from doing something by conditioning them—using divorce as the condition. To illustrate, the wife says: '*I will go shopping tonight*'. The husband says: '*No, you cannot*'. She insists. He then replies: '*If you go shopping tonight, you are divorced*'. If she *does* go shopping that night, the divorce automatically takes place, as divorce occurs when it is conditioned, even if it is articulated merely *orally*.

630. Divorcing: If a husband says to his wife *once*: '*I divorce you*', divorce then happens, since it is enough for divorce to happen if it is articulated *orally*. That said, since the husband says to his wife '*I divorce you*' only *once*, he can change his mind. That said, if he says '*I divorce you*' three times, there is no way back, and she is no longer his wife. Yet, for some, during her menstrual cycle, a woman cannot be divorced. That is, if he says '*I divorce you*' even three times, this divorce is invalid since it has happened during her menstrual cycle.

631. Best Friend: Some wives tell their husband so much about their (married) best friend, whether in a good or bad way. This is why if this friend gets a divorce, these wives stop being a friend with her, because they are worried that their husband might marry this friend as an additional wife or might divorce his wife and marry this friend, since the husband already knows a great deal about the friend.

632. Sisters: There is a saying: '*Your wife is like a shoe that can be discarded at any time. But your sister* [or any relative] *is like a part of your body that cannot be discarded*'. This saying is intended to encourage one to value his sister more than his wife.

633. Friendship: It is rare that a man deals (and can deal) with his wife as a 'friend'.

634. Chatting: Many men do not talk about their erotic life to their friends, because it is seen as a 'sin', 'wrong', 'a matter of privacy' and 'a lack of morality'.

635. Siblings-in-Law: Choosing a wife is not only about the wife herself (as an individual). Instead, one criterion for choosing a wife is that the wife has successful siblings. This criterion is made based on the belief that, if a wife's siblings are successful, this suggests that her children may become successful by association, as these children may become influenced by their successful uncles and see them as examples. A child is more likely to be around those uncles from their mother's side (more than those uncles from their father's side). This is because children are normally with their mother, who is normally with her family (including her siblings). This is how and why children get influenced most by their mother's siblings (i.e. by those uncles form their mother's side).

636. Shifts: Some women want to have their shift (and their classes) in the morning and hate having their shift (and their classes) in the evening. This is partly because they are housewives and partly because their parents or husbands do not feel comfortable about their daughters or wives being out at night. Because of this, in supermarkets, for example, female cashiers are assigned for the morning and afternoon and yet male cashiers for the evening and night. Likewise, female professors prefer to have their classes in the morning.

637. Prisons: In prisons, there are private rooms that prisoners can have temporarily to enjoy a 'legal *left-alone-with-a-spouse* time'. In these rooms, a prison is left alone with his wife for as much as they want. This is why prisoners may get children during their time in prison.

638. Luck: Since marriage is arranged through a third party, a widely common saying is: '*How good the wife that is chosen for one is a matter of luck*'.

639. Houses: <u>First</u>, there are normally no smoke detectors in houses. <u>Second</u>, one needs to push to enter a building, whereas in some other countries, one needs to pull to enter a building. <u>Third</u>, in some cities, the basement is called, literally, 'the bedroom' (using the English sound of the word).

640. Exoticness: <u>First</u>, if a Saudi's spouse is an 'exotic' foreigner (e.g. a white blonde person), he will, at times, be asked for approval of marriage in such places as car-checking points on highways. This is, of course, if the spouse's face and hair are uncovered, which is something that foreigners are allowed to do. <u>Second</u>, if a national tells others that s/he is married to a westerner, their fantasy lets them think of this spouse as 'hot', 'fit' 'blonde' and 'white', even though the spouse can be otherwise.

641. Wealth: Because of Saudi Arabia's association with oil and therefore wealth, some foreigners are accused of marrying Saudis for their wealth.

642. Travelling: Many women dislike that their husband travels without them (whether for fun or work). They would do many tricks and come up with reasons so as to ruin his plan to travel. Even if he travels anyway, they will be on his case and call him and claim that their child got so sick, asking him to arrange that someone takes the child to the hospital.

643. Family-in-Law: A man cares so much about establishing a lovely relationship with his families-in-law, because they intervene a lot, and if they like him, they will defend him against their daughter, and if they do not like him, they will try to cause trouble between him and their daughter and make his life difficult. In other words, a man's relationship with his family-in-law requires strategic planning.

644. Escaping: Some work hard, hang out with their friends or go to the gym just because they see these activities as good ways of running away and escaping from their noisy children, their marriage or their unpleasant wives. At times, even if they go home, they lock themselves in a room at their house.

645. There have been discussions about unconventional types of marriage:

646. Temporary Marriage: In this marriage, a woman marries herself to a man for an agreed-upon period of time (even for a few hours). This marriage is based on simply an oral contract articulated by the two parties. A man can start a new temporary marriage right after the previous one ends. But, a woman has to wait for three months before starting a new one. In this marriage, the wife loses the right in inheritance, housing and maintenance money. Besides, there is no need for consent from the father of the bride unless she is a virgin. Also, there is no need for witnesses in such a marriage; a key feature that allows the potential couples to keep it secret. Moreover, there is no 'divorce' in such a marriage, as the marriage simply ends when the contract is no longer valid.

647. Travelling Marriage. This marriage appears to be a permanent marriage, although either the groom or bride holds a secret intention that the marriage is temporary and will end at some point. Travelling marriage takes place when a woman wants to study abroad but cannot go without a male guardian. She then marries a man willing to act as her male guardian, since some sponsors or families do allow women to study abroad without a male guardian. Her *secret* intention is to divorce him once she is done with her studies.

648. Misyar Marriage: This marriage is a form of 'intercourse marriage' or a marriage of convenience. This marriage is similar to a Saudi typical marriage but with less commitment, fewer requirements and liberal conditions. In this marriage, the couple does not live together. He is not obliged to provide her with housing and maintenance money. She is not required to do housekeeping. For some, this kind of marriage helps poor men cope with the high cost of getting married. For some, this marriage is needed due to the nature of the culture where intercourse outside marriage is not allowed. Since the law allows a man to marry up to four women, this marriage (which does not cost much money) motivates one to marry more than one woman. Some women reject the idea of *Misyar Marriage*, seeing it to undermine the essence of marriage and downgrade the wife. For some, only women with serious medical and psychological problems and disabilities will accept this kind of marriage. Some believe that this marriage will lead to (and promote) prostitution and result in diseases and new social problems. Regardless of the kind of marriage that a man goes through, he has to pay the bride an agreed-upon amount of money, even if it is a small amount. Hence, some women have exploited this marriage as a business opportunity. They accept a *Misyar Marriage* offer and consequently get the money that is legally paid by the groom to the bride. Then, she asks for a divorce, seeking money from another *Misyar Marriage*. Some men go to Asian countries to have a *Misyar Marriage*. Male and female individuals offer online services that help with *Misyar Marriage*.

649. Foreign Marriage: To be allowed to marry a foreigner, one needs written legal permission, which can take up to a year to be granted. There are certain conditions that must be met in order for one to gain this permission. Here are some of these conditions. <u>First</u>, applying for permission to marry a foreigner must be done before the marriage takes place. <u>Second</u>, marrying a foreigner can be done only through both the state and tradition authorities. <u>Third</u>, the potential foreign wife must be Muslim. <u>Fourth</u>, one must be above 30 years old to be allowed to marry a foreigner.

650. Group Marriage: In order to achieve efficiency, reduce logistics and therefore encourage people to get married, group weddings (be they large-scale and small-scale) are organised by charities, associations, families or grooms themselves.

Giving Birth, Aging and Dying

651. There are certain norms and practices regarding pregnancy and birth:

652. Pressure to Have Children: <u>First</u>, once single men have a job, many are pressured to marry by parents and society. Their parents will promise them financial support in case they do not have enough money. <u>Second</u>, once men decide to get married, their female relatives quickly and easily find them a bride, regardless of how unmarriageable they are. <u>Third</u>, once men are married, social pressure is, at most times, placed on them to have children. If they have female children, pressure is, again, put on them to have a male child.

653. Pregnancy: <u>First</u>, once women get married, some want to become pregnant as quickly as possible. This is because some think of this as a clever and strategic way of preventing the husband from divorcing them. <u>Second</u>, it is common that parents know the gender of their potential baby, and yet, they, as a game, keep it secret and ask others to guess the gender. <u>Third</u>, normally, one's mother is the one who will act as a pregnancy consultant and a baby consultant for one, although in other cultures, this constancy is outsourced to the business sector and 'professionals'.

654. Intercourse: Intercourse is traditionally allowed during pregnancy.

655. Temporary Separation: <u>First</u>, after giving birth, many women stay at their mother's house for 40 days and welcome guests and presents (instead of resting). <u>Second</u>, it is culturally popular that guests hold new babies.

656. Hospitals: <u>First</u>, some men are not present while their wives giving birth. This is because they are careless and/or find it the act of giving birth 'disgusting'. Even if they are present, they wait outside the room in the waiting area. Some see the idea of watching one's wife giving birth is a western idea and therefore to be unwelcomed. <u>Second</u>, mixing up infants at the hospital was a problem in the past, which has been, however, addressed nowadays.

657. Breast-Feeding: <u>First</u>, in female-only spaces, women are, at times, allowed to reveal all different parts of their body (including breasts), except the area between the navel and the knee. This means that many women openly breastfeed in the presence of other women. <u>Second</u>, some women breast-feed their child in public (in the presence of other men) and yet from under the cloak. That is, the child is placed under the cloak for breast-feeding. In this case, no one will realise that the mother is breast-feeding.

658. Leave: At times, maternity leave is for merely a few weeks. The short length of this duration is believed to make sense for two reasons. <u>First</u>, women tend to have maids who take care of their newly born babies. <u>Second</u>, women give birth many times, meaning that, if they get, for example, six months for maternity leave, they will be, almost always, off work.

659. Baby Gender: There are various cultural rumours concerning the gender of the expected baby. Here are some examples. <u>First</u>, '*if a pregnant woman looks at ugly people, her child may look like one of them*'. <u>Second</u>, '*if the stomach of a pregnant woman is up, the baby is a boy. If it is down, the baby is a girl*'. <u>Third</u>, '*if a pregnant woman likes salt, the baby is a boy. If she likes sugar, the baby is a girl*'.

660. Walking: Some believe that, during the first eight months of pregnancy, women are not supposed to walk even for short distances, as this may kill the baby. That said, it is believed to be healthy that women go for a walk during the last (ninth) month of pregnancy.

661. Judging: In public daily life, it is difficult to tell if women are pregnant, given that women are fully covered in the traditional very loose cloak (and given that many women are overweight).

662. People tend to have a large number of relatives. This has certain advantages and disadvantages:

663. Missing Classes: If one's relative dies or is hospitalised, one may not come to the class. Yet, given the normally large number of relatives, this means that relatives die more often, meaning that students have to miss classes more often.

664. Gifts: People constantly need to buy presents given the large number of relatives, with whom they have to share gifts.

665. Shopping: Shopping trolleys and dishes are big given the large number of family members.

666. Fast Eaters: Some are fast eaters because they have grown up with many siblings (considering the large number of family members), so they are used to competing for food.

667. Seating: Despite the large number of family members, they, at times, want to sit next to each other on the plane or train without previous seating arrangements, begging other passengers to allow them to sit next to each other, thereby harassing others and causing chaos.

668. Driving: Many men do so much driving in the morning, for instance, driving their large number of children to school and eventually driving themselves to work. This so much driving takes a considerable amount of time. So, to reduce this time, some of these men drive fast, break many traffic rules, do various tricks to skip traffic queues and drive over pedestrian areas.

669. Large Cars: Having a large car makes many individuals feel powerful on the street. For many, a large car has enough space for the large number of children that many families have.

670. Travelling: Travelling as a family is difficult given the large number of children.

671. Quality Time: Because of the large number of extended families, it is difficult to have a quality time with any of them.

672. The culture has certain attitudes towards modern medical innovations and interventions:

673. Sperm Donation: Donating sperm is believed to be against the culture.

674. Organ Transplantation, Organ transplantation is believed to be culturally acceptable.

675. Abortion: <u>First</u>, having an abortion is illegal. It can be, however, done up to three months of pregnancy *only* to prevent harm (e.g. putting the mother's life in danger). <u>Second</u>, some women have abortions secretly and illegally by taking tablets, taking traditional herbs or having surgery outside the country. <u>Third</u>, there are websites that market abortion pills and traditional herbs. Abortion pills and herbs are delivered in person by mobile phone.

676. Artificial Insemination: The culture is still uncertain how to judge the innovation of artificial insemination.

677. Cloning: Cloning is culturally unacceptable.

678. Birth Control: Contraceptive pills are available at pharmacies. However, some believe that it is religiously not allowed to set a regulation that restricts the number of children. Despite taking contraceptive pills, there is so much unwanted pregnancy, for two possible reasons. <u>First</u>, contraceptive pills are believed not to work effectively with Arab ethnicity. <u>Second</u>, it is believed that there is so much unwanted pregnancy due to the non-existence of s*x education.

679. There are certain norms and practices regarding age:

680. Power: The hierarchical structure of Saudi society is, mostly, informed and influenced by age (and gender). In a car, many people let the oldest or the male to have the front seat as a sign of respect. Yet, if there are a female older than a male (in this case, gender versus age), then gender normally wins and therefore the male will have the front seat of the car.

681. Respect: Within many families, the level of respect varies from family member to family member based on age. First, during most gatherings, the eldest is held in high regard, receiving the bulk of conversation. Second, when eating together, it is seen by some as impolite to start eating before the oldest. Whenever the oldest starts eating, the rest follow. Third, a child is called 'the ignorant'.

682. Life Plan: The life of many men is well-structured. At the age of 17-18, their father gets them a car. At the age of 22-23, they graduate from university. At the age of 24-25, they get married after having saved money for two years. At the age of 25-26, they start having children. At the age of 30-35, they start designing and building their own house. At the age of 35-45, they finish building their house. Around the age of 70, they expect to die. For some, although such a life seems to be 'boring', it is so tempting to embrace it, as people living this life are seen to enjoy peace of mind.

683. Asking about Age: It is normal that one is asked about one's age, because age holds a social value. Based on age, one is judged. If one is older, one is expected to act wisely. If one is young, one is expected to act silly. One is expected to talk and be talked to according to one's age.

684. Older Siblings: <u>First</u>, for some, older siblings are more powerful than younger ones. At home, if one is sitting at the living room and got thirsty, one may ask one's younger siblings to bring one some water from the kitchen, instead of doing it oneself (i.e. bringing oneself some water). <u>Second</u>, for some, younger siblings are expected to be the one trying to keep in touch (e.g. by calling and visiting from time to time) with older ones; not the other way around.

685. Elderly: <u>First</u>, some of those in their 60s (or even 50s) consider themselves (and are considered by some) to be 'elderly'. They (especially women) stop dressing up and act as 'moral' advisors. They are allowed/asked to skip queues. In some supermarkets, there is a special till for them. They are at times called 'senior citizens'. <u>Second</u>, in this country, old people show weakness so that other people take care of them and do things for them. Yet, in some other countries, old people show fitness so as not to end up at the retirement home.

686. There are cases where one's marriageability becomes low. Here are some of them:

687. Being Old: First, many women are scared of 'spinsterhood' (a period that begins when an unmarried woman passes the marriageable age of around 27). Unmarried women, who are around 27 and above, might end up being additional wives. <u>Second</u>, once a single man passes the age of 30, his chance of getting married to a woman with particular characteristics becomes slimmer, because he is seen as old, and because women of his age cohort (particularly special women) are more likely to have already got married.

688. Being Unhealthy: <u>First</u>, Unhealthy children are sources of shame for some families. Because of their disabilities (e.g. developmental issues like having strong crossed eyes or real disabilities), some Saudi children are put into foster care by their family, whether inside or outside the country, because their children's disabilities will ruin the family's ability to be marriageable. Second, one must be above 30 years old to be allowed to marry a foreigner. In case that a man is under 30, he has to prove that he has tried to find a Saudi wife, but no one wants to marry him for certain reasons (e.g. disability). Actually, people with disabilities (e.g. Down Syndrome) are hardly seen in public.

689. Being Divorced: <u>Fourth</u>, A man cannot remarry a woman after divorcing her until she, after the divorce, marries another man and divorces him.

690. Studying Overseas: For one to get a state scholarship to study abroad, one must sign a statement affirming that one will not marry a non-Saudi woman *during* one's overseas studies. If one does so, the scholarship is no longer valid. This said, one can marry a foreigner *after* the scholarship is finished.

691. Arabism: <u>First</u>, knowing one's roots and having a large family tree are sources of pride and, moreover, encourage one to behave well and to work hard so as to sustain the reputation and honour of one's family. Many are proud to be Arabian and Saudi and to know their roots. Some are happy to come from a tribe, as tribes know well their roots. Many tribal people feel proud to come from a tribe that has an influential reputation in the country. <u>Second</u>, some citizens are proud to be Arabs. This means that a Saudi's decision to marry a non-Saudi and non-Arab is seen by some as problematic, with their children being only *half* Arabian, thus affecting the (Arab) ethnicity of their children.

692. There are certain norms, values and practices regarding children:

693. Child Quantity: First, the country is '*the Land of Kids*', wherein there are young children, babies and pregnant women everywhere. Second, it is normal that one is asked if one has children, because having children holds a social value. If one has been married without having had a child, people then assume that one has been struggling, trying to get a child. People do not assume that the couple, intentionally, do not want to have a child. Third, it is normal that one is, constantly, asked: '*do you have a child?*' If the answer is negative, one will, therefore, be told: '*ah, may God help you*'. Fourth, because the number of many family members is large, it takes them a very long time to get ready to leave the house.

694. Child Wildness: Many children are exceptionally 'wild'. To overcome this wildness, some parents use an app called '*Children's Policeman*'. It is an app that looks identical to the app that is normally used for making normal calls, except that the *Children's Policeman* app is false and makes fake calls and fake conversations with a policeman. The fake conversations with the policeman are well designed, in the sense that there are pauses throughout the conversations that allow parents to respond as if there is actually a real interaction between the caller and policeman. Also, the virtual policeman is designed to sound scary, angry and in a bad mood. There are in the app various options from which the parents can choose, so that the conversation can circle around the chosen option. Here are these options are. First is a child making the clothes dirty. Second is a child keeping crying. Third is a child lying. Fourth is a child not wanting to eat. Fifth is a child not wanting to study. Sixth is a child not wanting to take a shower. Seventh is a child not listening to the parents. Eighth is a child not wanting to go to school. <u>Ninth</u> is a child being naughty. If parents choose, for example, 'a child being naughty', the conversation will go the following direction: --> Policeman: 'Hello' --> *pause so that parents can respond* --> Policeman: 'What is wrong?' --> *pause so that parents can respond* --> Policeman: 'Really, your child is being naughty - where do you live?' --> *pause so that parents can respond* --> Policeman: 'Aha, I know that place - we will be there in ten minutes, is the child still being naughty?' --> *pause so that parents can respond* --> Policeman: 'Good to hear that the child is not being naughty any longer - if the child becomes naughty again, let us know'. By the end of the conversation, the child is scared and moreover hiding. This method has proved to be effective. Some parents have reported that this app is 'just magical', as it not only makes children disciplined but moreover hide underneath chairs out of fear.

695. Child Confidence: <u>First</u>, in public spaces, many families leave their children 'unattended', walking around and harassing others. This has, from a different perspective, a positive impact on children when they grow up, making them more confident in dealing with others during their adulthood. <u>Second</u>, men are raised to take care of and lead the female members of their family. Likewise, women are raised to be taken care of and be led. This is why many men end up being good at taking care and leading whereas many women end up being good at feeling the need for someone to take care of them and to lead them. Put simply, many men are good at leading, and many women are good at being led. <u>Third</u>, there is a remarkably large number of narcissists in the country, whether healthy or unhealthy narcissism.

696. Child Labour: It is normal to see children working or being used for work purposes——in non-official settings.

697. Child Tutoring: At times, a father employs a private tutor (who is normally a non-Saudi Arab) to tutor his children particularly in mathematics or English, for various reasons. First, parents are illiterate. Second, parents' literacy is limited. Third, their school teachers are not good. Fourth, parents do not have time. Fifth, parents are lazy. Normally, men tutor male children, and women tutor female children.

698. Child Wrapping: It is common that mothers wrap tightly with ropes their infants in blankets or similar clothes, which is believed to help their bones cohere.

699. Male Child: Many people show sympathy and pray for one if one has not had male children. One may marry an additional wife, since his current wife has given birth only to 'females'. Or, a woman may keep giving birth until she gives birth to a boy, which can mean that she has to give birth many times.

700. Child Abuse: Many parents shout at or even hit their children, to the extent that there are, from time to time, campaigns against the act of hitting children. If parents hit their children, they normally do not hit them on their face but rather on their butt, shoulder or back. This is because hitting one's face is culturally very sensitive, as the face is associated with honour and dignity.

701. Abandoned Child: First, mosque gates are common places where children are dumped and abandoned. The best time for baby dumping is just before people go to mosques for the first prayer (which is a few hours before sunrise). Abandoned children can be adopted and yet cannot take their adopted father's last name. They are given a random father's name and will be given no family name. A Saudi without a family name can mean that he is an abandoned child. Family name is a source of pride; hence, some abandoned children feel ashamed of having no family name. Second, some nationals marry foreigners, live in the country of these foreigners, have children with them and suddenly escape home, leaving the wife and children behind and ceasing all contacts. Third, some foreigners marry Saudis, move to Saudi Arabia, have children with these Saudis and suddenly escape to their home country, leaving the husband and children behind. At times, the wife leaves some of the children behind and at other times she takes all (or some of) the children with her. She would say that she would like to go to their home country for a visit, and then she never comes back.

702. Child Safety: First, safety standards for children are low, to the extent that it is normal to see people driving with a child in their lap. Second, it is normal to see children placing their head outside the car window while the car is in motion. Third, at times, adults are valued more than children. For example, in cars, only adult passengers count. Put differently, by Saudi standards, a normal car fits five passengers and yet an 'unlimited' number of children. Fourth, when the door is being knocked, the youngest child (male or female) is the one who opens the door and talks to the knocker, meaning that parents were not worried about safety. Fifth, older children (e.g. 8-year-old children) are allowed to carry younger children (e.g. 3-year-old children).

703. Child Aid: If one has a sick child (e.g. with a heart problem or sickle-cell disease), one then gets from the state a monthly financial allowance as support for the child. This is in addition to other financial and non-financial facilities.

704. Child's Friends: There are many reasons and social obligations why families have to act friendly. For example, a family has to act politely towards the friends or spouses of their children. This is not necessarily because they like them. Rather, they are socially obligated to be polite towards whoever their family members become friends with. This is done out of solidarity. Many mothers' greatest fear is to lose their son when expressing their real feelings against his wife. This is a game that is carefully played by mothers (and indeed by the rest of the family). On the other hand, when a family member dislikes someone, the whole family will dislike them by association so as to show family unity.

705. There are certain norms and practices regarding motherhood:

706. Child Quantity: <u>First</u>, having many children is seen positively by many mothers. For example, if one's husband becomes mean to her, she hopes that she gets protected by her many sons. <u>Second</u>, many women raise their child in a way that makes the child more sympathetic towards the mother than towards the father. This shows some aspects of power relations in spousehood, wherein children are used as a tool.

707. Adult Child: At times, a mother gets excited when her child hits the age when he is allowed to drive cars, because she has the power over him to ask him to drive her around anytime she wants. When a wife asks her husband to drive her around, he may say no to her. Yet, a child is least likely to say no to his mother when she asks him to drive her around. When a child grows old, and his younger brother reaches the age when he is allowed to drive, the older child outsources the responsibility to drive around the mother (and indeed other family female members) to this younger brother, as older brothers have power over younger brothers. The responsibility to drive around family female members is mostly outsourced to the youngest male child in the family. If there is a family consisting of five male children and four female children, then the youngest male child is the one who mostly drives around the four female children (and, of course, the mother).

708. Controlling: <u>First</u>, some mothers are controlling of their son——regardless of his age. <u>Second</u>, many men of all ages listen to their mothers' instructions and advice (e.g. when it comes to their marriage). <u>Third</u>, it is common that a man decides against his own decision to marry a particular woman because his mother has asked him not to marry her. <u>Fourth</u>, after marriage, it is common that there is tension between one's mother and one's wife, and one is normally confused whom to satisfy. A widely debated issue is whether a man's mother or wife should be seen as more important.

709. Loved Mothers: <u>First</u>, it is normal to hear a man saying: '*I am a mother person*' (a person close to his mother). It is common to hear that a man says that he is so close to his mother, to the extent that even if he is offered a job in a nearby city, he will turn it down, saying that he cannot take it because he needs to stay close to his mother. He says this proudly, and his mother is proud of him saying that. Second, in Saudi culture, a '*mother boy*' is someone whose mother is dependent on him. But, in other cultures, a '*mother boy*' seems to be someone who is dependent on his mother.

710. Loved Children: There is a saying that '*monkey is, in the eyes of his mother, a deer*'. In other words, an ugly person is always seen by his mother as handsome. This is used, for example, to stress how biased people can be towards what they belong to.

711. Child Care: A single man, normally, lives with his mother until he gets married and therefore moves with his wife——unless he, in-between these two events, has to study or work in a city that is different from where his mother lives. It is considered by many to be rude if a male single does not live with his parents, if all are located in the same city.

712. Old Mothers: It is common to see mothers in their 50s or more, being overweight, in a wheelchair and pushed around by their children.

713. There are certain norms and practices regarding fatherhood:

714. Child Quantity: Many men have many children, caring about quantity but not about quality. Men are known for liking to have many children. This is because, at times, when a father has many children, he feels and becomes powerful. When a stranger attacks a father, all his many sons will, more likely, protect him. Children are used (or even misused) by many fathers as a tool for protection. Many children fight any stranger if the stranger subjects their parents to humiliation.

715. Paying Back: A common reason why one has children is that they take care of one when one is elderly. Some parents explicitly tell that one key reason why they have decided to have children is that they want these children to take care of them at an old age. It is believed that, if one does not care about one's parents at their old age, it is likely that one's children will not take care of one at one's old age. So, what goes around comes around. Many people warn/remind one another of this belief, encouraging each other to take care of parents at their old age. Many individuals are concerned about having no one to take care of them when they are elderly and therefore unable. Because of the concern about having no one to take care of them at an old age, many individuals not only have many children but moreover maintain good relationship with the members of one's extended family who may take care of them in case their own children fail to do so.

716. Outsourcing: Some fathers get excited when their child hits the age when he is allowed to drive cars, because they will outsource to him the responsibility to drive around family female members. Some parents make their children take care of one another and therefore outsource parenting. That is, older children take care of younger children, including helping them with their homework.

717. Respect: <u>First</u>, in the presence of their father, some children do not cross legs, smoke, start a conversation before him, or argue with him, so as to show respect to him. <u>Second</u>, one does not confront one's parents or older family members. Moreover, if a father asks his children (including grown-up children) to do something, it is always seen by these children as an order with no space for doubt or questioning. It is socially exceptionally rude for one to question or doubt one's father and his requests. This applies to mothers as well. <u>Third</u>, there are online and offline campaigns and reminders on a regular basis that encourage one's to respect and serve one's parents.

718. Loved Daughters: <u>First</u>, it is believed that, when a man has two daughters and has been nice to them, he goes to heaven. <u>Second</u>, some fathers are too kind to their daughters, whereas many oldest brothers are mean to their sister. It is common that there is tension between a father and his oldest son, as the father tries to protect his daughter against her brother's maliciousness. Many brothers want to make sure that the privacy of their sisters is not damaged, since such damage will affect her marriageability and, more importantly, the reputation of the whole family.

719. Pretending: In the presence of their children, many fathers act as if they are religious, wise and conservative. They, however, act otherwise in their absence. Second, it is common that a group of male friends rent a room on a farm. Such a room is commonly called '*The Rest*'. Many men belong to a group of friends who have such a room. Some of them go to this room as often as they go home. In this room, some watch what they cannot watch home. Some go to this room to run away from their noisy children and their demanding wives. Some smoke shisha and cigarettes. Some play cards. In this room, some have a character that is completely different from that which they have with their wives and children.

720. There are certain norms, values and practices regarding familyhood:

721. Family Name: First, when people introduce themselves, many of them not only state their first names but moreover their family names as well. This is partly because many individuals are proud of their families and are proud to belong to a family. Second, it is common that, after introducing oneself (using one's first and family names), others respond '*what a great family*', even if they know nothing about this family——it is just a polite way of responding. Third, it is common that, after introducing oneself (using one's first and family names), one will be asked if one knows another person with the same family name. To illustrate, when one introduces himself as '*Abdul Al Lily*', one will be then asked '*Oh, do you know Muhammed Al Lily, with whom I work in Aramco?*' That is, one is expected to know as many as possible of those who have the same family name as one's.

722. Family Hostility: <u>First</u>, at times, members of a family act hostilely in relation to one another and, moreover, become the cruellest enemies. This is because of friction and ill-temper and because of concern over details (e.g. not being invited to an occasion). Also, people from different generations socialise closely with one another. Besides, many socialise extensively, to the extent that everyone knows the business of everyone and gossips about everyone. <u>Second</u>, family life is, at times, awash with drama, sorrow and unpleasantness. One's enemies await a weak moment in one's life to take advantage of it and use it for shaming. <u>Third</u>, in case of conflict among relatives, they may stop talking to one another, and there is more likely a mediator trying to bring them together again. Conflict among relatives does not last for a long time, and other relatives quickly intervene to eliminate this conflict. <u>Fourth</u>, many require firm consistency in the behaviour of their family members and friends, in the sense that they expect others to be always ready to assist them. When one does not greet, invite or stand by them, they direct harsh criticisms to him/her.

723. Family Retreat: There is a place named '*Centre for Family Development*', i.e. a help centre for couples. The Centre helps people (whether from inside or outside the country) to achieve and enhance family happiness, to overcome any problems among members of the immediate and extended families, to face barriers to getting married and to address any problems between the couple before deciding to get a divorce. If anyone has a family-related problem, s/he has three ways of contracting the Centre. <u>First</u>, one can *drop by* and meet with one of the Centre consultants in a private room. If the consultant is male and the client is female, her father, brother or son must be in presence too given that one cannot be left alone with anyone of the other gender unless he is a father, brother or son. Second, one can *call* the Centre, which will forward the call to an anonymous consultant. Third, one can *email* the Centre. The court sends family-related cases to the Centre, which then attempts to intervene to minimise the risk involved. If there is a case involving a potential divorce, the Centre may intervene to address the problems related and therefore help the couple to get back on track. The Centre trains fiancés and new and old couples in family skills. It also trains families with limited income in how to increase their income. It trains prisoners in social relationships. It offers family-related exhibitions, public lectures, seminars and workshops. It produces family-related leaflets, handouts, articles, cassettes and magazines and distributes them among society. It produces radio programmes.

724. Some are protective of (and loyal to) their family members. Family connection is strong, which can be seen in the following examples:

725. Family Venue: Some families own a venue, on which it is written the name of their families. This venue is dedicated to only the events and occasions of their families, such as weddings, engagement parties and the like.

726. Family Budgets: Some extended families have a lifelong family budget, into which family members constantly put money. Whenever a family member faces a financial challenge or wants to buy or build a house, s/he is given money from this budget. The budget is intended to promote family connections and to show the unity of family members. Such an idea of having a family budget is inspired by the widely common saying that '*one hand cannot clap*'. This saying stresses the value of (and the necessity for) collaboration and mutual interdependence.

727. Family Closeness: <u>First</u>, many people, who work or study away from their families, come over to see their families every weekend. This is done even if the distance is 400 kilometres. <u>Second</u>, many women cannot be away from her parents for a long time. They reject a marriage proposal from someone who lives in another city, since they are culturally expected to move to the city of their husband. They reject a marriage proposal from a man who plans to study abroad and wants them to go with him. Some women are criticised by some for not making sacrifices in order for their husband to succeed. <u>Third</u>, some Saudis, who want to study abroad, prefer to go to the UK (instead of the US, Australia, or Canada). This is partly because the UK is nearby, allowing one to come over to see one's family more often.

728. Loyalty: Among family members (and friends), devotion, sincerity, loyalty (particularly in difficult times) are sustained (and, moreover, are supposed to be sustained) at any price. If one cannot meet a family or friendship 'obligation' (for example, an invitation to an occasion), a straightforward, prompt and simple excuse is not accepted. Instead, an elaborate, convincing, twisted, long justification is expected to be articulated in a very emotional and careful way. Despite this justification, blame may still be put for not trying harder to meet the obligation.

729. Although some are protective of (and loyal to) their family members, they least care about wider society. Here are some examples to support this claim:

730. Lobbying: There are various sayings in this respect. First, '*I and my brother are against my cousin. I and my cousin are against the stranger*'. Second, '*relatives have priority over charity*'. It has the same meaning as '*charity begins at home*'.

731. Aggression: Many children and teenagers are aggressive, in various ways. First, the destruction of public facilities (e.g. restrooms, resorts, beach facilities and post boxes on house doors) is a common act. Second, when a father brings a toy to his sons, they, at times, destroy it and tear it apart. Third, some teachers at male-only schools have two cars (a fancy and decent car). They use the decent car to go to school because they are concerned that their students may ruin their cars. Fourth, a problem with many children is that, in public, some of them climb on almost everything, making a game out of everything (e.g. furniture).

732. Other Passengers: First, many train passengers use their phones to listen to audio and video clips without using headsets, showing no consideration for other passengers. Second, many men do not allow a stranger of the other gender to sit next to their partner. Such an attempt by families to reorganise their seating arrangements in line with gender-based considerations result in chaos and annoys other passengers.

733. Other Users: Some teachers and professors leave classrooms without erasing what they have written on whiteboards, showing no consideration of the teachers and professors coming after them to classrooms.

734. Other Drivers: First, when men drive their female relatives to a particular place (e.g. to school, work or a shopping mall), some of them stop in the middle of the street to drop these relatives by the gate, even if this results in a considerable delay in the traffic. Second, in traffic lights, cars in the right lane are allowed to go right even if the traffic light is red. Yet, it is common that, if there is a long queue in the middle and left lanes, a driver (who wants to go straight) skips the queue by taking the right lane, therefore blocking the whole lane and preventing other drivers from going right.

735. Others in Line: First, many individuals are not good with queuing; whether by foot or by cars. When queuing, many do their best and carry out different tricks to skip the queue, showing disrespect to others. Second, at the cashier, many customers want to order at the same time, so the cashier (especially if he is a foreigner) feels not only confused but also shocked by how messy it is. Third, some customers feel they can simply skip the queue just because they have only a few items.

736. Loudness: In public, many people speak loudly, whether on the phone or to the person beside them.

737. Blaming: At times, when one makes a mistake, one not only does not admit the mistake but moreover makes others feel as if they are the ones who have made the mistake. For example, one may stop in the middle of the street to talk to someone else, and if other drivers horn at him to remove his car so that they can drive through, he would open the car window and say '*be patient, be patient*', making them feel as if it is their fault. In this case, others may feel that they should apologise to him for not 'being patient'.

738. Left Trays: In fast-food shops (e.g. KFC and McDonald's), many individuals leave their tray beyond and do not themselves throw away their rubbish. They expect to be serviced in this respect.

Praying and Spiritualising

739. There are certain spatial issues related to praying. Here are some of them:

740. Public Mosques: People prayer collectively in places called 'mosques', which have a minaret and, at times, a dome. Prayers stand next to each other on lines facing a certain distant holy location. Hence, the ground of mosques is totally covered with carpets that have the pattern of striped lines. The distance between lines is around 1 metre. This distance is made to enable one (who stand on one line) to bend for prayer without hitting the person praying on the line in front of him. The thickness of each line is 5 cm. The line goes from the right side of the mosque all the way to the left. People stand on the first line at mosques, and once this line is full, people then start standing on the next line, and so on. People go to mosques to pray, to read (or learn how to read) and memorise the *Holy Book* and to listen to traditional, social, political and spiritual lectures. People can also prayer individually or even collectively outside mosques. Praying individually is not encouraged though. Praying outside the mosque is also not encouraged though. When prayer outside mosques, some pray on a mat-like carpet. Nowadays, there are memory-foam prayer mats. Such carpets are provided as part of the furniture in hospitals and hotels.

741. Private Mosques: In many workplaces, there is a main mosque, or at least a place designated for prayer. Many employees feel, socially, obligated to come to the mosque during prayer times so as to pray collectively with others, as their colleagues may gossip about them and criticise them for not showing up for prayer. Being criticised for not showing up for prayer causes one so much social trouble. It is rare that one does not show up for prayer in their organisation. Nationals unthinkingly see and treat all their fellow Saudis as believers, with no doubt that a Saudi can be a non-believer.

742. Sacred Places besides Mosques: <u>First</u>, besides mosques, there are other sacred places where there are held mainly religious lessons and sacred celebrations (e.g. the celebration of sacred birthdays and deathdays). <u>Second</u>, there are no churches.

743. Female Prayer Places: Given that mosques are located in the public domain, only men are *obligated* to go there for praying. Women normally do not prayer at mosques (i.e. in the public domain), but prayer in the domestic domain (e.g. at home).

744. Parking: Because there are no parking spaces, some prayers' cars are parked in the middle of the roads, thus blocking access.

745. Prayer Direction: <u>First</u>, people (whether at mosques or anywhere, such as parks and hotel rooms) must prayer towards a certain holy city located in the country (i.e. Makkah). For this reason, there are signs (with an arrow showing the direction towards this city) located almost everywhere, such as in parks and hotel rooms. <u>Second</u>, when one sits to defecate, one is not supposed to sit in the direction that points towards this city. Hence, toilets are designed not to point towards this city.

746. There are certain temporal issues related to praying. Here are some of them:

747. Prayer Times: People pray, collectively, at mosques (or anywhere) five times that are spread throughout the day. Prayer times are unfixed, in that they change throughout the year based on the sun. That is, <u>First Prayer</u> is a few hours before sunrise. <u>Second Prayer</u> is around noontime. This second prayer is treated differently on Fridays, in the sense that not all mosques hold this prayer. Rather, only large mosques hold this prayer and hence witness an exceptionally large number of prayers. There can be mini-markets on Fridays outside these large mosques where people trade, for example, fruit and vegetables. Such trading does not happen during the prayer but rather just after the prayer since trading is not allowed during prayer. During this prayer, people are more likely to give charity; hence, there can be people begging for money. <u>Third Prayer</u> is a few hours after noon. <u>Fourth Prayer</u> is around sunset. <u>Fifth Prayer</u> is a few hours after sunset. Some schedule deadlines, meetings and appointments *not* according to the clock, but rather according to the prayer times. To illustrate, one may say: '*I will meet you after the third prayer time*'. Or, '*I will get the job done by the second prayer time*'. People are supposed to pray on time; yet, if one misses a prayer time, one catches up by praying for the missing time. A common reason for missing a prayer time is sleeping.

748. Combined Prayer Times: When it is raining heavily, mobility becomes difficult; hence, prayer times are brought together. That is, instead of having five prayer times, people pray only three times. The first prayer stays as it is. The second prayer and the third prayer are brought together. The fourth prayer and the fifth prayer are combined.

749. No Business during Prayer Times: Shops must close during prayer times (i.e. four times throughout the day) for around 30 minutes. Tradition authorities drive around to ensure that shops are closed during prayer times. It is normal to see individuals begging a sale-person (who is locking the shop door for prayer) to let them get in the shop to quickly buy a small item. Tradition authorities, themselves, catch up with praying after prayer times are over. During prayer times, customers are asked to leave shops. In a large shop, customers can remain inside and continue shopping during prayer times. They, however, cannot check out or leave the shop as the gates are closed. That is, one is locked in. It is common to see customers begging a cashier to let them check out, as the prayer time is *just* due, or because there is actually *still* one minute left until the prayer time. For some employees, prayer times are used as smoke or leisure breaks or for lunch or dinner breaks. Although shops (including gas stations) close during prayer times, restrooms do not close during these times. Actually, restrooms need to remain open so that people use them to clean themselves to get ready for prayer. At times, at coffee shops and restaurants, when a prayer time is due, singles are asked to leave the shop, but couples and families can stay in. There are two justifications for this favouritism. <u>First</u>, mosques are normally only for men. So, if women are forced to leave coffee shops and restaurants, there will be no place for them to go. <u>Second</u>, some of these women *need* their partners to be with them since they do not feel comfortable being alone without a related male; hence, their partners are allowed to stay in as well.

750. Lateness: <u>First</u>, if one is late for a meeting, it is normal that one says that '*I was late because I was praying*'. This is an acceptable (and moreover preferable) practice (i.e. to give prayer priority over anything), and some people misuse it as an excuse for their lateness. It is also acceptable (and moreover preferable) that one leaves a meeting for ten minutes to pray and then comes back. <u>Second</u>, a few places (e.g. hospitals and academia) do not stop functioning for prayer. At times, the beginning of class-time clashes with a prayer time; hence, some students come to classes late because they were praying.

751. There are certain human resources issues related to praying. Here are some of them:

752. Prayer Employees: Prayer leaders, prayer callers and mosque-keepers are nationals, who get not only a monthly salary (around US$500, US$300 and US$250, respectively) but moreover sometimes free housing. This 'job' is normally beside their normal (professional) job, through which they get a salary as well.

753. Prayer Callers: First, in every small neighbourhood, there are large, decorated and elaborate mosques. There is a city (i.e. Al Ahsa) called '*the City of Mosques*', where there are often more than one mosque in every small neighbourhood. The distance between two mosques can be as little as 250 metres. <u>Second</u>, there is an officially employed 'prayer caller' for every mosque, who uses loudspeakers to call people in the surrounding neighbourhoods to come for prayer. This call involves singing certain sentences for almost one minute. These loudspeakers are located inside and outside the mosque. They are far-reaching, to the extent that, if one is sitting at home, one can overhear many prayer calls coming from different mosques. There is a friendly competition among local mosques to see who can be the loudest or be heard the most, especially since mosques are spaced so close together. These loudspeakers are used to deliver a weekly lecture that takes place on Friday around noon. The translated text of the prayer call is: '*God is the greatest, God is the greatest... God is the greatest, God is the greatest... I bear witness that there is no deity (worthy of worship) but God... I bear witness that there is no deity (worthy of worship) but God. I bear witness that Muhammad is God's Messenger... I bear witness that Muhammad is God's Messenger... Come to the prayer, come to the* *prayer… Come to prosperity, come to prosperity… God is the greatest, God is the greatest… There is no deity (worthy of worship) but God*. <u>Third</u>, announcement speakers in buildings (e.g. in supermarkets) are used for prayer calling. This prayer calling is automated. <u>Fourth</u>, people turn off music if they overhear a prayer call. It is disrespectful to have music playing during a prayer call. For example, if a driver is listening to music on the radio, and suddenly there is a prayer call, the driver will mute or turn off the music until the prayer call is over, and then s/he will unmute or turn on the music. <u>Fifth</u>, prayer speakers are not used for evacuation.

754. Prayer Leaders: There are certain roles for prayer leaders. <u>First</u>, people pray collectively at mosques, standing in lines behind a 'prayer leader' who stands at the front of them. All these people, including the prayer leader, stand towards a particular holy city in the country (i.e. Makkah). <u>Second</u>, the prayer leader uses loudspeakers to say the following statements: '*all the praises and thanks are [God's], the Lord of the [mankind, jinn and all that exists]… The most gracious, the most merciful…. The only owner of the [Day of Resurrection]… You we worship, and You we ask for help… Guide us to the Straight Way… The way of those on whom You have bestowed Your grace, not the way of those who earned Your anger, nor of those who went astray*'. These statements are read by the prayer leader twice or three times in every prayer, followed by reading a small part of the Holy Book. <u>Third</u>, when a man proposes to a woman, her family may want to ascertain his commitment to the faith, for example, by asking him to bring a written reference letter from the prayer leader in his neighbourhood, showing that he comes to the mosque for prayer. Being religious is seen to mean being honest, respectful, wise and good.

755. House-Keepers of Prayer Places: Some national mosque-keepers ask Asians to do the job of mosque-keeping on behalf of them. They then give these Asians a small share of their mosque-keeping salary and keep the rest (plus free housing) for themselves. In this case, these nationals do nothing and free themselves from the task of mosque-keeping.

756. There is limited consideration of safety in mosques. Here are some examples.

757. Extinguishers: There are normally no fire extinguishers in mosques.

758. Space Capacity: The number of prayers can be beyond the capacity of mosques. This is why some prayers, at times, stand outside the mosque on the street and pray using a carpet that they bring with them.

759. Driving: It is normal to see someone literally running and driving recklessly and aggressively to the mosque, as there are certain advantages based on when one arrives at mosques. Some drive 'wildly' (therefore exposing their own lives and the lives of others) just to make it on time to prayer.

760. In addition to the normal prayer, there are other forms of prayer:

761. War Prayer: Men pray collectively even during wars. During wars, collective praying is done slightly differently. During wars, when a prayer time is due, the army splits into two groups. Group 1 prays behind a prayer leader, whereas Group 2 faces the enemy. Once Group 1 completes half of the praying, they stop praying and go and swap with Group 2 to face the enemy, whereas the prayer leader continues the praying. Group 2 then comes back quickly to join the prayer leader so as to finish the second half of the praying.

762. Rain Prayer: in most parts of the country, it does not rain——except once or twice a year. If there has been no rain for a long time, the state officially announces that there will be a national collective praying for rain at particular places and at a particular time. Rain prayer is done around the winter season. Praying for rain takes place in the morning around the sunrise and is done by men only. Rain is perceived by many individuals in a positive way, to the extent that, when it starts raining, many shout: '*the goodness has come*'. When it rains, people feel happy, shout out of happiness and jump up and down. When it is raining (or even when there are sandstorms), school days get cancelled because the transportation system and the infrastructure are not designed against rain and sandstorms. That is, any decent rain can result in flooding. Buildings and streets are not constructed to be suitable for rain. When it rains, many streets, highways and buildings flood, and some buildings start to leak, with water going inside rooms and offices. There is no drainage in many streets and highways. Despite streets and highways being flooded, people carry on driving and go through flooded streets, to the extent that water gets inside their cars. Drivers drive fast through flooded streets, making the water fly up and away from the right and left sides of their cars. To take away the flood from streets, empty water-trucks pump the flood out of streets into the tank of the trucks. Some drivers try to go through flooded streets, but they get stuck as their cars break down because their cars are old and not water-proof. In this case, there are three solutions. First, the drivers leave their cars behind in the flood until the flood goes away. Second, the drivers (with the help of other people) push the cars to get them out of the flood. *Third*, the drivers connect their cars with other cars using strong cables, and then these other cars pull their cars out of the flood. Normally, it does not snow in the country (except for a few areas), but if it does, it is *not* snow but hail.

763. There are certain norms and values regarding praying:

764. Health: Obsessive-compulsive disorder (OCD) is widely known, discussed and common when it comes to religious practices. To illustrate, some people keep washing over and over again their body to get ready for prayer, hesitating whether their body is clean enough for praying——although washing the body once is enough.

765. Confusion: The culture is a complex mixture of traditional (e.g. Arabian, Saudi and tribal) and Islamic values to a degree that makes it difficult to distinguish between 'the social' and 'the religious'.

766. Liberalism: <u>First</u>, 'being liberal' is regarded as a 'movement' and 'ideology'. Hence, one may say '*I am liberal*', in the sense that s/he feels s/he belongs to this movement or ideology. <u>Second</u>, some do not know the meaning of liberalism and secularism. <u>Third</u>, being 'open-minded' and being 'liberal' are traits that are seen by some in a negative way. For example, one can be criticised for being open-minded or liberal. Some men do not want to marry open-minded or liberal women. <u>Fourth</u>, if one says '*I am not religious*', this does not mean '*I am a non-believer*'. It rather means '*I am not a strict follower*'. This is why it is normal to hear someone saying that '*I am not religious*'.

767. Beliefs: Although astrology is against tradition, it is common among women. Mentalism and divination are socially perceived.

768. Beads: Some use '*prayer beads*' for various purposes. <u>First</u>, some use prayer beads to count how many times they say certain religious sentences. That is, certain religious sentences are to be said for certain numbers of times (e.g. 100 times). Nowadays, as an alternative to prayer beads, some people have shifted to '*tally counter*' (a device that counts the number of times that one presses a bottom), pressing the bottom every time they say a particular religious sentence. Second, some individuals use prayer beads not for praying but for decoration. Third, for some individuals, prayer beads help calm their anxiety in unfamiliar situations, for example.

769. Religiosity: People tend to show more religiosity (e.g. listening to religious radio stations) in the morning than in the evening.

770. There are certain things that one is not supposed to do while praying:

771. Talking: While praying, one is supposed *not* to talk to others at all, *not* to respond to them and *not* even to look at them. One, while praying, must look *only* below at the ground.

772. Wearing Shorts: Individuals do not pray (and do not like to pray) in shorts, seeing this practice as religiously disrespectful.

773. Wearing Shoes: First, people do not pray wearing shoes or shorts. They take off their shoes before entering mosques. Second, because there are no shoe shelves, shoes are thrown in front of mosque doors. That is, when going into mosques, some leave their shoes on the ground by the entrance, since one is not supposed to wear shoes inside mosques. This is partly because mosques have carpeting. This disorganisation of shoes prevents those in wheelchairs from entering mosques. Third, a traditional shoe has two covering pieces. One covers only the big toe whereas the other covers the remaining four toes.

774. Wearing Nail Polish: To get ready for prayer, people wash their face, hands and other parts of the body in certain ways. If, however, one has nail polish, this washing is invalid. Since women do not pray during their menstrual cycles, women take advantage of this time and put on nail polish.

775. Wearing Make-Up: It is challenging to wear make-up given the five-a-day praying which involves washing one's face. To overcome this issue, women resort to the following three actions. <u>First</u>, they may apply waterproof make-up. <u>Second</u>, they may apply make-up after the last prayer which takes places a few hours after sunset. <u>Third</u>, they may find their menstrual cycle a good time to put on make-up since no prayer is required during their menstrual cycle.

776. Having Blood: <u>First</u>, some believe that, as long as there is blood coming out of the woman, she cannot pray, nor can they fast or have intercourse. <u>Second</u>, during their menstrual cycle, female students (and women in general) do not touch the Holy Book. So, they use gloves or cover their hands with tissues to be able to read it.

777. Shaking Hands: <u>First</u>, some refuse to shake hands with anyone with whom they are theoretically eligible to be in a marital relationship. If a male public figure dares shake female hands, severe and heavy criticism can consequently be directed against him. <u>Second</u>, people are supposed to wash (without soap) certain parts of their body to ready themselves for prayer. This readiness for prayer (as believed by some individuals) breaks if one touches a woman (e.g. through shaking her hand).

778. There are certain signs that show a man to be a strong believer:

779. Wearing Cords: The cord has a traditional meaning, as not wearing this cord is seen as a symbol of being a strong believer.

780. Wearing Cloaks above the Ankle: If the male cloak is *above* the ankle, this is an indication that the wearer is conservative and a strong believer. If, however, it is *below* the ankle, this can imply that the wear is non-conservative.

781. Having a Beard: First, the longer a man's beard is, the more society thinks of him as a strong believer and therefore as an honest, wise and truly good person. Having a long beard is a symbol of being loyal to the culture. People do not do anything against the faith in the presence of a man with a long beard, to show respect to him. A long beard is a representation of honesty, wisdom, goodness, respect and power. Second, the traditional image of people with a long beard is that they do not smoke cigarettes or shisha, as these two practices are against the culture. If people with a long beard smoke, this will be seen as insulting to the culture. Third, when a man has a beard, he takes care of it, to the extent that he may brush, blow-dry, put cologne on it and/or straighten it. Fourth, the fact that believers who have never shaved their beard means that they (as adults) have never seen their cheek skin (the one below their beard). Fifth, shaving the moustache and beard can be a sign of liberalism and/or wealth. Sixth, when religion individuals (with long beard) stop being religion, they do not shave their beard immediately, as this seen by some as socially embarrassing. They shave their beard gradually over years. Seventh, there has been lately a trend whereby men have short beards as a sign of beauty and fashion.

782. Having a White Face When Dying: There is a belief that, if the face of a person who has just died turns into black, this means this person is a sinner. If the face becomes white or there is a smile on the face, this means that the person is a good believer.

783. Being a Judge: <u>First</u>, all judges are supposed to be strong believers. In other words, one cannot be a judge unless one is a faith-specialised scholar and moreover a strong believer. <u>Second</u>, one must be religious (or, at least, pro-religion) to study religion.

784. Being a 'Scholar': The word 'scholar' is used to refer only to faith-specialised scholars. In other words, only faith-specialised scholars are considered and called 'scholars'. Individuals, organisations and authorities approach faith-specialised scholars and ask them how to handle public matters (for example, banking, economics, law and politics) and private matters (for example, marriage, divorce, intercourse, menstruation and pregnancy), since faith in the country regulates almost every aspect of public and private lives. Hence, being a faith scholar is demanding, requiring one to gain so much knowledge and to be always updated with social, cultural, political and economic affairs. Three presidents of the national council of senior scholars are blind.

785. There are certain signs that show a woman to be a strong believer:

786. Modest Clothing: At times, a man is judged by the veil of his wife (i.e. how covered she is and how modest her clothing is), thus symbolising the veil as a sign of reputation. One's wife is seen by some as a symbol of one's honour or one's reputation. If people talked about one's wife negatively, he would defensively respond 'Don't touch my honour!'.

787. Full Covering: <u>First</u>, if a woman is totally covered (wearing gloves and shoes and covering eyes, to the extent that one can find it difficult to figure out her skin colour and her age), this is a sign of her (and/or her husband) being a stronger believer. <u>Second</u>, many women do not want to be seen unveiled in the presence of non-related men, even if these men are physically far away, e.g. half a kilometre away.

788. Some veiled women try to look provocative, even though one purpose of the veil is not to attract men. Some of them like the attention, but they cannot simply stop wearing the veil as this might expose their imperfections or they can be harassed by tradition authorities and by the public. Despite the fact that women are fully covered, there are certain things which a woman does to make her appear provocative, engaging, non-conservative and/or expressive. Here are some of them:

789. Elaborated Cloaks: A veiled woman may make the traditionally black cloak sparkling, decorated and colourful. Instead of wearing a traditionally plain black cloak, some women have started to wear the cloak in various dark colours with adornments and accents, so as to put on show their beauty. A veiled woman may use her traditional veil and outfit as a tool to accent her best features and hide her imperfections (e.g. double chins, big brows, pimples on the forehead/chin or other flaws).

790. Elaborated Belongings: A veiled woman may have a fancy mobile phone, handbag and sunglasses to make her appear provocative, expressive and/or engaging. A manifestation of power for some women is to have a fancy handbag (although it is normally fake branded), as it is one of the few things with which they can show off, given that they are covered with the black cloak and the veil.

791. Elaborated Make-up: Some women cover their face except their eyes. Hence, a woman may perfect eye make-up, since eyes are the only part of her body that is exposed to the outside world and through which she shares with the outside world not only her feelings but also her beauty.

792. Fancy Perfume: First, to show and stress their beauty, some women wear a great deal of perfume (and yet they do not have a headache). They have perfume bottles in their handbag and refresh their smell from time to time. Second, when entering some classes in the female (or even male) campus, one feels as if one has just entered a perfume shop. It is common not only among women but moreover among men to wear perfume on a daily basis. Third, if a man smells like any female perfume that is not his wife's, this will bring him into question by the wife.

793. Colourful Lens: The typical female Saudi has black eyes or very dark brown eyes that look black. Nevertheless, some wear colourful lenses for events (e.g. weddings) so as to make the colour of their eyes match the colour of their dresses.

794. Sharped Shoulders: Conservative women wear the cloak in a way that goes over the head, therefore hiding their shoulders. That is, they appear not to have shoulders, as the cloak goes from the head down to the toe. Non-conservative women wear the cloak in a way that does not go over the head. They hang the cloak on their shoulder, revealing the shape of their shoulder. That is, the cloak goes from the shoulder (not from the head) down to the toe. Some men find it more 'provocative' when women wear the cloak from the shoulders instead of from the top of the head. Hence, some women display their beauty by wearing the cloak from the shoulders.

795. Branded Clothing: For example, the most popular brand for the veil is named '*Without Name*'.

796. Sashaying: To make her appear engaging, a veiled woman may sashay, swinging her hips and being light on her feet.

797. Shaking Buttocks: Men tend to find it provocative when a woman moves her buttocks up and down quickly and constantly. Hence, there are videos on social media wherein female users shake their buttocks. In general, Saudi men tend to fanaticise about female buttocks.

798. There are certain norms and practices regarding the Holy Book:

799. Frequent Reading: Reading frequently the Holy Book is part of the culture. It is normal to see a man or woman having in their handbag or in their pocket a copy of the Holy Book, which s/he takes out and reads on the go (e.g. on trains or planes). Nowadays, many individuals have the Holy Book as a phone application, which they use to read the Holy Book on the train, in the mosque or while resting.

800. Singing: When reading out the Holy Book, people 'sing' it (yet with no instrument). There are certain rules of how one sings the Holy Book.

801. School Day: At the very beginning of school day, part of the Holy Book is sung using loudspeakers, while male students are standing in lines, followed by students doing collective exercises guided by a sports educator and then collectively singing the National Anthem (without any instrument). Although teachers are present during this activity and ceremony, they neither exercise nor sing the National Anthem. The National Anthem is: '*Hasten... To glory and supremacy... Glorify the Creator of the sky... And raise the green flag... Carrying the written light-reflecting guidance... Repeat: God is great... O my country... My country... Live as the pride of Muslims... Long live the King... For the flag... And the homeland...*'.

802. Emotion: It is acceptable, normal and moreover preferable that a man cries (even in public) when reading or listening to the Holy Book. Such crying is interpreted positively as a sign of genuine engagement with what is written in the Holy Book.

803. Memorising: It is common that people read and moreover memorise word-for-word the whole Holy Book, which is around 80,000 words long. There are local and national competitions over how to memorise (and sing well) the Holy Book.

804. Schooling: There are primary, middle and high schools called '*Schools for the Memorisation of the Holy Book*'. These schools replace normal schools and focus on religious courses. Students of these schools, unlike other students, get a monthly allowance of US$70 (for primary school students), US$140 (for middle school students) and US$160 (for high school students).

805. Every year, people do not eat, drink, smoke, lick (e.g. licking ice-cream) or have intercourse during daylight hours for one month (i.e. the holy month). There are certain cultural norms and practices associated with this month:

806. Fasting: <u>First</u>, restaurants are closed during the daylight of the holy month. <u>Second</u>, during the daylight of the holy month, even non-believers are supposed *not* to eat in the presence of others and in public, so as to show <u>respect</u> to this month and to believers <u>Third</u>, although people are supposed to pray during the daylight of the holy month, most of them sleep once the sun rises and wake up once the sun sets. This helps these people not feel hungry during the day. That said, there is a recent phenomenon whereby people go for a walk or even run just before the sunset (when their hunger reaches a peak). Many think that this walk or run is particularly healthy. <u>Fourth</u>, travellers, sick people and women during their menstrual cycle do not have to fast during the daylight of the holy month. That said, the days that they have not fasted must be replaced at any time of the year. That is, they are supposed to fast for the same number of days as those of the holy month that they have not fasted. <u>Fifth</u>, once a child hits the age of 6-9, s/he will start practicing fasting (e.g. fasting merely for a few hours). If s/he hits the age of 9-12, s/he will try to fast for the whole day.

807. Functioning: <u>First</u>, despite not eating during the daylight of the holy month, employees still go to work, and students go to school and take exams. That said, working hours for most companies are reduced to only 6 hours of work per day during this month. <u>Second</u>, in some workplaces, working hours for believers are shorter by around two hours than those for non-believers. <u>Third</u>, pregnant women or breast-feeding mothers are supposed to fast during the daylight of the holy month unless they sense that fasting may cause risks to the baby. <u>Fourth</u>, some radio and TV channels stop broadcasting modern instrumental music and replace it with traditional one and acapella.

808. Marrying: There is no marriage or wedding during the holy month, for various reasons. First, there is a concern that, after having just got married, one may not help but have intercourse during daylight. Second, since one fasts, one feels weak to organise a wedding and give good first impressions to one's partner. Third, one is supposed to be busy praying and getting closer to God, not organising a wedding and spending one's time courting one's partner. Fourth, weddings can involve music and fun, thus affecting the divine spirit of this month. Given that there is no wedding during this month. Yet, soon after the month is over, there is an influx of weddings, to the extent that some get invited to more than one wedding in a single night.

809. Entertaining: First, during the holy month, it is normal that people stay up all night, eating, watching TV and hanging out with families and friends. Channels are normally busy throughout the year preparing shows for the holy month. Some of these shows are culture-oriented, but many of them are not. Second, because of the belief that modern music is sinful, some TV and radio channels stop playing modern music during the holy month; to show respect to its holy nature.

810. Desiring: First, if one has intercourse during the daylight of the holy month, this is a sin. To redress this sin, one has to fast during daylight hours for 60 consecutive days. If, however, one cannot do such fasting of 60 consecutive days, one feeds 60 poor people. Second, masturbation, in general, is not allowed. For some, if one masturbates during the daylight of the holy month, this will break one's fasting for that day. One has to compensate for this day at any time in the year. Third, during the holy month, there is a noticeable decline in how many times the Arabic word of 's*x' is looked up online, implying that the holiness of this month discourages some people from thinking about eroticism, at least during daylight hours. According to Google Trend, people look up the word 's*x' less during the holy month. There is, however, normally a peak on the first day after this month, perhaps because people are 'starved' for eroticism.

811. Eating: <u>First</u>, fathers have a special, generous budget for the food supplies of the holy month. Just before the holy month starts, people do intensive shopping, buying food supplies in preparation for this month. Mothers and sisters spend the whole day cooking and preparing for this feast. <u>Second</u>, although people do not eat during the daylight of the holy month, a great feast is served when the sun is set to break their fast. Many people over-eat once the sun is set. There are many cases where ambulances are called for those people who get sick or even pass out because they have over-eaten after fasting for the whole day. <u>Third</u>, outside the holy month, there is served only one tray that is full of rice, and there is meat on the rice. Yet, for the holy month, there is no such a tray, and instead, there are served many small plates, each of which has a different kind of food - more like tapas. <u>Fourth</u>, for the national celebration (the one which takes place right after the holy month and which is intended for celebrating that the holy month is over), people do not prepare a feast, although they are religiously expected to. Yet, they do prepare feasts for every day during the holy month, although they are religiously *not* supposed to, since a main aim of fasting during the holy month is to show consideration of the poor. Even the poor themselves feel pressured by society (and therefore by their children) to prepare feasts. Because of this pressure, the poor report sparing a special budget for this holy month and financially struggling particularly during this month.

812. Fast-Breaking: First, to break one's fast, one is supposed to eat three dates. This is why when one is at the restaurant and asks for any meal during the time of breaking one's fast, three dates come with the meal (normally for free). Second, during the time where people are supposed to be breaking their fast, there are some 'good people', standing by traffic lights and giving away packages of food to drivers. This initiative is appreciated by poor and non-poor drivers. During that time and on the train, these packages are also given to passengers for free. Third, it is common that people accidentally eat during daylight and yet either they remember and therefore stop immediately or those around them will remind them. They eat accidentally because they are not used to fasting. If one eats accidentally, one is forgiven. Fourth, some 'good people' build large tents next to mosques, where there are served feasts around the sunset, so that people can come and break their fast. Different people from different countries and ethnicities visit these tents. These tents are well-visited and can be large to the extent that there can be one tent for people with a common language. So, there can be a tent for those who can speak Filipino. There are activities and events inside these tents.

813. In daily life, one's mind is directed toward traditional and religious norms. What one sees in everyday life reminds one of traditional and religious values. The social atmosphere is tradition-oriented and religion-oriented. In daily life, one comes across and therefore sees a considerable number of instructions and reminders regarding tradition and religion. Here are some examples of these instructions and reminders:

814. Highways: First, when one drives on highways, there are road-signs throughout roads constantly reminding one of traditional and religious norms and values. Second, people stop on highways to pray in the open on the sidewalk. Some carry the prayer mats in their cars for this reason. People pray even in the desert.

815. Traffic Lights: When one stops at traffic lights, there are signs next to them reminding one of traditional and religious norms and values. Such signs are put up not by tradition authorities, but rather by citizens themselves. People are encouraged to do that because *every* time a driver reads the sign, they will get a holy reward.

816. Stickers: Some individuals print a very large number of stickers, on which is written something like: '*Do not forget God*'. On these stickers, there is a note: '*If you would like to get such stickers for free to distribute them, call this number XXX*'. These stickers are glued on walls, lifts, traffic lights, doors and others. The size of these stickers is 10cm × 5cm.

817. Graffiti: Graffiti displays traditional and religious values.

818. Messaging: First, it is widely common that one sends almost daily messages to one's contacts via social networks, reminding them of traditional and religious norms and values. Second, random text messages are sent by telecommunication operators or third parties reminding receivers of traditional and religious norms and values.

819. Tweeting: People tweet extensively in favour and support of traditional and religious norms and values.

820. Saying: While standing up or sitting, many individuals say in a heard voice: '*O' God*'.

821. Curriculum: A large component of the national curriculum is tradition-oriented.

822. Degree: A degree in Saudi tradition and religion is commonly held (especially by women).

823. Funding: It is easier for researchers to gain funding if their research is tradition-oriented.

824. Publications: Any form of written and verbal communication incorporates traditional and religious values. First, at the beginning of academic and non-academic books and letters, traditional terms or sentences are written, reminding one of traditional and religious norms and values. Second, in theses and dissertations, many graduates state and stress their loyalty to their tradition and religion, in the acknowledgements section. *Third*, many individuals include in any letter an extensive amount of religious wording and sentences, regardless of the letter is religious or non-religious and regardless of whether receivers are fellow Saudis or even foreigners.

825. Mosques: First, since mosques are widely spread throughout neighbourhoods, they act as consistent reminders of religion. Second, in most organisations and workplaces, there is a space dedicated to prayer.

826. Restaurants: In houses, restaurants and hotels, there are wall plaques in which traditional and religious sentences are written.

827. Rear-View Mirrors: It is common that people hang traditional and religious statements on the rear-view mirror.

828. Marriage: In the first year of marriage, some take their wives on a pilgrimage. For some of them, such a start would help bless their married life.

829. Discussing: During online written discussions in web-based forums, some people from time to time make a common that is *totally* irrelevant to the discussion. This comment aims to merely remind others of religion. Such a comment can be '*Do not forget God*'. Put differently, in threaded conversations, there are, at times, irrelevant messages that have nothing to do with the topic and yet are intended to remind converters of religious norms and values.

830. Naming: At times, streets and children are named after traditional and religious figures.

831. Tradition Authorities: Tradition authorities have their own cars, driving around to ensure the implementation of traditional norms. They have large fancy cars wherein there are a tradition agent, policeman and driver. They also walk on foot in public places to make sure everything is consistent with traditional and religious values.

832. Apps: Some have phone applications that orally remind them of prayer times and of traditional and religious values.

833. Much of what is heard in daily life directs one toward traditional and religious values and norms. Here are some examples.

834. Media: <u>First</u>, many acapella songs on the TV and radio stations remind one of traditional and religious values and norms. <u>Second</u>, there are live TV shows, wherein traditional and religious figures are present. The public calls these figures and enquiries about traditional matters. Third, there has been an intensive production, marketing and consumption of free audio files (which started as cassettes and now have taken a digital form) and books that encourage people to remain or become closer to traditional and religious values and norms.

835. Shops: First, there is a device attached to the door of some shops, which reminds one of traditional and religious values every time one opens the door. Second, in shops (e.g. garages, restaurants and juice shops), a religious TV or radio channel is turned on during working hours; reminding customers of traditional and religious values. This is also done because of the belief that having a religious voice in the background in the shop will make the shop blessed and therefore successful.

836. Train: First, at the beginning of a train or plane journey, there is an announcement reminding one of traditional and religious norms. Second, some people use their phones in public (e.g. on the train) to play traditional and religious audio and video clips without using headsets, so as to remind the public of traditional values and norms.

837. Cars: When turning on some cars, the player will turn itself on and articulate certain cultural and religious sentences, reminding drivers and passengers of cultural values.

838. Ringtones: Ringtones are, at times, used to remind the public of particular traditional and religious values and norms.

839. Companies: Telecommunication companies have launched a feature that enables the caller to hear a religion-oriented song instead of the normal dialtone.

840. Mothers: At their house, many mothers turn on a religious TV or radio channel and keep it in the background 24/7 even if no one is at the house, for various reasons. <u>First</u>, this is intended to constantly remind children of religious values and norms. <u>Second</u>, this is done because of the belief that having a religious voice in the background at the house will make the house blessed and make bad ghosts run away from the house. <u>Third</u>, this is done because potential thieves will think that there are some people at the house, even though there could be no one at the house.

841. Bookstores: There are a large number of tradition-focused and religion-focused sections at bookstores and libraries spread throughout cities. In generic bookstores, tradition-oriented and religion-oriented publications occupy so much space at the stores and their main areas. There are bookstores and libraries that are dedicated only to tradition-focused and religion-focused books. Moreover, religion-oriented books are given away to spread traditional and religious norms. They are passed around quite freely and can be found in various non-Arabic languages.

842. Affirmations: Traditionally and religiously positive public affirmations are acceptable, even when expressed randomly and out of context.

843. Schools: The school day starts with the reading of religious sentences.

844. Marriage: There is a welcome-to-married-life package that includes books and audio materials. This pack gives advice about married life from a traditional and religious perspective. However, it does not address eroticism.

845. Microphones: In any venue, when people test out microphones, many repeat '*in the name of God*'.

846. There are certain practices and norms regarding death:

847. Announcement: Once one dies, one's death is announced through two different channels. First, a text is written and shared through WhatsApp groups. In this text, it is written the name of the dead and their spouse, siblings and children. This is in addition to when and where the dead is collectively prayed for and buried. Second, graveyard organisations have Twitter accounts, tweeting about who has just died and when and where praying for the dead takes place.

848. Timing: When one dies, one's body is buried as soon as possible (which can be within a few hours), so the body is still 'warm'. This means that burying can take place during weekdays.

849. Cleaning: In some cities, there are a number of organisations that are in charge of cleaning dead people and make them ready to be burred. This service is done free of charge. The body is watered and washed (for free), and perfume is put on it. There is no make-up put on the body. There are associations that are in charge of washing dead people before they are put into graves. Dead people are to be washed in certain, detailed ways.

850. Viewing: The whole body is wrapped in white, excluding the face. Relatives can come from both genders to see the body and say goodbye.

851. Burning: The act of burning dead bodies is not allowed.

852. Coffins: There is no coffin. Rather, the dead is placed on a reusable large wood platter that has bars similar to ladders.

853. Praying: Just before burying, individuals pray in a mosque for the dead in an organised way. That is, a prayer leader (who can be anyone) stands behind the dead (who is placed in a platter that is borrowed for free, not rented or bought), and the rest of prayers stand behind the leader. This prayer takes around just two minutes. All prayers are men. Once the prayer is over, the dead is taken to the graveyard.

854. Shipping: It is normal to ship dead bodies to the holy mosque, for two reason. One is the special holiness of the mosque, assumingly making the dead get more holy rewards. The second is that the holy mosque has more prayers, meaning that more people will pray for the dead who will assumingly get accordingly more holy rewards.

855. Burying: Only male family members, friends, neighbours and colleagues are invited to bury the dead (normally in short notice, for example, just few hours before burying takes place). The dead is placed in a hole (its depth around one metre, its length less than two metres and its width less than one metre). Holes are made by a truck, before the arrival of the dead. The truck remains there during the time of burying and is not hidden. People use their hands and shovels to take the sand and throw it in the hole to bury the dead. The act of placing the dead body in the ground is a practice reserved only for men.

856. Landmarks: After the dead is buried, a stick or pipe is placed on the grave to identify the grave from other graves, in case that relatives want to come and visit the grave in the future. That is, one can come and visit graves——yet, only men are allowed in graveyards. One is not allowed to do anything elaborate with the grave (e.g. writing the name of the dead on the grave or placing special stones or flowers). Because of those sticks and pipes placed on graves, graveyards appear as 'landfill sites'. There are no flowers in graveyards. In other words, people do not bring flowers when visiting dead people. Tenth, no pictures (e.g. selfies) are taken at all, at any point of burying events. In the death certificate, the cause of death is not mentioned.

857. Ceremony: There is no speech, no preaching and no ceremony associated with death. That said, a farm or venue is rented, wherein the close relatives of the dead stay for certain hours (e.g. from 4:00 pm to 8:00 pm) for a few days (e.g. three days) and wherein guests come over to share their condolences. The number of guests is between 1500 and 3000. Guests come over for a few minutes and throughout the visiting hours. Guests are not only the relatives, friends and colleagues of the dead but, moreover, the friends and colleagues of the dead's relatives. They come over not necessarily to honour the dead but to support the relatives of the dead.

858. Gender: Although women are not allowed in graveyards, they are allowed in the farm or venue where condolences are shared. That is, in the farm, there can be a section for men and a section for women. Normally, only female non-virgins attend, whereas female virgins stay at home and take care of children since children are not allowed to attend. Male virgins and non-virgins can attend. During the event, some male close relatives cry but normally quietly for a short time. Many women (whether they are relatives or non-relatives) cry (whether genuinely or falsely) and normally loudly for a long time. Women remain in their black outfit (including covering their hair in black) for the whole event, even though there are no men in presence among them. Men are in their white traditional outfit. It is particularly socially unacceptable to come to these events in non-traditional outfit (e.g. trousers).

859. Dining: At times, dinner is served at the venue. Apart from the cost of the venue (between US$300 and US$1000) and dinner (between US$300 and US$700), death ceremony costs hardly anything.

860. Inheritance: <u>First,</u> because women tend to be dependent on men, many women inherit hardly anything, except a few gold necklaces, rings and bracelets. <u>Second,</u> people are not excited about keeping some of the dead's stuff for memory. <u>Third,</u> many families use the money of the dead to build a mosque or make a water well in Africa (a place that many nationals associate with poverty).

861. Condolence Phrases: <u>First,</u> there are no memorials. <u>Second,</u> to offer condolences to others, some would say: *'May God make your reward great/multiply'*. Others would then respond: *'Our reward, and your reward'*. Phrases for offering condolences are *'May God have mercy on him/her and pardon him/her'*, *'May God let him/her live in His spacious gardens'* and *'The continuation/rest is in your head'*.

862. Shocks: The death of fathers is perceived by many children as an emotional shock, even if these children are old (e.g. in their 40s).

863. Car Accidents: Death due to accidents has become so common to the extent that some take such death for granted. If a teacher tells his students about the death of their peer due to an accident, that may not trigger a reaction from these peers since they are used to such death stories. The problem is not only that the rate of accidents is high, but moreover that accidents are dramatic and severe.

864. Ghosts: Some believe that *'one may die if one takes pictures of ghosts, and if one stares at the dark, one will be killed by a host who will think that one has seen the ghost'*.

865. Intercourse: <u>First</u>, after the death of her husband, a woman can get married again after a few months——or once she gives birth if she is pregnant. During these months, she cannot leave the house unless it is necessary. That said, men can get married immediately after the death of their wives. <u>Second</u>, for one particular sacred deathday, some people hate having intercourse on this day. <u>Third</u>, a man is allowed to marry his sister-in-law only if his wife is dead. In other words, he cannot be married to two sisters who are both alive. If one's wife passes away, one can then marry her sister.

866. Writing: <u>First</u>, even in a non-religious (e.g. academic) book, letter and talk, when a dead person is mentioned, the phrase *'May God be merciful to him/her'* is at times placed after his/her name. <u>Second</u>, when an important person is mentioned, the phrase 'May God protect him/her' is at times placed after his/her name. In other words, if the phrase *'May God be merciful to him/her'* is placed after the name of a person, this means that this person is dead. <u>Third</u>, if the phrase *'May God protect him/her'* is placed after the name of a person, this means that this person is still alive.

867. There are certain norms and practices regarding hygiene and cleanness:

868. Highways: Although many people travel extensively by car within the country, they, however, do not have a 'rest-places' *culture* on roads. Indeed, there are gas stations on roads with facilities, but most of these facilities are limited, disorganised and dirty. Hygiene in public spaces and facilities is low. For example, gas stations are dirty and disgusting places. Restrooms at gas stations (and public places) are very dirty and smelly. Moreover, the ground of gas stations is full of potholes. Supermarkets at gas stations normally look unsophisticated and old.

869. Cleanness: Many men and women wear a great quantity of cologne and moreover dress up whenever they go out. Many maintain a high level of cleanness, not only in terms of dressing well and wearing cologne but moreover in terms of shaving their underarm hair on a regular basis.

870. Bins: <u>First</u>, in many households, taking out the trash is the duty of men. <u>Second</u>, ghosts are believed by some individuals to be located around/at bins. Hence, some are worried that they may accidentally hit (and therefore upset) a ghost while throwing rubbish into bins. For this reason, some say '*In the Name of God*' while throwing rubbish into bins, so as to be protected against ghosts.

871. Windows: There is no cleaning-window culture. The windows of many buildings (e.g. the windows of houses and shops) do not get cleaned, whether from the inside or outside.

872. Throat: Some (particularly old) Saudis constantly clean their throat and spit in public. Yet, blowing one's nose, in public, whether for men or women, is not preferable.

873. Pollution: Concern about car pollution is limited. For example, having BBQs and picnic can take place on highways, with no consideration of car pollution (and safety).

874. Teeth: Many individuals use a piece of a tree (which is twice the length of a finger and is slightly smaller than one's little, pinky finger) to brush their teeth. They use this piece of a tree while socialising (e.g. while walking, talking and during meetings)——this practice is socially acceptable (and moreover preferable).

875. Laptop: Men and women's laptops tend to be exceptionally dirty. They do not clean them, just as they do not clean their house or shop windows.

876. There are certain norms and values regarding celebration:

877. Values: Having fun (and, indeed, *how* to have fun) is not a traditional value. Many have negative attitudes towards fun. For some individuals, fun is 'a waste of time' and 'is for kids'. Some do not have fun because they are 'lazy', conventional or conservative. Fun is seen by some individuals as something 'bad' and something that comes from 'the devil'. Free time (i.e. when one is not busy with something productive and serious) is seen negatively by many, who believe that such time is more likely to be misused by humans to do something bad, since humans are seen by some to be, essentially, bad. For some, having fun makes one look 'stupid' and makes others laugh at one. Even for major occasions (e.g. national celebrations and national days), there are limited institutionally-organised fun activities. National celebrations are not socially seen by many individuals as fun-oriented activities, but rather as events wherein one exchanges visits with one's very extended families. National celebrations involve limited institutionally-organised fun activities.

878. Camel Celebration: There is an annual 'Camel Festival', which is believed to be the largest camel festival in the world. It involves two competitions. <u>First Competition</u> is a competition for the most beautiful camels. Individuals can participate in the competition with 100 camels, 50 camels, 30 camels, 20 camels or single camels. The categorisation of camels is based on colour: white, yellow, between yellow and red, red and black. There is a committee judging the beauty of these camels. There are 10 winners for each category. The first, second and third winners get US$260,000 each, and the rest get US$26,000 each. Some owners inject the lip of their camels with a particular protein to make their lip look more attractive to judges. Some illegal drugs are given to camels so as to make them faster in the contest. <u>Second Competition</u> is for the fastest camels, with many camels competing in courses. There are side activities, such as exhibitions showing the tallest camel, the shortest camel and a camel that has dots (as if it is a cow). This is in addition to a traditional market and a theatre with musical concerts and plays.

879. Literary Days: There are 16 literary clubs in various cities. They exist as official associations, each of which has a board of directors. Some have their large building with modern interior design and a large theatre hall. They hold literary contests (e.g. for the best poem or artwork) and events in celebration of '*World Poetry Day*', '*World Book Day*' and '*International Arabic Language Day*'. They feature important cultural figures or towns (e.g. poets, short stories, novelists and travellers). They feature books or act as a publisher and therefore publish people's books. They organise academic and non-academic talks, conferences and seminars. They hold 'Poetry Evenings' and 'Storytelling Evenings'. They sponsor visual arts exhibitions. They exist within the traditional boundaries. They used to be for men. However, an initiative has been taken to welcome women to these clubs, but there have been campaigns against such an initiative. Despite these campaigns, some clubs have formed a 'female committee'. Other clubs have gone further and included women in their board of directors.

880. Wedding Anniversary: Celebrating a wedding anniversary is not part of the culture and is even seen by some as a sin. There have been campaigns intended to discourage people from thinking about celebrating their wedding anniversary. The campaigns argue that such a celebration is a western value and is therefore not to be done and followed.

881. Birthday Celebration: Everyone has two birthdays a year: according to Arabic and English calendars. Yet, some celebrate neither of them, since such celebration is seen by some as a foreign value. There is a concern among some that, if the idea of birthdays becomes common in the country, the consequences will be dire, for various reasons. First, one's life will be full of birthday celebrations, as Saudis have many friends, connections, siblings and cousins. Second, turning down one's invitation is rude and results in deep social complications. Third, a celebration of birthdays will be very expensive and time-consuming, given that many Saudis like and expect elaborate parties and fancy presents.

882. Deathday Celebration: An ideological minority celebrate around 30 sacred birthdays and deathdays. For certain sacred birthdays and deathdays, there are themes, involving some kind of dramas. For example, a sacred figure was killed on his wedding day. So, when people gather for his deathday, the occasion starts with a sense of happiness simulating the happiness of his wedding. Then, the atmosphere suddenly promotes a sense of sadness, simulating his sudden death during his wedding. To enhance this simulation, there are candelas that attendants move around. For sacred deathdays (and birthdays), an ideological minority gather to read out and sing poems and/or listen to lectures. Poems are not sung using instruments, since using instruments is a culturally sensitive issue. On the one hand, if it is a sacred birthday, the read poems promote a sense of happiness, and the lectures show how the person was born. On the other hand, if it is a sacred deathday, the read poems promote a sense of sadness, and the lectures show how the person died. At the end of sacred birthday and deathday celebrations, food is served.

883. Valentine's Day: Tradition authorities ensure that shops, on Valentine's Day, do not sell anything red, preventing citizens and residents from celebrating this Day. The celebration of Valentine's Day is rejected by many for various reasons. <u>First</u>, this celebration is a value of other faiths. <u>Second</u>, love between lovers should be exchanged throughout the year; not only on this Day. <u>Third</u>, Valentine's Day is merely a business idea promoted by the business sector to get money out of people. Some are active on social networks warning their fellow Saudis not to make a religious mistake by celebrating Valentine's Day. Many brochures and handouts are distributed against the celebration of Valentine's Day. That said, there can be, accidentally, sold at shops Christmas decorations given the lack of understanding among tradition authorities and even shop-owners regarding what are (and are not) considered Christmas decorations.

884. Christmas and New Year: In social media and communication applications, many campaigns against Christmas and New Year's celebrations, which come from other faiths. Many Saudis do not recognise the difference between Christmas and New Year's celebrations; yet, they campaign against them. During foreign occasions (e.g. Christmas), the Saudi customs become strict, in the sense that they do not allow in anything that is in line with these occasions. To illustrate, during Christmas' time, no passenger is allowed to bring into the country anything red. To go around this restriction, some non-Saudis (and Saudis) go to Bahrain to buy some Christmas decorations and get them wrapped as 'presents' so as to prevent the Saudi customs from knowing what these presents actually are. These Saudis buy Christmas decorations and use (or 'misuse') them for their own celebrations, since these decorations are seen to look 'nice' and 'flashy'.

885. Religious Celebrations: There are two religious (national) celebrations a year. The first celebration is right after the holy month. The other is almost two months after the first celebration. For these celebrations, people wake up before the sunrise, collectively pray during the sunrise, start exchanging visits during the morning, take a long nap during the afternoon and then continue exchanging visits in the evening until late at night. For these celebrations, it is common that people exchange messages with fancy wording, wishing others happy celebrations. These messages are normally not genuine, as their wording is 'stolen' from the Internet. People merely copy an existing text, select all their contacts and send the text to them.

886. Family-Pride Celebration: Intellectual practices are attributed not only to individuals but moreover to their whole extended family. That is, some extended families celebrate and feel proud when one of their members makes an achievement. Some of them organise very large parties (with hundreds of invitees) in celebration of a family member obtaining a master's degree or having a managerial position, for example.

887. Children Celebration: In some towns, some parents hold a special party for their infants and small children that takes place in the middle of the holy months. They produce elaborate packs of sweets and nuts. They invite other children to the party. At times, children knock on house doors, singing and asking for sweets.

888. Mother's Day: There is a campaign again Mother's Day. This campaign is popularised through social networks, where texts, hashtags and posters against this Day are shared and exchanged. Some campaigners argue that this Day is for those 'losers' who remember their mother only once a year but know nothing about her for the rest of the year.

889. Remarks: <u>First</u>, many are unproductive at work, as they are distracted by many social events throughout the year. Saudis first get ready for the 'holy month', then a national celebration, then the national day, then another national celebration, then summer, then a mid-term break, then a mid-year break, then a mid-term break, etc——actually, mid-term breaks have been cancelled in 2017. <u>Second</u>, turning 60 (or 30) years old does not hold any particular value. Hence, people do *not* throw a particular party for these ages or engage in any form of celebration. <u>Third</u>, female-only beauty salons offer 'henna', which women use to make artistic decorations on their hands and feet for weddings and celebrations. At times, almost the entire palm and/or the whole bottom of the feet are dipped in henna, making henna look as if one has gone with her feet and hands through mud. <u>Third</u>, when something good has happened to one, one is the one is expected to organise a party for others in celebration. This is even though in some other cultures, when something good has happened to one, others are the ones who are expected to organise a party for one in celebration.

890. There are certain norms and practices regarding resting and sleeping:

891. Yawning: When yawning, one is culturally supposed to put one's palm against one's open mouth.

892. Saying: '*Sleep is a Sultan whose orders are executed*'.

893. Professional Life: In general, it is common that workers come home in the afternoon and take a nap for around one hour. That said, many individuals, throughout the year and regardless of their age, normally have unusual and inconsistent sleeping hours and patterns. This is particularly true for women (who normally have no jobs), for students (who sleep during their classes) and for employees (who sleep during their work).

894. Dorm Rooms: There are hardly any female backpackers, since many norms and values of backpacking do not go well with the social nature of Saudi women. Saudi women would not normally accept to sleep on a bunk bed in a shared dorm room, especially if it is mixed-gender.

Interval

40 Saudi single men were asked: '*Have you ever flirted with a girl?*' 14 flirted with a girl. One did, but 'the experience was awful; full of pathetic dramas'. One did 'for four years. I have been still suffering from this. While praying or studying or before falling asleep, I get distracted by the kisses and foreplays I had with the girls. This scares me, as one day someone will do this to my sisters or daughters. God forbid'. One 'flirted with girls in various ways. At the beginning is love, and at the end is leaving'. Another respondent 'did it once and got caught by tradition authorities who asked me to sign that I would not do it again'. One did, but 'the experience was sh*t'.

For one participant, the experience was 'beautiful and unique'. For another, 'it was more like an experiment out of curiosity. I lost interest the moment the girl took my number. I only wanted to see if the girl was attracted to me'. One stated: 'Yes, but I quickly regretted'. One did it 'because of erotic desire and because we are religiously weak. I did this through WhatsApp and BBM, which caused a destruction of our families. I wish we did not know phones and flirtation'.

The rest (26 participants) had not flirted with a girl, as 'I see it as lack of propriety'. Flirtation 'can destroy the honour of the family's the woman being flirted with'. One is 'scared that one sees me flirting with a woman, and this will cause me a lot of trouble'. For some, it is 'wrong', 'harassment' and 'a sin'. One replied: 'No, no one tried to flirt with me'. One had 'no friends encouraging me to do this, thank God'. One does 'not want to put myself in a critical situation with a girl'. One does not 'have feelings for girls so much'. One fears 'God, and it is not part of my morality'.

Genitals

Gendering

895. There are certain norms and practices that vary based on whether one is female:

896. Reputation: Some believe that, when a 'female' makes a moral mistake, the reputation of the whole family consequently suffers. If she has a reputation for being a 'bad girl', all her male and female siblings are then at risk of being unmarriageable. On the other hand, if a 'male' makes the same mistake, he is the only one whose reputation suffers. Bearing these two contradicting social attitudes, when tradition authorities catch an unrelated male and female hanging out together, they normally arrest the male and release the female so as not to ruin her family's reputation.

897. Gum: The act of chewing gum is seen by some individuals as a sign of femininity. For this reason, some men avoid (and/or are criticised for) chewing gum in public.

898. Lies: It is believed that the following ten sentences are the most common lies among women. First, 'my children do not eat so much'. Second, 'my husband loves me so much'. Third, 'since the morning, I have not eaten any food'. Fourth, 'pregnancy has ruined the shape of my body'. Fifth, 'no one has as much patience as the patience I have'. Sixth, 'whenever I go to a wedding, mothers want me to be a wife for their sons'. Seventh, 'whoever sees me thinks I am young'. Eighth, 'no one believes that she is my daughter'. <u>Ninth,</u> 'I slept only for an hour last night'. <u>Tenth,</u> 'I got pregnant by mistake'.

899. Interests: 'Females' are made fun of for being into: make-up, shopping malls, shops, fashion, restaurants, TV shows, brands, clothes, gatherings, McDonald's and communication with friends via social media.

900. Blood Donation: There are blood donation events and campaigns. That said, blood donation is more common among men than women, based on a common belief that blood donation is not healthy for women.

901. Ear-Piercing: Ear-piercing is for women only and done when one is an infant.

902. Salaries: There is, in the public sector, no difference between male and female salaries.

903. Breasts: Some women try to make their breasts bigger. They do so by drinking rose water for a week or soymilk for three weeks.

904. Dresses: For weddings, wearing the same dress twice is embarrassing for many women. Many women have a large number of dresses. Many women design their own dresses. They have good design skills. Once the design of the dress is finished, they send it to a shop to turn this design into a reality. For weddings, man women's favourite dress designs are big, wide and long with many decorations and adornments. That is, they wear (elaborated) ballroom dresses. Short dresses (e.g. cocktail dresses) are discouraged even at female-only events and occasions, as they are short and therefore seen as inappropriate. However, a few women still wear them.

905. Jewellery: <u>First</u>, whereas in other countries, only 14 KT gold (which is less expensive and less valuable), in Saudi Arabia, it is common to find 18, 21, 22 KT gold, which is more valuable and better for trading and thus for investment. <u>Second</u>, one is not supposed to eat with gold or silver utensils. <u>Third</u>, for some, a man is not to wear any gold (be it yellow or white gold), including engagement and wedding rings. This is because if a man wears gold, this is believed to go against masculinity and religion. Normally, men wear only silver rings (not gold ones). Some believe that wearing gold increases female hormones and decreases male hormones. For some, when gold is worn on the skin, it is assumed to send its atoms into the blood. Such atoms cause serious medical problems. The female body, though, is believed to have the ability to get rid of such atoms through menstrual cycles. Some believe that wearing gold for a woman helps with the enhancement of the blood circulation in her body——this, however, does not apply to men.

906. Female Businesses: There are limited places where women can work. Because of this limitation, some women have tried to come up with their own business ideas. Some female businesses take place during parties and family gatherings. For example, many extended families gather together once a week at the houses of families' oldest members, or there is a hosting roster among the family members. Some women run a small business during their family gatherings; selling snacks, drinks and/or ice-cream. Some women run such businesses merely for fun (not really for profit).

907. Joints: At times, the skin of the female body's joints (i.e. knees, elbows, the back of the neck and moreover the genitals) is darker than the skin of the rest of the body, which is seen by many men as unattractive. Some think that the reason why the skin of the female genitals is darker is because women use water to clean their genitals, yet they do not dry these areas after using water, which consequently, in the long run, turns the skin of these areas into a darker skin.

908. 'True woman' is a social label that many women would like to win. This label is granted to those women who hold and practice the following cardinal virtues:

909. Religiousness: Hence, women tend to be (or act) more religious than men. They are normally the 'religion reinforcer' in the house.

910. Virginity: The life of particularly single women is restricted not only in terms of their exposure to men but moreover in terms of doing those activities (e.g. football, ice-skating and horse-riding) that are believed to possibly result in lost virginity by accident. Sport is seen by some as a risk to female virginity. Female virginity is crucial, as most single men want to marry a virgin woman for their first marriage.

911. Submission: Being obedient is a quality that many men look for in their potential spouse. Moreover, women are socially supposed to show erotic availability. That is, a woman is to say yes whenever her husband wants her for intercourse. If she says no, angels keep saying to her '*damn you*' until she accepts.

912. Domesticity: Hence, the term 'home' (or 'family') can mean 'one's wife', showing a sense of domesticity. In public, one's wife is normally referred to in general terms using such words as 'home' or 'family'. If a man asks his friend '*Where were you?*' he might reply '*I was out with my family*' or '*the home wanted me to do something*'. For many male marriage-seekers and their mothers, cooking is a key skill that a potential wife must have. It is the duty of 'good' mothers to train (from an early age) their female children to be good cooks. Normally, men do not cook for themselves, nor can they be found in the kitchen. Normally, men do not wash dishes. If people know of a man going to the kitchen (cooking and washing dishes), they may think of him as being dominated by his wife and may laugh at him.

913. Shyness: Being, or at least acting as, shy is seen by many as a good feature of women.

914. At times, Saudi society is organised in favour of women. Here are some examples:

915. Leave: Mothers can take parental leave whereas fathers cannot.

916. Delivery: In some universities, the cars of take-away shops and restaurants always go into the female campus to deliver food and supplies to students. This phenomenon, however, hardly exists in the male campus. Besides, local grocery stores offer delivery to houses (i.e. to women), as long as the bill is at least US$2.5. Women call local grocery stores and ask for delivery even chocolate bars. The common delivery services to the domestic domain are appreciated particularly by women, for four reasons. First, many women do not walk even for short distances. Second, female accessibility to the public domain is limited. Third, some women feel neither comfortable nor confident going to grocery stores, even if these stores are in their neighbourhood. Fourth, some men prevent their female family members to go alone to even nearby grocery stores or restaurants. This prevention is as a consequence of 'male authoritarianism', or because these men are worried that these women may get harassed by male strangers.

917. Travelling: When going out or travelling with their families, men normally pay for everything and for everyone. Even if the wife has a salary that is higher than her husband's, he has the legal obligation to pay her expenses.

918. Marriage: Getting married costs women nothing and yet costs men a considerable amount of money. A groom gives a bride around US$10,000 in cash. This amount of money varies based on families' reputation and wealth. At times, money is given by a groom to a bride in an elaborate way. He may design a tree model, shapes the money in the form of leaves and hangs these 'leaves' on the tree. Brides spend, in a few weeks or months, the US$10,000 given to them by grooms. They spend them on gold, clothes and accessories in preparation for their new married life. Some brides buy 'portable cosmetics beauty cases'. A husband pays his wife US$10,000 (or half the amount) to divorce her. A woman can divorce her husband, but she has to pay him back the money he paid her to marry her. Families see the act of men giving away money for marriage and divorce as essential, making men take marriage and divorce seriously. There have been unsuccessful campaigns stressing the necessity for reducing the money given by grooms to brides.

919. Gifts: Some grooms buy jewellery for brides' mothers; not their fathers. They buy brides jewellery and pay for the wedding, honeymoon, flat rent and furniture. Furniture is designed to be exceptionally heavy and therefore difficult to be moved around. Despite such heaviness, many families constantly move around the pieces of furniture at their places. Furniture and decoration tend to be elaborated and have so many flowers and patterns.

920. Escorting: When a man is in the company of a woman, he gets various advantages. First, in some shopping malls at certain times, although a woman can get in alone, a man cannot get in unless he is escorted by a woman. Second, between cities and even inside cities, there are checkpoints. In these checkpoints, if there is a woman in the car, the driver is less likely to get stopped, because policemen are afraid of being accused of looking at another man's wife. Third, if a man wants to cross a street, no driver normally stops to let him cross. If, however, there is a woman with him, drivers more likely stop to let her cross.

921. Prayer: Men, unlike women, are supposed to wake up a few hours before sunrise and walk to the mosque to pray.

922. Education: There is a whole university that is dedicated to women. Another whole university had been dedicated to men until 2018, when women have been allowed to register. This means that, whereas there is a female-only university, there is no longer a male-only university.

923. There are certain norms and practices that vary based on whether one is male:

924. Help: A male's masculinity depends on how helpful he is to his female relatives. For example, a 'male' would not be considered 'man' if he did not carry the bags of his female relatives. The more a man makes his female relatives comfortable and less tired, the more of a 'man' he becomes.

925. Protection: First, a male's masculinity comes into question if anything bad happens to a woman, and he could not protect her. Second, the masculinity of a 'male' is questioned if a female relative of his has done anything immoral or traditionally inappropriate. Third, most men consider themselves to be protectors of any female. To illustrate, if a random woman on the street shouts out saying that the male stranger next to her is harassing her, all the men on the street (whether they know her or not) would take violent action against the harasser. Fourth, many Saudi men trust their fellow male Saudis a lot, but not when it comes to women (e.g. their female family members such as their wives, mothers and sisters). For instance, a man would trust his friend with his life, but not when it comes to his wife.

926. Bromance: 'Bromance' is a norm, with many men having close, emotionally intense bonds. It can be achieved, for example, through holding hands, hugging one another tightly, putting one's hand on another's shoulder, calling each other '*honey*', '*my love*', '*moon*' '*my lover*' or '*the lover of my heart*', travelling together and being 'there' for one another anytime. If a friend stays overnight at his (male) friend's place, it is acceptable if both share the same bed. That said, some Saudis are worried that, for some reason, their friends become their enemies who would use their secrets and weaknesses against them. This is why there is a saying that '*Beware of your enemies once and of your friends a thousand times*'.

927. Circumcision: Only men get circumcised. Circumcision happens normally during infanthood or childhood.

928. Touching Genitals: It is common to see men touching their genitals from time to time because of itchiness. Itchiness is, at times, related to the soap one uses and/or to the type of underpants. No observation is recorded of women touching their genitals.

929. Language: <u>First</u>, the Arabic word for a 'p*nis' is used to refer to a 'male'. In other words, the same word is used to speak of a 'male genital organ' or a 'male being'. <u>Second</u>, a man refers to his gentle as 'the equipment'.

930. Hairlessness: If a man has no hair on his skin, this is seen by some as a symbol of beauty and yet also as undermining one's masculinity.

931. At times, Saudi society is organised around gender in favour of men. Below are some examples:

932. Employment: <u>First</u>, many university majors and jobs (e.g. working as taxi drivers, judges, police and army) are exclusive to men. <u>Second</u>, if a woman works as a taxi driver, she is treated by men (and by other women) as if she has gone above societies, crossed moral boundaries, undertaken a 'cultural crime' and acted in a masculine way, thus becoming an outcast. <u>Third</u>, there are hardly any Saudi flight attendants. <u>Fourth</u>, some individuals do not like their female family members to work as nurses or medical doctors, since, in hospitals, the two genders socialise closely and loosely. Despite such an attitude, many men ask that their female family members to be checked by female nurses and female medical doctors; and yet, these men do not allow their female family members to work as nurses or medical doctors. This is why there are many *foreign* nurses and medical doctors. <u>Fifth</u>, women can work as teachers but not engineers, and there is no engineering degree for women. Those women who went abroad to study engineering cannot find a job at their country after they come back home and moreover are undermined by men and local companies. Many individuals believe that teaching, nursing and medicine are jobs that fit the 'nature' of women. Hence, many women work as teachers, nurses, medical doctors and at the female section of banks. Lately, some women have begun to work as security guards (yet within female-only sections), as receptionists, as cashiers and as salespeople. If a man works as a chef or nurse, he used to be seen by women as feminine and treated in a bullying way.

933. Salaries: Some men get all the salary of their wives and give them merely part of it. At times, wives' salary is transferred directly to husbands' account. In this case, wives get money from their salary only through their husbands. At times, some men want to marry women who work as teachers, because they are interested in these women's salary.

934. Weddings: Many wedding invitations display only the groom's name and the name of the bride's father.

935. Family Trees: Many families keep track of their family tree using a 'snake chart' representing family relationships in a conventional tree structure. This tree, in most cases, includes only male members.

936. Family Pictures: Many family pictures, or any public pictures, include only male family members.

937. Guardianship: Many employers ask women to bring a letter from their male guardian that states that he allows her to work. Every woman has to have a male guardian, who is her father. If a woman marries, her male guardianship is transferred from her father to her husband. The father loses complete guardianship rights to his daughter. If a woman's father and husband are dead, her oldest son takes over her guardianship. Some women complain about their son acting as an authoritative guardian.

938. Decisions: Many important (family and public) decisions are (to be) made by 'males'.

939. Events: Normally, when there is a public invitation to a public lecture, it is, by default, for men unless it is explicitly stated otherwise, e.g. unless it is stated that it is for families also/only.

940. Places: Many places (e.g. many restaurants and many coffee shops) are for men only. There are a limited number of coffee shops for women alone. There are youth hostels, including facilities such as table tennis and swimming pools. Youth hostels are only for men. There are a few hostels (i.e. around 20 hostels) in the country, with there being only one single hostel per main city. All these hostels belong to the *Youth Hostels Association* (YHA), and a membership is required for one to be allowed to book a bed. In other words, there are no *non-*YHA hostels. Some stay in hostels for months because they are cheaper (US$8 per bed). One must pay cash *daily* even if one is staying for months. The regulation is that one is not supposed to stay for more than 15 days, but this regulation is not strictly implemented.

941. Nobility: When people want to compliment a woman for being noble, they refer to her as *'the sister of noble men'*. So, the compliment does not go directly to her, but rather it goes *through her brothers* to her.

942. At events or public places, there are mostly two separate sections: for singles and for families. Here are some norms and practices regarding such a separation:

943. Terminology: The term 'family' refers to two types. Type 1 is any group that consists of two or more related people from different genders. Type 2 is any individual woman, whether her marital status is single or married. The term 'single' refers to all *individual* men, whether their marital status is single or married. Any man, who is not accompanied by a woman, is considered single, even if he is actually married. The singles' section is for single *males*. Single women go to the family section, even though they are actually single. A married man is considered a single as long as he is not escorted by women——the presence of any related woman (e.g. a sister) is believed to prevent many men from acting as 'bad boys' and flirting with women. If there is an event for singles only, women are not allowed, as the word 'singles' normally refers to single *men* alone.

944. Architecture: The norm is that there are singles' and families' section at restaurants, for example. At times, the families' section is divided into small rooms with a closed door or curtain. That is, there is a room per family. The waiter (i.e. a male one as there are no waitresses) does not enter a room before permission is given by the family inside the room. Every time the waiter wants to enter the room to deliver food or drink, he knocks on the door and waits until the women in the room re-cover their faces, and then the man of the family will let him in. At times, there are no such rooms at the families' sections, and rather tables are exposed to one another. In this case, the restaurant offers movable, flexible, non-transparent and long partitions which are provided based on requests. Customers can use these partitions to build walls all around their table so as to prevent other customers from seeing those sitting at the table. Once partitions are built all around the table, veiled women sitting at this table feel free to reveal their face, as no other customers can see them thanks to the partitions. Inside the small room at the restaurant, the way in which family members sit at the dining table is organised in a certain way, considering that some male family members are still not to see the face of some female family members (e.g. brothers are not to see the face of their sisters-in-law). In this case, although brothers and sisters-in-law sit at the same table, brothers are placed on certain chairs in a way that does not allow them to see the face of their sisters-in-law. For example, a brother will sit at the beginning of the dining table on the left whereas the sister-in-law will sit at the end of this table on the left, thus making it difficult for him to see her face. In this sitting position, the sister-in-law can, therefore, take off *only part* of her face-cover in a way that the brother cannot see her face. She shapes her face-cover in a way that makes it not possible for her brother-in-law to see her face. The husband of the sister-in-law will be located on the chair facing the chair of his wife, and therefore he can see her face and easily communicate with her.

945. Waiting: <u>First</u>, if a man drops by a governmental department for a particular matter, his wife waits at the car. She does not come with him, as women do not enter many governmental departments. He, moreover, rushes and places pressure on the employee to sort out his matter as quickly as possible, and the justification for such a rush and pressure is that his wife is being at the car. <u>Second</u>, when a couple or a family stops by a take-away shop, the wife stays at the car, and the husband goes to the shop and makes the order and then collects it. That is, most women do not feel comfortable going inside take-away shops because these shops are populated by male customers and because they, at times, do not have a section for female customers or even families.

946. At times, there are advantages and preferences for 'families' over 'singles'. Here are some examples.

947. Parks: At times, some parks are dedicated to families only, and no single men are allowed. That said, single women are allowed.

948. Train: On the train, it is announced that priority is given to families when leaving the train.

949. Threat: Married people see singles as threats to their partners.

950. Romance: Singles are presumed to become emotionally distressed when exposed to romantic and erotic happenings. It is unacceptable that, in public, a couple kisses (or holds hands, in some towns) so as not to hurt the feelings of singles. Any public expression of affection and love between spouses, between parents and children and between lovers is unacceptable in some areas.

951. Clothing: At times, only those men accompanied by women are allowed in female-specific clothing shops. This means that a married man cannot enter these shops to buy a surprising female-specific present for his wife, unless he is accompanied by his sister, mother or auntie.

952. Noise: Some forms of 'discrimination' against singles, at times, turn out to be good for them. For example, some singles like the fact that singles' and families' sections are separate, as this separation excludes families' *noisy* children.

Toileting

953. There are certain norms and practices regarding restrooms:

954. Stay: People are supposed to spend as little time as possible at restrooms because they are believed to be places where devils live.

955. Articulation: People are supposed to say certain sentences when going into and coming out of the restroom.

956. Tissue: There are no tissue papers at restrooms. People use water from a hose to clean their genitals. In some countries, restrooms do not offer water; so many Saudis take a bottle of water with them.

957. Drying: Although people use water to clean their genitals, they do not dry their watery genitals, which can cause a water spot on their clothes that the public can see. To overcome this problem (having a public wet spot on their clothes), people wear two layers of underwear that are intended to absorb this water, thus preventing others from noticing how wet one's bottom is after leaving restrooms.

958. Left Hand: People use their left hand for cleaning their genitals using water. Hence, people are supposed to use their right hand for eating or drinking. The right hand is to be used for clean stuff, whereas the left has is to be used for dirty stuff.

959. Left Leg: One is supposed to enter bad places with the left leg (e.g. restrooms) and in good places (e.g. mosques and houses) with the right leg. In contrast, one is supposed to exit bad places (e.g. restrooms) using the right leg.

960. Washing: People normally wash their hands after visiting the restroom.

961. Sitting: Normally, the two genders sit down for urination.

962. Holiness: People do not go to the restroom with anything that contains any sacred terms or sentences. Hence, they leave their bags outside the restroom, just in case their bags include something that consists of any sacred term or sentence. It is likely that belongings will _not_ be stolen if they are left outside the restroom, as people trust each other to a decent degree.

963. Tipping: Charges (or tips) for the use of restrooms do not exist. Some visitors to restrooms give money to restroom-keepers (i.e. Asians). This money is seen by these individuals _not_ as a charge or tip, but rather as a charity.

964. Teachers: In the presence of students, some teachers and professors avoid not only going to the restroom but moreover drinking water, because such acts are seen to undermine their profession. At times, teachers have their own restroom at school.

965. Shower: Some believe that one is, culturally, supposed to take a shower after intercourse.

966. Changing Rooms: Changing rooms are rare, because of social concern over hidden cameras. Hence, women normally take their newly purchased clothes to the nearest restroom to try them on. That said, there is no concern among people that there could be hidden cameras at restrooms as well.

967. Floor: The floor and sink of restrooms are always wet and dirty, because of the following reasons. First, people show little courtesy for the next occupant. Second, people wash their hands and feet for the five-a-day prayer. Third, people use water to clean their anus. After urinating or getting rid of solid waste matter from their body, one uses water to wash one's organ or bottom. This makes one's organ and bottom wet. However, because it is normally hot, they get dry quickly.

968. Knee: Knee problems are a common medical condition, because people put pressure on them through the following practices. <u>First</u>, people squat for resting, defecation and micturition. <u>Second</u>, for the five-a-day prayer, people bend their knees. <u>Third</u>, for eating and socialising, people sit on the ground and bend their knees. The most common way of sitting is sitting on the floor while bending the knees. Sitting with bent legs is done by crossing them over each other. The lower part of both legs is folded towards the body, crossing each other at the calf, with both ankles on the floor, with the feet tucked under the thighs.

969. Markings: Many markings in restrooms show erotic desire. Here are some of these markings. <u>First</u>, 'She is crazy, but I love her'. <u>Second</u>, 'I die for you'. <u>Third</u>, 'How come you love me, and you love somebody else? How come you have at your heart two people at the same time?' <u>Fourth</u>, 'One can see how much one misses one from the eye. Tears are the left memories among lovers. I am tired of loving him. When they ask me if I love him, I reply: I love him'. <u>Fifth</u>, 'I am announcing that, in [Name of City], there is a heart that sings and suffers for her'. <u>Sixth</u>, 'If crying makes the heart of the lover cool down, I swear I would make it flooding with tears'.

970. Toilet Types: In many male restrooms, there are flush squat toilets, sitting toilets (normally for westerners, people with disabilities and the elderly) and urinals (*not* used by nationals). That said, urinals never exist in mosque restrooms, since they do not meet a certain hygiene standard required by the religion.

971. Location: If one is out of the house and would like to visit the restroom, the first thing that comes to one's mind is normally to look for a mosque, since mosques are everywhere (that is, almost within a kilometre, there is a mosque) and are attached to them restrooms that are open to the public almost 24/7. Almost in every gas station, there is a mosque, and the restroom is attached to the mosque (not to the supermarket, as it is the case in some countries). One does not have to go through mosques to reach restrooms, since restrooms have doors that are independent of mosques and that can be accessed directly from streets. This means that, whereas in some other countries, restrooms are difficult to find (and hence people 'crash' coffee shops or go to malls), this is not an issue in Saudi Arabia.

972. Cleaning: Even if a Saudi man helps with housework, he would more likely not go as far as cleaning the restroom, as this is too much against the feeling of 'pride' that he has been fed into his mind.

973. Child Rearing: First, for many, child-rearing is a female responsibility. Second, baby-changing rooms are located within women's restrooms——an act that implies that only women deal with children and that such a task will never be done by a man even if he is a single father. Considering this belief, at times, when a man's wife dies, he rushes into getting married again as he needs a woman who can deal with his children. Third, men do not teach in kindergartens nor specialise in childhood education. Fourth, once children hit the age of three, they start taking care of (and even carrying) younger children, taking up responsibility, 'nursing' and 'parenthood' at an early age.

974. Signs: There are signs by restroom doors reminding one of religious norms and values when going into and coming out of the restroom.

975. Belongings: It is common to see belongings left unattended, because their owner has gone to the restroom (or to pray). This is why some Saudis get into trouble abroad for their belongings unattended; something that is normal in their Saudi culture and mentality. In general, it is safe in terms of burglary (and, of course, murder). Some do not lock their belongings at the gym.

976. Flushing: Although a dual-flush toilet (which has two buttons that enables one to flush light and heavy amounts of water) exists, people normally do not use this feature, nor do they even know the difference between the two buttons and why such a difference exists.

977. Scale: It is not part of the culture to have a scale in restrooms.

Desiring

978. There are a few spaces wherein emotional feelings are expressed. Here are some of them:

979. Literature: Literature (e.g. poems and novels) is a place where people go for erotic expression. Many Saudi novels have become popular and successful, and one reason for this popularity and success is that they talk about and dealt with eroticism. There has been an increase in the number of erotic novels——an issue that has become a source of discussion in newspapers and Literary Clubs.

980. Stickers: Although men and women do not show love and emotions in public (e.g. by holding hands), men show love and emotional frustrations through the stickers they put on their car window. Some individuals use the car window to communicate with their lovers. One writing on the windows of a car is: '*All what I wish for is to become as we were when we first met*'. Another writing is: '*May God bless her and protect her from herself*'. Others express their own ideologies on the surface of their cars, by putting ideological stickers. Other car stickers show a sense of belonging to the country: '*May God protect my nation*'. Other stickers show a sense of religion: '*I believe that there is no God except God, and Mohammed is his prophet*'. Other car stickers show a concern about one's belongings: '*May God protect the car from the bad spirit*'.

981. Social Media: The online world is a place where some express their emotions. Some write (whether as their status in social networks, or in public web-based forums and online groups) emotional words, phrases or poetic sentences. There have emerged various online groups where romantic Saudis hang out and exchange such sentences. In these groups, they share romantic pictures with romantic sentences written on these pictures. Some of these sentences are written by the ones who post them. But, other sentences are taken from Arabic literature or copied from somewhere on the Internet. Here are some of these sentences. <u>First</u>, 'Calmness and loneliness are her style'. <u>Second</u>, 'She keeps silent despite the thousands of tales in her heart'. <u>Third</u>, 'She likes masks; they hide sorrows'. <u>Fourth</u>, 'She believes it takes a few days to love a man, but forever to forget this love'. <u>Fifth</u>, 'If life is measured by happiness, then write on my tomb: "She died before birth" '. <u>Sixth</u>, 'Love is a word she heard of, liked and tried, but which ended up killing her'. <u>Seventh</u>, 'He feels jealous even of her hands when they touch her own body'. <u>Eighth</u>, 'He loves her because she is a female with the full enormity of femininity'. Ninth, 'He asked her not to buy an expensive pillow as she would end up sleeping in his lap'. Tenth, 'Love is like a war – easy to start, difficult to stop, and impossible to forget'. Eleventh, 'Loving the wrong person is fate but to continue with this love is stupidity'. Twelfth, 'Jealousy to love is like water to a flower; a little amount refreshes it, but a great amount kills it'. Thirteenth, 'Behind every disappointed woman is a man'. Fourteenth, 'The game is over; he lost his mask and she lost her heart'. Fifteenth, 'All she wishes is that the wind takes her to his lap'. Sixteenth, 'He sometimes calls her other women's names, but she calls all other men by his name'. Seventeenth, 'Suddenly, I loved someone I never thought I could even stand'. Eighteenth, 'I did not love him as a person but as a home'. Nineteenth, 'He does not love me, but he loves my style of loving him'. Twentieth, 'I am surprised to find love to be necessarily a combination of agony, pain, purity, loyalty, adoration, awe, separation and longing'. Twenty-First, 'Inside him, I have found a home in which I have not been allowed to dwell'. Twenty-Second, 'Each absentee has an excuse except him; he has my heart'. Twenty-Third, 'It is very difficult for her to erase him from her life; after all, he has been her life'. Twenty-Fourth, 'She has promised to continue dreaming of him until destiny gets sick of this insistence and allows them to get together'. Twenty-Fifth, 'For me, the luckiest women are those going to bed with a heart devoid of love'. Twenty-Sixth, 'The man is a silent creature, but in his eyes is a language that can be understood only by a lover'. Twenty-Seventh, 'The female forgives her enemies but not that who breaks her heart'. Twenty-Eighth, 'A tip for a man: If you want to kill a woman, colonise her heart and leave'. Twenty-Ninth, 'It is difficult to be in love with someone she can kiss only in her dreams'. Thirtieth, 'For me, there are two kinds of people who cannot feel the taste of love: a man with a new woman every day, and a woman tempting men through her beauty'. <u>Thirty-First</u>, 'For me, there is nothing worse than hearing a voice similar to that of my absent lover'.

982. There are certain norms and practices regarding desire and intercourse:

983. Love: Some single men and women listen to love music. They dream of love. They talk about love. They watch love movies and series. They read about love. They wish for love. They write about love. They cite poems about love. In short, they are into the idea of love, to the extent that many single drivers hang a heart-shaped object on the rear mirror. Despite their passion for love, they end up getting married through arranged marriage where a decision is made *for* them rather than *by* them. In liberal countries, there is normally a story behind how a couple have met, but in Saudi Arabia, there is no such a story since marriage is arranged. Two nationals might agree to get together through arranged marriage in the hope that they will eventually fall in love. If it turns out that they have not been able to fall in love, there are two scenarios. <u>First</u>, if the couple fail to fall in love after their arranged marriage, they might choose to merely get a divorce. <u>Second</u>, if the couple fail to fall in love after their arranged marriage, they, more likely, get 'stuck' with this marriage since divorce is financially, socially and culturally difficult. In this case, the husband will use his wife simply for children and intercourse and spend most of his time at work and with friends. The wife will spend most of her time on domestic life, following fashion, attending or organising social gatherings and hanging out with her girlfriends.

984. Eroticism: <u>First</u>, although eroticism seems one of the most sensitive issues, it is the least formally conversed and documented. Particularly unmarried women are not to talk about eroticism. Eroticism is not taught at educational institutions, or anywhere else. Second, no scholarly publication talks about eroticism——as if it does not exist. Eroticism is seen by sociologists as an off-limits topic. Libraries and bookstores are full of books on everything within married life except eroticism. Even if publications address eroticism, they provide general, vague and faith-based information. There are no sociological books (beyond novels and poems) that talk about eroticism openly. Third, if parents watch something on the TV together with their child, some of them will immediately cover with their hand the eye of the child if there is any kissing on the TV. This would be, however, infeasible if parents have so many children watching the TV with them. Fourth, in the past, there used to be concern among parents and educators that school students would exchange erotic videos via CDs. Nowadays, it is common that students (and adults) share erotic videos via social networks and communication applications.

985. Organ Adjustment: If one has both male and female organs, nothing is done until one is an adult. During adulthood, if this person starts to experience female-specific issues (e.g. menstrual cycles), this person will be considered a woman, and her male organ will be removed medically.

986. Organ Transplantation: The culture is still uncertain how to perceive the innovation of organ transplantation.

987. Group Intercourse: Some believe that the male and female members of a faith-based minority gather together on a particular night, turn off the lights and start having group intercourse. Whoever is born due to the intercourse that night becomes a spiritual guide. This belief is, however, false.

988. Stores: There are no 'pleasure stores'. Some shops sell underwear and bras made of sweets or chocolate. They are not displayed. One can ask discreetly if sellers have them.

989. Thigh: There are certain parts of the male body that are believed by some women to be provocative, for example, thigh. Men cover their thighs, whether in the presence of women or even other men. Security does not allow one to enter shopping malls if one wears a short that reveals any part of one's thigh. Tradition authorities may stop a man wearing shorts above the knees and advise him against it. Men normally cover their thigh even in male-only gyms.

990. Covering: In male-only spaces, men are allowed to reveal all different parts of their body, except the area between the navel and the knee.

991. Arms: The upper part of arms is believed to be provocative for women. For this reason, wearing tank tops for men is seen by some as inappropriate.

992. Trousers: until recently, the culture did not like it when a man wears Western trousers and t-shirts, which were seen by some as symbols of Westernisation. Many nationals nowadays wear shirts with English writings, and yet they do not know the meaning of these writings. At times, these people are told that the meaning of these writings is something that shows 'hatred against us'.

993. Nudity: There are no revealing pictures of the female body at museums. People are not exposed to any erotic or nudity-related objects, whether in museums or in educational settings. Nudity is not part of the culture, to the extent that a child does not see his/her parents naked, regardless of how little s/he is. Children do not get naked despite how little they are. If a child walks around naked, his siblings may start embarrassing him/her by saying *'woo, shame on you, shame on you'*.

994. Romance: The online world is a place where some express their emotions. Some have a collection of romantic digital pictures where a couple kiss or hold each other romantically. They display these pictures on their Instagram account and use them as their profile pictures.

995. Oral Intercourse: Oral intercourse is discussed. Some report having oral intercourse. Others see oral intercourse as disgusting and inconsistent with high standards of living and pride. They see oral intercourse as a practice done by animals, non-believers and pornography.

996. Anal Intercourse: Anal intercourse is discussed. Many enquiries about anal intercourse have been directed to tradition authorities. Some such enquirers have already had anal intercourse. Others wonder if it is OK to do so. Tradition authorities inform them that it is not allowed. Emergency departments have encountered female patients admitted due to bleeding as a result of slight tears in the colonic lining as a result of anal intercourse. These patients inform their doctors that their husbands insist that their wives have anal intercourse with them. Some women have divorced their husbands because of their persistence in carrying out anal intercourse. Many individuals become interested in anal intercourse particularly after their wife gives birth for the first time. After giving birth, the organ of some women becomes permanently wider and looser. For this reason, husbands seek an alternative that is tighter, going for anal intercourse.

997. Slaves: Some believe that, if, theoretically, slavery exists, one is allowed to have intercourse with one's slaves, regardless of how many slaves one has.

998. Unstoppable: Some believe that, once one has intercourse for the first, one cannot stop. This is why when getting a divorce, some rush into getting married again.

999. Adultery: Some believe in what is called 'eye-adultery'——a concept that refers to the practice of staring (or even just looking) at a woman, even if she is fully covered.

1000.   Minors: First, some believe that, in a local ideological community, it is allowed that a spiritual guide has intercourse with a baby. This intercourse is in the form of either moving his genital between her thighs or on the top of her genitals. This belief is false. Second, there is no law for the minimum age of marriage for women. Many agree with marriage to anyone above 9 years old, as long as she and her male guardian do not mind. For some, a woman should be allowed to get married whenever she wants, regardless of her age. If a woman gets married at an early age, this is believed by some to help prevent her from having intercourse before marriage.

1001.   Harassment: First, there have been campaigns that aim to raise social consciousness about minors being erotically touched and harassed by adults. Many minors report being erotically harassed by adults. At times, some male school teachers are accused of having an intimate relationship with their male minor students. Second, it is believed that, if a child keeps pulling down his shirt while walking, this suggests that he suffers from a traumatic experience whereby he has got harassed. Third, in the streets of some towns, one does not talk to people of the other gender, e.g. to ask for directions. That is, a man asks only men for directions. Likewise, a woman asks only women for directions. If a man talks to a woman on the street, this could be interpreted as 'harassment'. A violent action might be taken by the public against him. Also, he can be in trouble if he gets caught by tradition authorities. Fourth, some men used to call random numbers, hoping to reach a woman. When reaching a woman, he used to show her interest and beg her not to hang up, insisting until she accepts him. For this reason, when receiving a call from an unknown number, some do not pick up the phone, or they pass the phone to their brother, father or husband to answer and therefore scare away the harasser. Fifth, some women complain about the physical or oral harassment committed by some native and foreign male doctors, who, for example, over-touch them while doing a check-up and keep calling them 'beautiful'. Sixth, oral harassment of women is a common practice. Such harassment is normally not physical but quick oral outbursts that consist of a few words such as 'Hey Pretty'. There have been social campaigns against such harassment. Seventh, at specific times, Saudi single men are not allowed to enter shopping malls, because of the concern that they may harass 'families' (i.e. women). This rule of forbidding single men from entering shopping malls sometimes does not apply to *foreign* single men, based on the belief that they (unlike Saudi singles) do not harass women.

1002.   There are certain norms and practices regarding same-gender activities:

1003.   Law: The penalty for female-female intercourse is lashing. The penalty for male-male intercourse is the execution of the two. This is regardless of whether they are married or single. Same-gender intercourse has to be witnessed by four in order for the penalty to take place. Finding witnesses is unfeasible, making actors unworried about punishment.

1004.   Convenience: Some singles have intercourse with others of the same gender just out of convenience and because access to the other gender is restricted. It is practically easy for men to have a 'boyfriend' since it is traditionally acceptable if two men are alone in a closed room or even hold hands and put their hands on each other's shoulder in public.

1005.   Pigeons: In the past, it used to be believed that, 'if a man takes care of pigeons, he is into boys'. Taking care of pigeons used to take place in the rooftop. This is why when a man offers a boy to see his pigeons in the rooftop, this is not a genuine invitation.

1006.   Foreigners: It is believed that, non-Saudis, who are interested in the same gender, may like to come to Saudi Arabia to work and live, given gender separation whereby one sees in daily life only people of the same gender, and given that men can hang out with other men with hardly any suspicion that they are erotically interested in one another.

1007.   Wording: The English word 'gay' is known by the average Saudi.

1008.   Swearing: It is common that one uses swearing (or defence) that shows one's interest in same-gender intercourse. For instance, one day on the bus, a man said to his friend: *'get out of my way or I will push you'*. The friend responded: '*If you push me, I will push it [i.e. his genital] into you*'.

1009. **Walls:** Restroom walls are places where people write about their interest in same-gender intercourse. Writings in restrooms show interest in male-male intercourse. One writing, for example, is: '*I am a plus and am seeking a minus,* [his number]'. A plus is a man who likes to give (i.e. make love) and a minus is a man who likes to take (i.e. be made love to). This plus–minus terminology is popular among the young generation. It is believed that, if a young male is made love to, his buttocks will then become bigger.

1010. **Owing to gender separation and therefore the limited exposure to women, little women-related things (e.g. making general jokes regarding eroticism) can 'satisfy' many men and make them pleased. This erotic desperation can be seen in the following cases:**

1011.Joking: Citing (directly or indirectly) anything related to intercourse makes many men laugh and is considered by them to be funny. Making jokes about eroticism is a common practice among men (be they single or married, liberal or conservative, young or old, ordinary or elite). They extensively exchange these jokes in their daily face-to-face and digital conversations (e.g. through WhatsApp groups). Making jokes about eroticism puts a smile on the face of many men. These jokes are general, not personal. That is, married people normally do not talk to their friends about their *own* intimate relationship, because such talk is seen as a sin and reflects a lack of morality. Here are some such jokes. First, 'It is said that, if intercourse was on Mars, the Arabs would have been the first to make rockets'. Second, 'A stoned man sent his wife a picture of himself on a horse, with the following caption: *"I'm on top!!!"*. <u>Third</u>, 'One said to his wife: *"I want to call you Flower, but flowers wither. I want to call you Moon, but the Moon cannot be seen during the day. So, I have decided to call you Pen*s as it is also attached to me"'*. <u>Fourth</u>, 'An old woman went to a pleasure shop and asked the sale-man: How much is the red toy over there? The salesman replied: *"I am afraid that thing is a fire extinguisher!"'*.

1012.   Hinting: Male chit-chatting is full of erotic innuendos. Here are two examples to illustrate the point. <u>First</u>, one would say to friends: *'I went to work this morning, but I forgot my glasses, so I went all the way back home to get them'*. The friends would then comment: *'Aha, so you went all the way! Ha-ha'*. So, the friends here restate the phrase *'all the way'* hinting at the concept of intercourse. <u>Second</u>, if people tell someone taking a test: *'Good luck'*, he may respond: *'Are you wishing me good luck for the day or for the night?'*, therefore directing the meaning here towards 'intercourse' (which is something that is socially associated with night).

1013.   Describing: At times, when nationals hang out together outside the country, they feel good by describing and commenting on the elements of the women that they run into.

1014.   Wording: Fresh juice is a large market, to the extent that there are many shops dedicated only to fresh juice, serving elaborate forms of juice. There is a section on the menu of some such shops called, for example, *'For Married People'*. In this section, there are offered various types of juice that include kinds of fruit that are believed to enhance one's desire. These types of juice are called *'honey money'*, *'Viagra'*, *'late night'*, *'the night when the couple see each other for the first time privately in their room'*. Some believe that natural remedies (i.e. avocado, mango, nuts and arugula) make one perform better erotically. Some shops serve a drink called '*Married People's Drink*' that consists of all these items.

1015.   Singing: Some listen to songs, the texts of which are erotically provocative. To illustrate, one song is entitled: '*I am just a little girl*'. Its lyrics are: '*She came to whisper in my ear, and I asked her what is wrong. She said I find it painful because I am just a little girl. I, therefore, asked her to widely open her legs and make them as apart as possible, so I can put it easily inside her. She asked me to put it in slowly, slowly and begged me to put only its glans. I then apologised that mine went all the way until my balls hit.*'

1016.   A man can marry up to four women. There are certain norms and practices regarding this kind of marriage:

1017.   Reasons: There are various reasons why a man has an additional wife. <u>First</u>, a common reason why an old man wants to marry an additional wife is to '*feel young again*' and/or '*kill boredom*'. <u>Second</u>, if one's wife cannot give birth at all or cannot give birth to males, he may marry an additional woman. <u>Third</u>, a common reason why a man wants to marry an additional wife is that his first wife cannot understand them or that she has become disabled or permanently sick. So, the solution is (from his perspective) is to keep her (instead of divorcing her and therefore breaking her heart) but get married to an additional wife. <u>Fourth</u>, some men would marry a woman that no one wants to marry just to do her a favour. Divorced women or old women may not be marriageable except as additional wives. <u>Fifth</u>, if one's wife is having her menstrual cycle, he can have intercourse with another wife. Some, however, believe that women, in close proximity, cycle together. Hence, the wives of one man have separate housing to avoid cycling together, and, indeed, to avoid any tension between the wives.

1018.   Reaction: If one has a second wife, this does not mean that the first wife approves of the second marriage. Also, the two wives do not normally become friends with one another. Multi-marriage is full of politics exercised by wives against each other. Some women are relaxed about their husband marrying an additional woman, because their father has done the same with her mother. Also, their sisters and cousins have gone through the same thing. Moreover, some women want their husband to have an additional wife because they want to miss him and therefore be happy to see him again. Besides, for some women, multi-wife marriages improve the quality of their relationship, because the wives compete over who pleases the husband most. It becomes a competition for the husband's preference. Some women want their husband to have an additional wife because they want to have days off to clean the house and make themselves beautiful (e.g. waxing).

1019.   Management: Managing more than one wife depends on how good the husband is at management. The husband normally provides each wife with her own flat. He ensures the children of one wife gets along with those of the other wives.

1020.   Travelling: The law of some countries approves marriage to only one wife. When going there to these countries (e.g. for tourism or to study), Saudi men, with multi-wives, face the problem that they are not allowed to be accompanied by more than one wife. As a solution, these women, therefore, take turns travelling with their husband.

1021. **Phones:** Smartphones allow one to have more than one contact under the category 'Spouse', showing sensitivity to the national rule of multi-wives.

1022. **Group Intercourse:** A man is not allowed to have intercourse with his multi-wives at the same time. A man's wife is not to see his other wives undressed.

1023. **Embarrassment:** If a man marries an additional wife, this will make the first wife embarrassed and criticised by others for not satisfying him.

1024. **Flirting:** In a non-Saudi context, when two people flirt with one another, but one of them figures out that the other person is married, this may be the end of the game. But, in Saudi Arabia, it is different. That is, if the woman figures out that the man is married, this information is not dangerous since he can legally marry an additional wife. The man may not even feel bad about flirting with another woman and may not even call it cheating since the law allows him to marry an additional wife.

1025. **History:** Multi-wife marriage used to be common in the past. Currently, it seldom happens, for various reasons. <u>First</u>, many women have become stronger, asking for divorce if their husbands marry an additional woman. <u>Second</u>, it is expensive, especially given that the cost of living has started to increase. <u>Third</u>, a man, who is married to a relative, may not be able to marry another woman because the whole family may disapprove of his action. <u>Fourth</u>, a man's adult children from his first wife may dissuade him not to marry a woman in addition to their mother.

1026.   Conditioning: The potential first wife can state in the marriage contract that her husband cannot marry any woman apart from her.

1027.   Talking: Some women do not show others that they are happily married. This is because they are worried that others may seek a relationship with their husband, whether legally or illegally, whether as an additional wife or a lover.

1028.   Joking: It is common among men to joke (whether with their wife or their friends) about their intention to marry an additional wife.

1029.   There are certain norms, values and practices regarding jealousy:

1030.   Value: Male (and female) jealousy is seen by many men and women as a 'good' social value. Because of male jealousy, some male drivers do not talk to a male stranger (e.g. a policeman in a checkpoint or a cashier in drive-thru boots) through the window of the passenger front-seat if a female relative of theirs is sitting on that seat. This is why either this stranger walks around towards the window of drivers to talk to them from the driver window, or drivers get out of the car to talk to this stranger.

1031.   Pride: Jealousy is a source of pride for many individuals. The more jealous many husbands feel, the prouder of themselves they become. For some individuals, masculinity is measured *not* mainly according to how muscular and tough a man is, but more importantly according to how jealous and protective he is of his female relatives. Male jealousy is actually a source of appreciation by some women. For some women, the more jealous a husband is, the more appreciated it is by the wife and the more loved and cared about she feels.

1032.   Shame: A man, who does not show jealousy for his wife (for example, by allowing her to socialise with men), is socially labelled as 'cuckold'.

1033.   News Reporters: Some Saudi wives hate that many Arab women on the TV do not act professionally; talking and moving their body in extremely feminine ways. Some Saudi wives do not allow their partner to watch TV news reported by Arab women. They, however, do not mind him watching TV news reported by a non-Arab woman given her professionalism.

1034.   Friendship: because   of   jealousy,   most individuals do not allow their partner to have friends of the other gender. In many towns, partners work hard to limit one another's exposure to the other gender. If a married person has a friend of the other gender, this is seen by some as 'cheating', even if these two friends have never met (or even can meet) in the flesh, and the friendship is totally virtual and technology-based. Despite this norm, there are many 'cheaters', who spend, virtually, a lot of time together. Some of these people do not have the intention of having intercourse with their female contacts. Rather, they just enjoy flirting and talking to women. Or, they do that out of boredom, or because of their belief that a man needs to have female friends.

1035.   Fight: Because of men's jealousy for their families, some men may get into a fight with any stranger who targets their families' reputation or family members, be they male or female.

1036.   Maids: Some wives are jealous of their maid. They are fearful that their husband may have an affair with her. At times, if a family has a maid, the husband cannot be topless at home, as the wife will be jealous. Wives may refuse an offer by the husband to employ a maid to help them. To avoid such jealousy, some families employ an old and unattractive maid. Or, they may hire a couple: a *married* female maid and a male driver. Most maids have limited beauty and old, and this is because many agents (which are in charge of bringing maids from outside Saudi Arabia for employment inside the country) are believed to base their selection criterion of maids on how old and unattractive maids are.

1037.   Drivers: <u>First</u>, the wives of some ridesharing drivers are uncomfortable with their husbands working as ridesharing drivers and therefore being exposed to women (i.e. female passengers) all the time. <u>Second</u>, some Saudi ridesharing drivers are worried that they may be beaten up by the husband of their female costumers because of his jealousy. <u>Third</u>, some ridesharing drivers complain that, at times, their female costumers ask them to drive them home, and yet these women ask these drivers to lie if their husband asks these drivers where their wives have come from.

1038.   Immorality: Some individuals believe that failing to maintain gender separation can lead to jealousy (and sexual discrimination, harassment, rape, distraction).

1039.   Security: Many women do not feel secure in their relationship, because they are constantly worried that their husband may marry an additional woman. Many women act very jealous and will do their best to prevent their husband from having any contact (be it friendship or colleagueship) with any female, as this contact might encourage him to marry this woman as an additional wife.

1040. There are certain times when desire is supposed to be dysfunctional:

1041. **Mosque**: A practice is that one stays in a mosque for a certain number of days, devoting oneself to worship and staying away from worldly affairs. During these days, one is not allowed to go out of the mosque nor have intercourse.

1042. **Pilgrimage:** One cannot have intercourse during pilgrimage. If one had intercourse during pilgrimage, the pilgrimage would be invalid. One would have to make a sacrifice. For some, masturbation does not invalidate one's pilgrimage, although it is still a sin.

1043. **Non-marital Intercourse:** The penalties for those who have non-marital intercourse range from just whipping (for those who do not have spouses) to execution (for those who have spouses). These penalties can be implemented *only* if the act of non-marital intercourse is witnessed by four people, which is practically almost impossible. If there is evidence by four witnesses that a woman had an affair, the sentence is to be stoned to death. These witnesses must be male and Muslim and are known for being trustworthy. If a man accuses a woman of having an affair (yet without having four witnesses), the accuser will be sentenced to 80 lashes. If the husband accuses his wife of having an affair but the wife denies and there is no evidence the man, at the court, swears to God four times that he is telling the truth and then says that God damn him if he is lying. The wife, however, can protect herself by swearing to God four times that he is lying and then by saying that God damn her if he is telling the truth. In this case, the sentence is that the couple get separated from one another forever and can never re-marry each other.

1044. **Menstruation:** A woman does not have intercourse during her menstrual cycle; hence, her husband may have a roundabout form of 'intercourse' with the wife, either moving his genital between her thighs or on the top of her genitals.

1045. **Outside Bedrooms:** Romance happens only inside the house, to be specific, inside the bedroom. One normally does not show romance in front of one's children. Couples do not kiss in the presence of others, including their children. Instead, words of affirmation are exchanged between them.

1046. **Pleasure:** Some women think that, if they show their husbands that they enjoy intercourse, it could create suspicion (*'showing pleasure'* --> *'she loves that'* --> *'she loves men'* --> *'she is a bad girl'* --> *'she will maybe cheat on me to have pleasure with other men'*).

1047. **Post-Divorce:** After leaving her husband, a woman can get married again only after having her period a few times——or a few months later, if she does not have her period because of her young or old age.

1048. **Concerning beauty, there are three forms of make-up that some wear:**

1049. **Western Make-Up:** Most women wear 'western' make-up. There are various issues here. <u>First</u>, some women put on a great amount of make-up, and their skin is strong enough to survive it. <u>Second</u>, for many women, it takes a lot of time to do make-up for one event.

1050. **Traditional Make-Up:** Some women wear traditional eye make-up (i.e. a black liner for the eyes) not only for beauty but moreover for health purposes. Some men wear this kind of make-up——a practice that is socially acceptable.

Interval

Ten single Saudi women were asked if they had ever had any friendship with men. Only one had actually had, and her family knew about it. The rest, however, pointed out that they never had, as it 'is a sin'. A woman's friends 'must be only her father, brothers and husband'. One does 'not believe in such friendship'. One cites the well-known belief that, 'when two people of different genders meet up, the devil shall automatically be their third'. For one, 'the friendship with women is better'. These women were, moreover, asked to write down what they thought about female masturbation. Only one sometimes masturbated: 'It is better than having intercourse'. The rest did not masturbate, as 'it is a sin and unhealthy' and 'a bad habit'. Another reply was: 'No, thank God. It results in little happiness but massive sinfulness'.

16 married Saudi women were asked to write what they thought about 'the American woman'. She 'is like any other woman'. She 'is fun and helps others'. One likes 'her rationality, her way of thinking and her organisation'. One likes 'her beauty'. She 'is modest'. Another likes 'only Muslim Americans'. She is 'pretty but stupid sometimes'. She 'no longer follows the right path'. She 'is just like a product in America'. She 'is a trouble-maker and has, to a large extent, a male character'. Her real femininity 'is taken away from her'. One hates 'that she accepts to lose her dignity and modesty'. She 'is simple and lacks knowledge except on what surrounds her'. Another hates 'her immorality, equality with men and independence and how she sells herself to anyone that pays more'. She 'cannot be a mother for our children'. One does not like 'how dominant on her partner and how she cheats on him'. Most of the times, she 'is overweight and not devoted'.

Extremities

Exercising, Driving and Travelling

1051. There are certain practices regarding sports:

1052.   Female Sport: There is limited 'sports culture' among women. Here are some examples. Example 1, women do not teach sports nor specialise in sports education. Besides, at the beginning of school day, male students stand in lines and do a collective exercise guided by a 'sports-educator'——this sports activity, however, is *not* done in female schools. Example 2, normally, only men go to football clubs and public swimming pools. Sports arenas are common but mostly among men. In general, sports facilities tend to be only for men. Example 3, the female outfit (being a cloak and therefore wrapping the whole body) limits one's mobility, preventing one from doing any form of sport activity in public. Besides, it is difficult to maintain the veil when doing sports (or when it is windy).

1053.   Culturally Adjusted Sports: Sports must be adjusted to be in line with the culture. Here are some examples. Example 1, at times, female faces, female arms and female legs on imported products (e.g. imported gym machines) are pixelated or obscured using black pens or tape. Example 2, since music is culturally controversial, there can be no music in many public places, such as restaurants, shops and gyms. At gyms, although there are choreographed group-fitness classes (which are supposed to be exercise-to-music), music may not be played during many of these classes given the traditional sensitivity towards music. Example 3, at gyms, men are not allowed to get naked in front of one another, meaning that there are private small changing rooms which a man gets in and locks himself to get changed. Example 4, many men cover their thigh even in male-only gyms, because it is believed by some people that men are not allowed to expose their thigh to one another.

1054.   Public Work-Out: Some avoid exercising in public (e.g. at gyms or parks). They do not do activities in public (for example, they do not exercise in public or go to gyms) because they are anxious about 'the evil eye' and are afraid of being exposed to it. The evil eye is a look that is given based on jealousy. If those working out get hit with the evil eye, they may, consequently, permanently lose interest in work-out and moreover make them lose their fitness.

1055.   University Life: Sport is not part of university life. At many universities, there are limited sports-related clubs (except for football clubs). That said, some universities have established on their male campus 'outdoor gyms' and 'cycle stations' that enable students to go from one place to another inside the campus——there are no such facilities on the female campus. Hardly anyone uses these facilities, partly because universities force students into wearing the traditional outfit (i.e. the long, loose, white cloak), which cannot be used for workout and cycling as the equipment is dirty (being out all day long and affected by others' sweat) and therefore make the white cloak dirty.

1056.   There are certain norms and practices regarding female gyms:

1057.   Law: From 2018 onwards, there have been established proper female-only gyms. There used to be hardly any gyms for women. If gyms existed for women, they used to be mostly associated with hospitals and/or five-star hotels. Hence, when women went to gyms, it used to be done out of necessity, for example, because these women were sick and were asked by their doctors to do certain exercises in order for them to be healed. In other words, women, typically, did not use to go to gyms for general fitness.

1058. **Socialising**: Many women come to gyms to socialise with their friends. Other gym members are on their phones all the time. At the gym's swimming pool, women just stand and chat and barely move.

1059. **Couple Fitness:** A couple cannot go to the gym together. Because of the separation between the two genders, activities which couples can do together (e.g. going to the gym with one's partner) are limited. That said, for expats, there are gyms inside their compounds where men and women can work out together since these compounds are strictly private and are normally exclusive to expats. At these gyms, female expats can wear 'western' gym outfits.

1060. **Parking:** Outside the female gym, there are many cars (with a male Asian driver inside these cars) waiting for women to get out of the gym so as to drive them back home. These Asians are the drivers of these women's families. At times, these drivers are husbands, fathers or brothers.

1061. **The culture responds differently to different sports:**

1062. **Football:** Football is exceptionally common among male nationals (whether to watch or play). As for watching, many people watch and follow closely international football teams and are knowledgeable about them. Men watch and discuss football matches extensively and read a lot about them on the Internet, even during working hours. The football teams that nationals follow most are *Real Madrid* and *Barcelona*. Some members of tradition authorities, however, disapprove of the widely common practice of supporting *international* football teams and players for two reasons. <u>Reason 1</u>, one is not supposed to support players from another faith. <u>Reason 2</u>, football players' thighs are shown. As for playing, some young people play football on the street and use their shoes to show where the beginning and end of the goal are. Some adults make a large sandy space within their neighbourhood where they gather in late evenings to play football matches.

1063.   Swimming. There are resorts, even though outdoor activities (e.g. swimming) tend to be for children and men (not women), since women's mobility is limited due to the nature of their traditional outfit. Swimming is normally for children. Swimming pools (e.g. in farms, resorts or compounds) are dominated by children. Adults are at the pool just to entertain their children. Fathers (not mothers) are normally the ones with the children at the swimming pool——swimming is one of the few times where fathers (not mothers) are the ones who take care of the children. It is difficult for one to use the swimming pool for exercise since children are everywhere. Normally, people do not have the culture of using the swimming pool for exercise. When going to a swimming pool, some bring with them shampoo. If they have not brought shampoo, they may ask a random person to borrow his shampoo.

1064.   Cycling: Cycling is not part of the culture. Most men (and indeed women) do not ride a bike for transport, since this is seen to undermine them. Cycling for transport is viewed by many as being for 'foolish', 'cheap' or 'low-class' people. A few individuals have tried to encourage the idea of cycling for health. This initiative has had a limited effect, given the hot weather and irresponsible driving style and because there are no lanes for cycling. Recently, a few women have promoted female cycling (for fitness), being the first Saudi female cyclists and 'cycling activists'. From time to time, there are marathons for cyclists or runners. These events are a recent phenomenon and are used to be for men. Since 2018, there have been female-only marathons for female runners, who run in their black traditional outfit. There have been no marathons for female cyclists yet. Although there are no lanes for cycling, a few lanes exist and are located by the corniche. The problem is that these lanes are short and form merely loops. This means that cycling cannot be used for transportation and for the pleasure of going from one place to another.

1065.   Horse-Riding: Horse-riding is not a formally-organised activity, even though it is common. It is done casually, and there is no clubs and formally organised activities and institutions for horse-riding. At times, horse-riding training is offered as part of some 'summer clubs', where young people learn skills (e.g. computing and learning English) and engage in fun activities (e.g. travelling and horse-riding). There is no outdoor horse-riding for women. A saying is: 'teach your children archery, swimming and horse riding' – yet, archery does not exist in the culture.

1066.   Walking: <u>First</u>, many do not go for a walk, to the extent that it is common that one says '*let us go for a walk*' to mean '*let us cruise by car*'. So, cruising by car is culturally considered 'walking'. Whereas people outside Saudi Arabia go for a walk in parks or mountains, many Saudis go for a walk in shopping malls or on sidewalks by roads. Some retired people go, in the morning, for a walk on a regular basis in shopping malls. Second, because some women are covered in black, when they walk on the street, it is difficult for drivers to notice them, especially at night. Third, because women normally do not drive, they tend not to realise the dynamics, logic and danger of traffic; hence, when they walk on the street, they are not careful enough of car traffic. Fourth, many teenagers walk femininely in slow motion (and speak in a 'Mickey-mouse voice').

1067.   Motorbiking: First, men do not ride a motorbike for transport, as this is seen to undermine them. There are just a few who have fancy motorbikes and use them just for fun and in mornings on weekends when there is no traffic. Riding a motorbike is seen by some as a sign of being a bad or wild person. Second, there are no designated parking spaces for bikes and motorbikes. Third, there are policemen on motorbikes.

1068.   There are certain norms and practices regarding driving:

1069.   Roundabouts: There are many roundabouts. Almost in every roundabout, there is a massive, elaborated sculpture.

1070.   Foot: It is not illegal to drive with flipflops. One can even drive barefoot.

1071.   Hand: Some drivers put their hand out of the car window while driving. They leave their hand out of the car window hanging.

1072.   Bumps: First, there is an exceptionally large number of speed bumps. Most of these bumps are not highlighted, are high, are not logically located and/or serve no obvious purpose. Ideally, bumps are located in areas where the maximum speed is 30. Yet, in Saudi Arabia, on highways and roads (where the speed can be up to 100), drivers may suddenly face a bump. Bumps are, at times, large, to the extent that some of them hit the bottom of cars. One reason why it is common for older Saudis to suffer from back pain is the nature of bumps. Pregnant women are seen by some as being at risk from these aggressive bumps. Some choose to buy a big car, based on their belief that big cars are robust against such illogical and aggressive bumps and to avoid the damage these bumps may cause to cars. Besides, having a big car is seen by some as a source of power. Second, at times, while one is driving, one's multi-sport watch (which has the feature of countering stairs) starts counting stairs, thinking that one is actually taking the stairs. This is because some roads are bumpy, making multi-sport matches think that one must be taking the stairs.

1073. **Tyres:** First, the car tyre business is populated by Yemenis. Many Saudis do not trust many Yemeni workers, who are known for trickery, for charging more than the actual charge and for claiming that they can fix something that they cannot actually fix properly. Second, some drivers have no spare tyres. Hence, when some have a flat tyre, they struggle. They either call a car-carrying trailer, a taxi or a friend to help them.

1074. **Garage:** When one leaves one's car in the garage, garage workers may sneakily and secretly use one's car for their own benefit during and outside working hours.

1075. **Safety:** First, some are good at multitasking. For example, some drivers eat or are on their phone while driving. Another example is that many receptionists and customer services representatives serve more than one customer at the same time. <u>Second</u>, irresponsible car racing is common on public roads. <u>Third</u>, many drivers do not indicate when wanting to turn right or left or make a U-turn. <u>Fourth</u>, many Saudi drivers are good at handling the unexpected while driving. This is because they are used to driving into unexpected things. For example, a street or road may suddenly deviate to the left or to the right. Likewise, drivers may run into a bump on a highway. <u>Fifth</u>, while driving, some keep one of their legs up against their chest.

1076.   Traffic Lights: <u>First</u>, while waiting for the traffic light to be green, some drivers get out of the car, go to the boot to get something and then return to the car. <u>Second</u>, in a three-lane road, it is normal at a traffic light to see a driver on the *right* lane wanting to turn *left* or even make a *U-turn*. So, he tries hard to squeeze his car to turn, despite the possibility of causing an accident. <u>Third</u>, at the intersections with no traffic lights, the rule is whoever goes first goes first. Hence, drivers compete on who goes first.

1077.   Family Gathering: Some immediate families meet once every week at their fathers' house. The neighbourhood where this house is located becomes full of cars during the gathering, for two reasons. <u>First</u>, the norm is to have large families, averaging seven children. So, if every one of these seven children has seven children of their own, the number of grandchildren will be 49. <u>Second</u>, almost every adult man has his own car.

1078.   Traffic Instructions: <u>First</u>, many people are good observers and followers of traditional instructions. However, they are 'bad' observers and followers of non-traditional instructions (e.g. traffic ones), showing a lack of concern for social order. Chaos and accidents in streets and roads are the norms. When there is traffic, drivers always want to go first and will do various tricks to prevent other drivers from going first. <u>Second</u>, people drive too close to each other. <u>Third</u>, in some towns, although traffic can be hectic, it always moves, and it is rare to see 'road rage'. Some like the lack of too many rules, thinking that having too many rules takes the fun out of driving.

1079.   Roads: <u>First</u>, the left and right lanes are the most dangerous, as people overtake from the right and from the left. The middle lane is relatively the safest. <u>Second</u>, some streets and highways have no lanes or have lanes that are difficult to see. <u>Third</u>, on streets and highways, there is always an extra lane that some make for themselves; a lane that is not supposed to be there and is risky to make. If a street has two lanes, some create a third lane out of nothing. <u>Fourth</u>, when approaching a roundabout, one is supposed to give way to all vehicles already on the roundabout. Yet, many do not follow this traffic rule. <u>Fifth</u>, one roadwork sign is a mannequin that is dressed as if it is a real roadworker. The left hand of this mannequin automatically keeps waving so as to warn drivers of roadworks. <u>Sixth</u>, theoretically, curvy roads exist so as to avoid mountains, for example. Yet, in Saudi Arabia, curvy roads exist in the desert where roads can be made easily straight since the landscape is flat. <u>Seventh</u>, it is common to see a driver who wants to exit a highway and then suddenly changes his mind and therefore makes a dramatic move to get back to the highway. <u>Eighth</u>, highways suffer from sand creep, meaning that small sandy hills are constantly generated on highways. Sometimes, thick liquid is placed on the sides of highways so as to make sand heavy and therefore prevent it from moving. Besides, bulldozers are used to push sandy hills sand away from highways.

1080.   Distance: If a driver leaves a distance of more than half a metre between his car and the car in front of his, then another driver will try to sneak in. This is why drivers keep a very short distance between their cars and the car in front of them and become aggressive when another driver tries to sneak in.

1081.   Irresponsibility: First, particularly in the morning (when professionals and students go to work and school), traffic is exceptionally dangerous and chaotic. Second, many people go beyond the speed limit, even though they know that there are radars, and that they will be caught by radars. That said, some of these people know the exact location of the radars; hence, they slow down *just* before the radar and then speed up *immediately* once they pass the radar. When there is a new radar, people spread the word via WhatsApp, warning their fellow drivers against this new radar. Third, it is not only drivers of small cars who drive irresponsibly, but also drivers of trucks. Fourth, indeed, traffic can be messy in many countries. However, what makes traffic in Saudi Arabia particularly 'unique' is that many people drive aggressively. Fifth, some drive recklessly even in the presence of their female family member, and she, more likely, does not say anything. Even if she comments on his irresponsible driving, he may tell her that it is not her business. Yet, if an accident happens, the victim is the female passenger who cannot drive herself and therefore is to be driven by men. Accidents are caused by men, yet and female passengers are merely victims, who have to put up with irresponsible male drivers. Sixth, it is not only Saudi drivers who tend to drive irresponsibly, but also many foreign drivers. Many foreign drivers drive irresponsibly for various reasons. For example, they are influenced by citizens. Besides, they feel that they have to drive irresponsibly so as to 'survive'. Driving responsibly (in Saudi society which normally drives irresponsibly) makes one get nowhere. Also, driving responsibly in Saudi society can be dangerous, and at times, it is actually safer to drive irresponsibly. Seventh, other drivers get annoyed if one follows traffic instructions. For example, if one stops because there is a stop sign, other drivers will overtake one.

1082.   Drifting: Unsafe drifting is a common outdoor activity among young people. There are two main places where drifting takes place. First, some young people gather publicly in wide *streets and roads* where drivers come to drift. At times, these drivers cover the ground of these areas with diesel, which intensifies the smoking coming from the types while drifting. Second, some young people gather publicly in the *desert* where some drivers of 4*4 cars come to drift on sandy hills. These drivers go fast up and down these hills. If they want to spice it up, they drive on the side of these hills.

1083.   Checkpoints: The police create checkpoints in random streets and roads to check documents (such as driving licences) and to check whether drivers and passengers are wearing seatbelts. Many do not wear a seatbelt. When some of them approach a checkpoint, they wear the seatbelt, and once they pass the checkpoint, they take it off. To disable a seatbelt alarm, many individuals use 'seatbelt alarm stoppers'——small clips that can be inserted into the receptacle. Or, they fasten their seatbelt and yet sit _on_ it. In general, many do not wear seatbelts. Yet, from time to time, the police become strict about seatbelts and issue many fines for not wearing seatbelts; accordingly, people start wearing seatbelts and warning each other via. social networks about the fines for not wearing seatbelts. Yet, when the police stop being strict about seatbelts, many people stop wearing them.

1084.   Cruise: <u>First</u>, some young people have the tendency to fix the speed even for a short distance (e.g. for a few kilometres). When fixing the speed, they try not to disconnect it *by any mean*, even if this means that they make 'crazy' moves to overtake. At times, if other drivers do not let one overtake them, one may go left *beyond* the left lane to overtake anyway. When overtaking from the left beyond the left lane (which is normally full of small stones), this results in these stones flying away and hitting the windows of other cars and possibly breaking these windows. At times, the stone causes merely a crack that starts small and continues to grow and spread across the glass. To stop the crack from growing, people create a small circular border around the crack. This has been proven to be effective. <u>Second</u>, cruising up and down streets inside one's town is a common practice. It is done out of boredom. <u>Third</u>, there is no minimum speed limit, meaning that those cruising (or some Asians) drive slowly on highways.

1085.   Overtaking: If a man is driving behind another car, he may try to overtake one anyway, even if the other driver cannot let him overtake because it is crowded and/or because there is a car on the right. He may keep flashing fast and constantly at the driver and get exceptionally very close to the other car to place pressure on the other driver to let him overtake. This is even though he may not be actually in a rush, but this is his driving style.

1086.   Rushing: Rushing is a norm. Here are two examples. <u>First</u>, nationals tend to drive as if they are in a rush——although (or because) they are always late for meetings, gatherings and appointments. <u>Second</u>, people normally eat quickly as if they are in a rush, although they are not.

1087. **Car Types:** The culture is dominated by Toyota, Chevrolet/Ford, Hyundai and Nissan cars.

1088. **New Cars:** Some believe that, during the first 1,000 km, new cars are supposed not to be driven for long distances and not to go over 80 km, as new engines need to be 'trained'.

1089. **Wrapping:** First, some drivers cover the above-dash area (i.e. the flat space above the dashboard and below the front window) with fabric or leather, so as to prevent it from being destroyed by sunshine. Second, when buying a new car, some drivers cover the seats of the car with fabric or leather. They take off this cover when selling the car, so that the seats look new to the potential buyer.

1090. **Gas Stations:** First, in gas stations, there is a male worker standing by the petrol machines, serving customers. He holds all the cash in their pocket. It is so much cash (around US$2,000). He is not scared of being mugged. Customers pay him directly. When he gives customers change, he takes all the cash out of his pocket and gives them the change. Second, some gas stations offer free tissue boxes for those who get their car filled with petrol. Many individuals get attracted to this offer. Third, in gas stations, people fill up their car tank. It is not common that people fill only a quarter or half of their car tank.

1091. **Insurance:** There was social resistance to the innovation of insurance (e.g. car insurance). This is because some thought that it was unfair that one would get less than or even more than what one would have given, as it would be the case with insurance.

1092.   Pickup Trucks: Pickup trucks are widely common. There is, however, a cultural problem when a truck has only three seats that are next to each other. This cultural problem is illustrated in the following scenario. A male driver is with his male friend in a truck. However, he wants to pick up his female relative to drop her somewhere. In this case, the sister will have to sit next to his friend, which is culturally unacceptable. That is, the following two seating structures are not culturally appropriate: [*Seated Brother*] [*Seated Friend*] [*Seated Sister*] OR [*Seated Brother*] [*Seated Sister*] [*Seated Friend*]. To address this cultural problem, there are normally two roundabout alternatives. <u>Alternative 1</u> is that the friend sits in the open cargo deck, leaving the brother and his sister alone inside the car. <u>Alternative 2</u> is that the brother asks his friend to drive the car, then the brother sits next to his friend, and his sister sits next to the brother. So, the car structure will be like this: [*Seated Friend*] [*Seated Brother*] [*Seated Sister*]. In this case, the brother acts as a physical (and thus moral) barrier between the friend and the sister.

1093.   Ambulances: In daily life, one sees hardly any ambulances. This is perhaps because everyone has a car and drives oneself and one's family members to the hospital.

1094.   Potholes: While driving, it is normal to run into deep and wide potholes that may tear tyres. Particularly when it rains, streets, roads and highways become full of potholes. The potholes are big and deep, to the extent that, if a tyre hits a pothole, it, at times, breaks.

1095.   Horn: Many men use their car horn in various ways to convey different meanings. <u>First</u>, if one beeps for one second only once, this means that one is merely saying 'hi' or 'thanks', and the other driver is expected to beep for one second twice as a way of saying 'hi' in return or 'you're welcome'. Second, if one beeps for three seconds twice, this means that he is informing a person inside a building of his arrival and that he wants this person to come out to meet him. Third, if one beeps for seven seconds once, this means that he is angry at someone, who may beep back for ten seconds to defend himself. Fourth, some beep continually *en route* to weddings. Fifth, some give two quick beeps when approaching an intersection to warn other drivers of their approach——they do that because they ignore the '*Give Way*' sign.

1096.   The Art of Messiness: In some towns, although traffic can be messy, there is an art of this messiness. For example, if one parks one's car in a way that blocks other parked cars and prevents these cars from leaving, one is expected to leave one's number on the window of these cars, so that when the drivers of these cars want to leave, they can call one to come and move one's car. Alternatively, if one does not leave one's number, one is expected to constantly watch one's car from a distance, and whenever the drivers of these cars come and want to leave, one should come quickly and move one's car. When one moves one's car to let these drivers leave, one is supposed to beep (for one second) at the other drivers, and this beeping is meant as a 'thank-you'. On the contrary, in other towns, some park without any kind of regards to others, in a messy, disorganised way. At times, one gets stuck in front of a shop, having to honk loudly for someone to, finally, realise that s/he is blocking the way. Moreover, some may scratch one's parked car and never leave a number so that they can pay for the damage.

1097.   Car Maintenance: Many cars on streets are not supposed to be on streets, as they are too old and poorly maintained, having, for example, no side-mirror and/or no rear lights.

1098. **Help:** It is normal that, when a driver asks other drivers for direction to a particular location, they will ask him to follow them, and then they will take him to the exact location even if this requires that they drive for 10 minutes and even if the location is not on their way.

1099. **Stuck Cars:** Drivers tend to like to take shortcuts even if this means going through sandy areas. Because they, at times, underestimate how fluffy the sand of an area is, their car gets stuck. This is why, from time to time, one sees cars being stuck in sandy areas.

1100. **Disabilities:** Deaf people drive, and one may have a taxi driver who is deaf.

1101. There are certain norms and practices regarding women driving:

1102. **Law:** Although women are allowed to drive since 2018, only a few of them drive. Driving (and the street, in general) is still male-dominated.

1103. **Hours:** Female drivers tend to avoid busy times when driving becomes aggressive.

1104. **Cycling:** Women do not ride a bike or motorbike.

1105. **Fancy Cars:** For an outsider, it seems that women drive only fancy cars. But, if one looks at it closely, one will notice that female drivers tend to be liberal (and, hence, they have agreed to drive), and liberal women tend to come from wealthy families, and wealthy families can afford buying their male and female members fancy cars.

1106.   Taxing: There are hardly any female taxi drivers and ridesharing drivers.

1107.   Trucks: Women do not drive trucks, buses and mini-buses. Hence, some Saudis abroad find it strange when seeing female drivers of buses.

1108.   Pick-up Cars: Women do not drive pick-up cars, as pick-up cars are seen for hard work and toughness.

1109.   There are certain norms and practices regarding parking:

1110. Ineligibility: Despite their ineligibility, some park their car in spaces designated for the disabled.

1111. In-between Parking: Some park their car in-between two parking spaces, therefore occupying two or even three spaces.

1112. Trolleys: Having bought supplies from a supermarket and transferred the supplies from the trolley to their car, some shoppers leave the trolley behind in places where other cars can park.

1113. Cleaners: In a parking area, when a driver is parking (or, leaving), the Asian cleaner of the parking area normally comes close to the car, cleans (or pretends to clean) around the car and shows a sense of poverty so as to attract the sympathy of the driver and passengers in the hope that they may give him charity.

1114. Drop-off: When driving somewhere, men first drop off their women by the gate and then go and park the car. When going to the airport, men drop women by the terminal gate and then go to park the car. Most women do not walk from the parking area to the main building. When going back home, most men drop women by the house door and then go and park the car. Many male drivers drop off their female relatives as close to the gate as possible for various reasons. <u>First</u>, it is because many women do not want to walk (from the parking area to the gate) since they are unfit and/or considering that the weather is hot and therefore destroys their make-up. That is, it is challenging to wear make-up in the hot and humid areas of the country. <u>Second</u>, it is seen by some men as a way of respecting women.

1115. Parking Backwards: Parking backwards (by reversing into a parking spot) is common.

1116. Parking Areas: <u>First</u>, there is normally no designated parking for wedding venues. This is even though hundreds of guests are invited, and guests come to weddings with cars. This is why the way in which guests park outside wedding venues is messy, with people double-parking and parking in the middle of streets. This also applies to mosques, which normally have no designated parking as well. <u>Second</u>, on highways, there are normally no designated spaces for pulling over. One can pull over only in gas stations or by going off-road.

1117. There are various ways of selling a used car:

1118. For-Sale Sign: It is to put a *'For Sale'* sign on the car, with the phone number of the car owner and possibly the price.

1119. Online Advertising: It is to advertise it online, through websites where a seller sets a price, and others negotiate the price. There are almost ten such websites, some of which are nation-wise, and others cover various Arab countries. As part of the registration process for some of these websites is to confirm that '*I swear to God that I will transfer 1% of the car price if the car is sold via our website*'.

1120. Car Exhibition: It is to go to the Car Exhibition, where there are only men, and which is full of what are called 'Bargainers'. Bargainers are male. They are old and young Saudis and non-Saudis. Many of them negotiate the price with car-owners in 'aggressive' and 'unethical' ways. The activity of many Bargainers is like an 'organised crime', with them working secretly together and playing different psychological and political games (e.g. the lobbying game) to influence the decision of car-owners, for example, by subjecting one's car to some form of 'humiliation' by exaggerating the weaknesses of the car. The Car Exhibition could be named '*the Land of Trickery*', to the extent that car-owners (who have come to sell their cars) know for sure that they have been aggressively ripped off. Some of these car-owners (especially foreigners) psychologically suffer from this trauma of selling a car at the Car Exhibition; a trauma that lasts days after leaving the Exhibition. Bargainers warn car-owners not to trust other Bargainers and that other Bargainers are liars and cannot be trusted. If car-owners display their phone numbers on the 'For-Sale' sign of their car, they may get text messages from anonymous strangers during the auction stating, for example, that '*I know you do not know me, and you do not know my name, but I am someone who likes good things for you, so do not trust these Bargainers*'. The *Car Exhibition* consists of two areas. Area 1 consists of shops where used and new cars are displayed. Area 2 is for auctions where Bargainers make bids on cars. Making bids on cars is what many of these Bargainers do for living, so this is why they are (or at least, they think they are) good at bidding and tricking people. Bargainers do not call this trickery, but '*the politics of work*'. Bargainers do not buy cars for themselves, but they buy it and re-sell it immediately or buy it to exhibit it with a higher price at their used-car shops. The auction area is over-crowded with a zero-safety standard. In the auction area, it is messy, in terms of the way people organise themselves and walk around and in terms of the way in which cars are organised and are moved around. Bargainers have a small blue device which they move around the car to check if any part of the car has been repaired because of an accident or if any part of the car has been painted. Many Bargainers ask a customer if they can drive the car around, even though they know that they will not buy it. They promise a customer that they will buy the car, and they let him go through a whole complicated administrative process, and then just before the payment time, they flake and change their mind about buying the car.

1121. Inside cities, there are limited public transportation facilities, beyond legal and illegal taxis and school buses. There are certain norms and practices regarding public transportation:

1122.   Train: There is a train that runs between cities, which women use to commute to university or work. The male relatives of these female students drive them to and from the train station. Because women do not drive and do not feel comfortable living (or, are not allowed by their family to live) in a different city, many women commute by train. In the morning and in the late afternoon, the number of female passengers on the train is way higher than that of male passengers, because of these female commuters.

1123. **Bus:** First, there are travel agencies throughout the country offering the service of taking people (even just for weekends) by bus (or plane) to the holy cities for pilgrimage or visiting. Going by bus to the holy cities is cheap. Second, there are no buses inside some universities even though these universities are very large, and the weather can be extreme. Third, no one is allowed to get on a public bus (or train) unless one has a ticket that specifies one's seat. In other words, everyone on a bus or train has to have a seat, as standing (because one has no seat) is not allowed. During the annual pilgrimage in Makkah, the whole city welcomes more than 2 million pilgrims. It becomes full of 50-passenger buses. The air smells like diesel because of these buses.

1124. **Plane:** First, flights to the country are normally full of men. Second, on some planes, there is a '*Ladies Only*' section. Some critics see this as an example of how the culture encourages one to be too conscious of one's sexual orientation. It is believed by others that adding this function to the booking options will make men's lives easier when they take a flight, as this means that there is no need for male passengers to stand up waiting for the flight attendant to rearrange passengers' seats because of some women's discomfort with sitting next to a male stranger. Some male passengers refer to occasions where they are asked to take another seat because they happen to be sitting next to a woman that is not comfortable to have a man sitting next to her.

1125. **Private Drivers:** Although social life relies on cars, women normally do not drive, and their male relatives must drive them around. Many husbands, fathers or brothers drop their female relative at school or work before they themselves go to work. Then, they use their lunch break to pick up these women from school or work. For other families, their female members go to school or work using school buses or by private vans, minibuses or small cars which drive one women or a couple of women to and from school or work. At times, some families have their own (normally Asian) driver who lives with them in the house and drives around female members of their immediate families, extended families, their neighbours and their friends.

1126.   There are certain practices associated with taxiing.

1127.   Harassing: <u>First</u>, formal taxi service is not civilised, in the sense that taxi drivers cruise around in the hope of running into potential passengers, or they stand in crowded areas and fight (or lobby) for potential customers. <u>Second</u>, if one is a female passenger, she may be matched with a female ridesharing driver, if available.

1128.   Beeping: If one stands or walks on streets or roads, passing taxis drivers (whether legal taxi drivers or not) will beep at one to offer their services. These drivers are, at times, pushy.

1129.   Employing: The fact that women normally do not drive and therefore have to be driven has encouraged not only legal but illegal taxi drivers, who are normally male students, unemployed citizens or those Saudi workers who wish to increase their income by doing an extra (illegal) job besides their legal one.

1130.   Driving: The most irresponsible drivers are taxi-drivers and delivery-food drivers.

1131.Insulting: Some taxi drivers would be insulted if a passenger put on the seat belt, partly because s/he is 'insulting his driving'.

1132.   Entertaining: Some taxi drivers keep on tradition-oriented radio channels, reminding passengers of traditional and religious values.

1133.   Seating: First, in a taxi, female passengers may not be allowed (by male drivers) to sit in the front, since the seat next to the driver is, culturally speaking, is *only* for a woman who is related to the driver. This means that if there are a group of four women taking a five-seat taxi, they all have to squeeze in the backseat even though the front seat is free. Second, when a male passenger sits in the backseat of a taxi, the taxi driver, at times, thinks of him as trying to be a westerniser or to follow the western style, or, at least, someone who must have studied abroad.

1134.   Ridesharing: Some ridesharing drivers are worried that the police may stop them and accuse them of being with an unrelated woman, especially given that the ridesharing company does not protect them from this accusation and does not provide them with an ID. The ridesharing company warns their drivers against the act of picking up customers from female-only places (i.e. female-only campuses), so as to minimise the possibility of these drivers being caught by the police for picking up unrelated women. Some ridesharing drivers feel uncomfortable the first time they had a female stranger (i.e. a female passenger) at their cars. Many ridesharing drivers never allow their female passengers to sit next to them (in the seat next to the driver's seat), as culturally speaking, only female relatives can sit next to the driver. Some female passengers (who want to be socially perceived as 'good women') do not use ridesharing services alone. They are rather escorted by their male relatives or their female friends/relatives. Some ridesharing drivers (especially those who do not feel comfortable around women) like it when female passengers are escorted by male relatives. Some women never agree to take a ridesharing service.

1135.   Many national drivers seek services from inside their car (i.e. through the car window). They communicate with the outside world through the car window. Here are some examples:

1136.   Gas Stations: Some drivers go to gas stations, open the car window, tell the worker how much petrol to fill the car with, and then pay him through the car window.

1137.   Supermarkets: Some drivers stop by the door of a supermarket, call the cashier using the car horn, open the car window and ask him to bring what they want from the supermarket. The cashier then goes back to the supermarket, brings the order and gives it to the drivers through the car window.

1138.   ATMs: Drive-thru services are common for food and cash from ATMs. There is over-supply of drive-thru cashpoints, and yet under-maintenance of them.

1139.   Entertaining: Some children get half of their body out of the car window while the car is in motion, seeing this as a means of entertainment.

1140.   There are certain norms and values concerning travelling:

1141. Sin: Up until almost two decades ago, travelling was promoted as sinful. Travelling has been criticised by some for exposing Saudis to other conflicting ideologies, making them question their own ideology. The culture does not like any means (e.g. travelling to other countries) that help raise one's consciousness, as this will make one questions one's traditional norms. In the last decade, there has been a considerable change in this belief. Many Saudis started going abroad for tourism. The countries that many Saudis go to include: Bahrain, United Arab Emirates, Egypt, Turkey, Malaysia, Indonesia, the UK, Spain, Balkans, Germany, Austria, Philippines, Sri Lanka, Thailand, the Maldives, Tunisia, Syria, Lebanon, Switzerland, India, Bosnia, Azerbaijan, Georgia and the Czech Republic. Recently, there has been a change in this list due to some events.

1142.   Neighbour Countries: Bahrain is a small island nearby Saudi Arabia. There is no way to drive to Bahrain except through Saudi Arabia, as there is a short causeway connecting the two countries. There is an app, informing people how crowded it is at the border of Bahrain. It informs people how long it will take to cross the border, whether from Saudi Arabia to Bahrain or from Bahrain to Saudi Arabia. It offers statistics about how crowded it has been throughout the week. During weekends, it is most busy, taking people an average of two hours to cross the border. It is particularly busy during the weakened of the week when people get paid——normally, people get paid in the last week of every month. Many Saudis drive particularly 'insane' in Bahrain customs. Cars queue in lanes to get through Bahrain customs, and drivers compete to skip queues and to get through the customs as quickly as possible even if this means driving irresponsibly with a high chance of having accidents. Many Saudis (and of course, non-Saudis,) go to Bahrain for cinemas, drinks and/or intimacy. That said, the establishment of cinemas in Saudi Arabia discouraged some from going to Bahrain for cinemas. Some non-Saudi women (and Saudi women) go to Bahrain on a *'girls' night out'*. They ask a taxi-driver (or their own drivers) to take them to Bahrain, escort them there for the whole day and eventually bring them back to Saudi Arabia. The taxi driver normally charges them around US$140.

1143.   Customs: In some non-Saudi customs (e.g. Lebanon, Egypt and Sri Lanka), when officers know the traveller is a Saudi, they call him 'prince' and ask him for money or a 'gift' (as they sometimes call it). Some Saudis give them what they ask for.

1144.   Souvenir: An ideological minority go to certain countries to visit the graves of sacred figures and get blessed. They visit ideologically important mosques or graves there, using fabric to wipe the mosques or graves for blessing. They cut this fabric into small pieces and give them to others as presents. These pieces are worn for blessing.

1145.   Solo Travelling: Some husbands, at times, travel without their wives. They rather travel with their friends. Some women try to prevent their partners from travelling abroad without them, because they are worried about three things. First, their husband may engage in emotional or intimate activities. Second, their husband may have a female masseuse. Third, their husband may come back with an additional wife.

1146.   Sponsors: Every foreigner needs a sponsor to come to the country.

1147.   Visa: Expats cannot exit (whether temporarily or for good) the country without what is called an 'exit-visa' issued by their sponsors. This exit-visa can be multi-exit or single-exit.

1148.   Middle Class: In the past, only upper-middle-class people (and above) were the one travelling abroad. But, nowadays, also middle-class people travel and yet they spend a lot of money and do not go on a budget trip. For them, it takes a long time to financially recover from their previous trip.

1149.   There are certain norms and values concerning tourism (and fun in general):

1150.   Attitudes: Many men (especially older ones) are criticised for being 'sad creatures', taking life seriously and moreover seeing amusement to undermine maleness. They are socially expected not to be light-hearted. Women are, likewise, expected by some to follow the strictest rules of society and engage in limited entertainment. Fun and entertainment have limited space in the social fabric and mentality of the culture. Many have a stoic way of life and choose not to have a pleasure-oriented lifestyle. For them, happiness is not an objective. When taking a group picture, many look 'grumpy', not because they are actually grumpy, but rather because they are worried that smiling in pictures undermines them and makes them look 'stupid' or 'crazy'.

1151. Cost: First, many think that tourism inside the country is expensive; hence, they choose to travel abroad (or not travel at all). There are no tour buses——except a few that have been made in 2017 available in the capital. There are no tourism agents. There are no tourist information centres. There are merely limited institutionally-organised touristic activities for foreigners (and nationals). Second, many are not into tourism *inside* the country, because they think that domestic flights and services (e.g. accommodation, food and activities) are expensive in the touristic areas of their country.

1152.   Needs: This society tends to judge and accept things *not* based on whether society *wants* or even *likes* them, but rather based on whether society *needs* them.

This is why fun is resisted in the country; because society does not *need* fun. For many, society should function based on *need* (not with *luxury*). For example, if one was asked '*Why are you resisting this?*', one would reply '*We do not need it*'. To further illustrate, if one was asked '*Why has Saudi society resisted the ideas of music education or sports education for women?*', one would answer '*because society does not need these ideas*'.

1153. **Hierarchy:** In some festivals, there is a VIP section which only invited people can enter.

1154. **Lottery:** Lottery is not part of the culture, because some believe that it is against the culture.

1155. **Tourism:** Travellers and backpackers cannot freely come to the country. In other words, there is no real tourism inside the country for outsiders. Hence, the structure of the society is not set for international tourism, and the locals have no concept of such tourism and how to handle potential international tourists. International tourism and tourists have not influenced the society, whether financially or culturally.

1156. **There are certain norms and values concerning international cultural exchange:**

1157. **Proselytising:** People have the tendency to pride themselves on proselytising others to their faith. Many families attempt to make their maid convert. It is a traditional norm that a Saudi gets excited about making others convert, and this excitement is partly because Saudis are raised this way by their family and as part of their education. Many Saudis see any non-Muslim as a subject to be invited to Islam, even if these Saudis are 'bad' Muslims or even do not practice Islam. This is why many Saudi readers of this book have criticised the author for *not* trying to invite (*through* the book) non-Muslim readers to Islam. Of course, this book is written purely for the sake of international communication (*not* for religious reasons), with neither religious nor political agendas.

1158.   Cultural Agents: There is a cultural agent, whose effort has been outstanding and yet oriented towards religion. This agent is called, literally, '*The Centre for Raising the Awareness of Foreign Communities*'. What is meant by 'awareness' here is 'religious awareness'. The Centre has branches in almost every major city, with male and female sections. It aims to invite foreigners to religion, organise religion-oriented (serious and fun) activities, organise social gatherings for converts, teach foreigners Arabic with religious orientation and distribute religion-oriented handouts, leaflets and books in their own languages. It has been active in translating religion publications from Arabic into many different languages. In one branch of the Centre, for example, there are 10 preachers, 16 support staff, 3 drivers and thousands of volunteers. In only one year, the branch recorded 933 converts, including 7 Kenyans, 11 Ethiopians, 2 Americans, 1 Syrian, 2 Ghanaians, 2 British people, 2 Ugandans, and 1 Madagascan. The branch carried out 8,347 activities, including 2,932 lessons, 549 lectures, 54 open days, 449 discussions, 2,380 field tours, 380 translated lectures, 204 induction courses, 249 Islamic courses, 425 meetings, 35 general activities, 30 seminars and 124 other activities. This is in addition to 86 football competitions, many reaching-out activities, 25,000 gift packages (consisting of food and/or clothes) and 2 exhibitions. Besides, the branch organised dinner gatherings, to which 122,120 people came. During these dinner gatherings, there were 252 lessons, 83,400 participants, 232 games and 50,855 participants in these games.

1159. **Treatment and Favour:** First, it is normal to hear that one has decided (or one's family has decided for one) to go to the west or to India for medical treatment. Second, it is common that, when a family member travels abroad for study, work or tourism, other family members ask him/her to buy them a certain thing that is cheaper and of better quality in the travelled-to country.

1160. **Employment:** It is rare to see Saudis working outside their home country, for various reasons. First, many Saudis are attached to their culture and family. Second, Saudi culture is very different from any other cultures in the world; hence, Saudis find it difficult to adapt to any other culture. Third, there is a belief that '*the Saudi is like a fish that cannot live outside its aquarium*'. Fourth, it is not competitive in the Saudi employment market, meaning that anyone can easily be socially and professionally outstanding, with just little effort. Fifth, the financial status of the country has been excellent, and therefore the country affords to import, not export, workforce. Sixth, the standard of living is high whereas the cost of living is relatively reasonable.

1161. Defence: At the international level, many Saudis are protective of their own tradition. They are sensitive to anything that might somehow affect their cultural norms and values. Many Saudis interpret (or misinterpret) any act by western culture toward their own culture. They explain this act as a conspiracy against their traditional norms. Boycotting is a common social practice. If any country or company missteps Saudi traditional values, nationals may boycott against its products in the hope that this will teach them a 'lesson'. Many Saudis twist a text or picture written or designed by a western figure to make it look as if it is a conspiracy against Saudi culture. Many Saudis think that their tradition is always good, and others want to attack their traditional norms and values.

1162. **Decoration:** There are campaigns against shoes with decorative soles that are shaped in the form of religious terms. This decoration is seen as humiliation of religion, since this decoration (and therefore the religious terms) is associated with the ground. In general, any association with the ground is seen as humiliation; hence, many do not like it when one sits in a way that exposes the back of one's feet or shoes to their face, perceiving this as undermining and humiliating. Many avoid participating in any practice that could undermine or humiliate them.

1163. **Signs:** The sign of the *Red Cross* does not exist. If this sign is shown on products (e.g. British flag t-shirts or jewellery), there will be campaigns against them.

1164. **Dualism:** There is a common belief: '*sh*t in a country that is not yours*'. Many Saudis play dual roles. They act conservatively within Saudi borders, while acting 'liberal' (in other words, 'sh*tting') outside Saudi Arabia. Many Saudis proactively seek to keep their society closed and pure. For them, 'dirt' should remain outside the country. They have sought to prevent many foreign values from being imported, initiating real and virtual campaigns against Valentine's Day, Mother's Day, birthdays, Christmas, New Year's celebrations.

1165. **Interaction outside the Country:** When studying abroad, the interaction of some Saudi students with others is limited, for various reasons. First, many Saudi students abroad are adults, who travel with their spouses and children and lead a quiet law-abiding life, concentrating on their studies, taking care of their wife and many children, nurturing their ambitions and making plans for their professional life back in Saudi. This lifestyle of many Saudis abroad has limited their interaction with others. Second, there are various 'politicised' events, stories and 'stereotypes' that have presented 'the Saudi' as wild, loud, strange, terrorist, wealthy, closed, conservative, religious, Muslim, difficult to understand, odd, funny, womaniser, repressed, repressing, dominant, erotically harassing, hating women, erotically depressed, mean, manic, erotically illiterate, living in the desert, a prince, a racist, loving cars, riding camels, living in tents, wasting money, etc. Such negative 'stereotypes' have discouraged some from interacting with Saudis abroad. <u>Third</u>, when Saudis go abroad to study, some of them become members of a Saudi community in the city where they are studying. In many cities outside Saudi Arabia, there are Saudi communities that are financially sponsored by the Saudi authorities. In these communities, members gather together, for example, to celebrate Saudi national events, to welcome and help recently arrived fellow Saudis and to play football. Such communities have limited many Saudis' interaction with others. <u>Fourth</u>, there is a lack of Saudis working abroad, which has reduced the opportunity for foreigners to get to know them. Because of such reasons, 'the Saudi' is presented to the outside world to be concerned with confusion and puzzlement.

1166.   Interaction inside the Country: Many westerners are housed in compounds sheltered by extensive concrete walls with barbed wire and protected by security (at times, double-security provided jointly by a private force and the Saudi national force). Many facilities are provided inside such compounds (for example, swimming pools, gyms, tennis courts, green fields and restaurants), which encourages those living there to merely stay within their compound. Some westerners could live poorly back in the west and could not moreover find a job, but when they have come to Saudi Arabia, they now have a good job, are well-treated, have their own (yet shared) swimming pool and are protected by double-security. Nationals are normally not allowed within these compounds, limiting the exposure of those living in compounds to Saudi culture and to nationals themselves. Many nationals report not seeing westerners except in supermarkets.

Asking, Begging and Giving

1167. **There are certain issues that are related to poor Saudis and charitable work:**

1168. **Charity Quantity:** There are around 150 registered private charities and around 650 public charities.

1169. **Charity Names:** Most of these charities are named after male or female rich people and outstanding figures. In the name of some of these charities, the full name of these people (that is, their first name, their father's name and their family name) is included. At times, a name can be formed in the following way: '*Dr Abdul bin Essa Al Lily, his Wife, his Parents, his Brothers and his Offspring*'. In short, some charity names are long.

1170. **Charity Work:** Charities tend to focus on the following issues: orphans, women, widows, the disabled, the poor, those in need, youth and religion. There seems not to be other issues, such as animals or the environment. One may wonder why orphans, widows and the disabled constitute main issues and where these (seemingly many) orphans and disable individuals come from.

1171.Donation: It is common to see one donating a building, plot of land or other assets for charitable purposes with no intention of reclaiming the assets. There is a foundation dedicated to this endowment.

1172.   Wording: Many poor people do not like to be called '*poor*', but rather '*people with limited income*'. Many charities do not call those poor people that they help '*poor people*', and instead they call them '*beneficiaries*' or '*the needy*'.

1173.   Charity Day: On the last day of the holy month, residents in poor neighbourhoods stand by their house waiting for others to give them charity (food and money). This is the day when most people give charity and help others.

1174.   Mentality of the Poor: Many show a sense of belonging to the middle class, although they are poor. They take a loan to buy a new fancy car. Actually, because of the country's association with oil, outsiders do not realise that many people are poor.

1175.   Mosques   in   Poor   Areas: In   poor neighbourhoods, although houses are in a bad condition, mosques are at times in a good condition and, moreover, fancy.

1176.   Wealth   in   Poor   Areas: In   poor neighbourhoods, one may run into an outstanding, fancy, large house with a fancy car next to it.

1177.   Accommodation: Regardless how poor one is, people live in concrete-made accommodation.

1178.   The Poor's Children: There are many children in poor houses, for four possible reasons. <u>First</u>, they could not effort contraceptive pills. <u>Second</u>, there was a limited awareness of birth control. <u>Third</u>, they gave birth to many children in the hope that at least one child might become successful and therefore get the family out of poverty. Fourth, that was to ensure that at least one of the children would take the responsibility to take care of them in the old age. Fifth, more than one family live in one house.

1179. **Skin**: The skin of poor people in the Eastern Province is darker than the skin colour of the average Saudi. Skin colour could be related to the fact that most poor families come to the Eastern Province from the Southern Province where darker skin is the norm. In other words, skin colour cannot be misinterpreted as a form of racism.

1180. **Value**: A common belief is that 'poverty is not shame'.

1181. There are certain practices regarding the acts of asking, begging and giving:

1182. **Murder**: One can get away with murder through begging and emotion. In theory, it is the law that, if one deliberately kills someone, the killer is handled in one of the following three ways. First, the killer is to be killed by the court. Second, the killer is to be pardoned by the family of the killed. Third, the killer is to pay money to this family. It is up to the family of the killed to choose among these three options. If the family of the murdered chooses the death penalty for the murder, society will put an exceptionally large amount of pressure on this family to change their mind. Outstanding figures, neighbours and relatives will keep calling and/or coming to the house of the family of the killed, begging them to change their mind. It is shameful and against Arab, tribal and Bedouin chivalry if one turns down somebody begging one for something. If the family changes their mind and asks the murderer to alternatively pay them money, but the murderer cannot afford this money, members of society, charities, business people and outstanding figures will help him/her. All this is considered to be an aspect of social solidarity.

1183. **Begging:** <u>First</u>, begging is illegal. There is an 'Anti-Begging Office'. <u>Second</u>, nationals normally do not beg for money, perhaps because of social pride. If there are beggars, they are normally foreigners. <u>Third</u>, it is normal to see women begging for money in car parks and next to traffic lights. It is difficult to know the nationalities of female beggars since they are fully covered and because they speak quietly. Many beggars are women, who carry a baby in their arm to gain sympathy. They use anything at their disposal in exchange for money. Young people also beg for money. <u>Fourth</u>, it is common that one asks others (family members and friends) to lend one money. Yet, some refuse to pay back the money that they have been lent. <u>Fifth</u>, common places where people beg for money are mosque gates, traffic lights and parking areas.

1184. **Alms:** People are obligated (faithfully, not legally) to annually give alms. Alms-giving is a private and voluntary decision. The amount of alms is specific, i.e. a particular small percentage of one's possessions, calculated based on the worth of all these possessions. Alms-giving is enforced not by law but rather by peer pressure, ideological reasons and/or personal feelings. Alms are given to certain categories of people, including poor people, alms-collectors, potential or new converts and those fighting for certain causes.

1185. **Good News:** When someone brings you a piece of good news, you are expected to give one in return something (money or an invitation to dinner).

1186.   Mutual Benefit: Mutual benefit is a key norm among family members and friends. The spirit behind this is well expressed in the following formula: *'If you help me now, I help you later, but if you turn me down now, I turn you down later'*. Mutual benefit can include looking after one another's children, keeping one another company in the absence of the husband and using one another's driver and maid. If one asks a family member or a friend for help, one expects a swift and energetic response full of enthusiasm. When one offers a service or help, one already becomes preoccupied with expected returns and is sure of being repaid. A father or a mother expects his/her children to pay him/her back for the effort that s/he has put into raising them and spending money on them during their childhood. When a favour is returned, one makes it clear that one is now free of any obligation. If one fails to return a favour, one will be taunted. Nationals are normally occupied with the idea of 'giving and taking': that is, offering services to family members and friends and collecting services from them in return. They are good at remembering and keeping count of what they owe others and what is due to them. If one is taught by someone, one is then expected to show (as a form of repayment) respect and gratefulness for this teacher for the rest of one's life. The typical Saudi shows keenness to protect others from any harm or risk and to volunteer out of pride and honour. One needs to merely call for saving from a potential risk, and others will surely not hesitate to give one all support.

1187.   Declining: Even if they like what is offered to them (e.g. a meal), some decline (and are socially expected to decline) the offer a couple of times before accepting it. This is seen as a polite way of handling an offer. For this reason, it is not easy to figure out whether a Saudi really means it when saying 'no' to an offer. Likewise, nationals normally expect others to make an offer many times before they accept it.

1188.   Money: Many think that all the world money is worth gold that is reserved in Switzerland.

1189.   Generosity and hospitality are well-established norms and are sources of pride for nationals. Here are some practices associated with these norms:

1190.   Generosity: The culture is structured around the concept of generosity. Being seen as generous is an important value. Guests' hospitality expectation is high. Many expect so much from the host. They get offended when not so much effort has been put into hospitality. They start gossiping and telling other people that this person is 'cheap'. Being seen as cheap is humiliating and a big shame.

1191. Visits: <u>First</u>, it is not only that visits are unexpected (or arranged spontaneously at short notice), but that visits last long. At times, one does not (nor can one) decline visitors, even if one is occupied or even unwell and sick. <u>Second</u>, at times (e.g. having a new baby, returning from a trip, being sick, death, weddings), visits are compulsory. Not making it to a compulsory visit is harshly criticised. By the same token, refusal to receive visitors is also harshly criticised. <u>Third</u>, nationals normally do not like a cold reception. They expect a generous and warm welcome and to be well taken care of. <u>Fourth</u>, Saudi homes are normally known for their hospitality, whereby guests are all the time expected. <u>Fifth</u>, regardless of how quick a visit is, guests are not permitted to go away before they are offered drinks and food or snacks. <u>Sixth</u>, some hosts serve so much food (beyond what invitees can eat), in an attempt to avoid being seen as cheap. They keep insisting on eating more even if invitees insist that they are full.

1192.   Food Serving: First, when one is visited at one's office, one normally serves visitors tea, dates, chocolate and/or biscuits. Second, in some workplaces, someone is employed *only* to make tea and coffee and serve them to employees and customers. Third, during meetings, a 'tea server' offers tea to participants. Fourth, in weddings, individuals are employed to serve tea and dates to guests. Fifth, in social gatherings, the youngest child of the host is the one serving tea and coffee to all guests. Sixth, nationals serve tea and coffee in two containers (one container for tea and the other for coffee) that are identical. Although the two containers are identical, the container for tea is slightly longer than the container for coffee. This is how people differentiate between the container for tea and the container for coffee——with the larger container being for tea.

1193.   Incense: Nationals use something similar to a 'vaporiser', which takes the shape of an upside-down triangle. At the top of this vaporiser, there are burning coals. Small pieces of wood are placed on these coals to slowly burn and, therefore, produce so much smoking that reportedly smells 'nice'. Such vaporisers are served at the end of social gatherings. Guests pass around these vaporisers, placing them under their arms, beard and headwear, letting the smoking going through their body and clothes. Serving these vaporisers is seen as a sign of generosity. These vaporisers are made of metal and wood and have elaborate patterns. Firefighters warn employees not to use these vaporisers in their workplace if their workplace is supplied with fire alarms as the smoking coming out of these vaporisers trigger fire alarms.

1194. **Pressure to Eat:** Gatherings involve so much food of different kinds (snacks, starters, mains and dessert). So, if one is on a diet, one feels bad after leaving a gathering. To show a sense of generosity, hosts place so much pressure on guests to eat more and more even if guests say that they are totally full. Hosts keep insisting on guests to eat more. Not eating so much can be seen as rude, as it can be interpreted by hosts as a sign of the food tasting bad.

1195. **Paying:** In restaurants, it is normal that nationals get into a heated argument, with each offering to pay the bill so as to show generosity.

1196. **There are certain norms and practices regarding accommodation:**

1197. **Hidden Cameras:** Some individuals are worried about possible hidden cameras in hotel rooms.

1198. **Gender:** <u>First</u>, in hotels, one does not over-hear other neighbour guests making love, as lovers keep quiet. <u>Second</u>, in some towns, unrelated people of different genders cannot rent a hotel room. <u>Third</u>, in some towns, a woman cannot rent a hotel room—except when it is a fancy hotel. A related man must be present during booking so as to make the booking for her. This implies that the concept of 'online booking' is inapplicable in these towns.

1199. **Hospitalisation:** It is normal that pregnant women are asked to leave the hospital within 24 hours after giving birth. This is because of the large number of women giving birth, which makes it difficult for hospitals to accommodate and hospitalise them for more than 24 hours.

1200. **Security:** <u>First</u>, fancy hotels and resorts have gates with security examining cars including their boots. <u>Second</u>, it is normal that a gate security in hotels stops working for a few minutes so as to pray. Meanwhile, anyone who wants to go through the gate has to wait until the security finishes praying.

1201. **Breakfast**: Although breakfast is included, some hotels do not have a buffet, nor do they have a restaurant. Instead, they serve breakfast at the room.

1202. **Smoking**: It is rare to find a hotel room or a car for rental that does not smell like cigarettes.

1203. **Size**: Hotels more likely offer apartments (than rooms), with kitchen and living rooms.

1204. **International Companies**: Chains of fancy hotels companies exist. Chains of non-fancy hotels (e.g. ibid) hardly exist.

Shopping, Serving and House-Keeping

1205. **There are certain practices regarding shopping:**

1206. **Shopping Malls**: <u>First</u>, the country is full of shopping malls that follow the latest aspects of fashion. For a date with their partners, some go to shopping malls. <u>Second</u>, the *Push and Pull* signs on shop doors are limited.

1207. **Shopping Categories:** <u>First</u>, at times, shops are categorised, grouped and therefore located based on what they sell. For example, shops that sell bags are located in one specific area. In other words, in one street, one finds a lot of shops that sell bags. Likewise, shops that sell jewellery are located in one specific area. <u>Second</u>, at times, shops are categorised, grouped and therefore located based on gender. For example, shops that sell female clothes are located in one region. In other words, in one street, one finds a lot of shops that sell female clothes. Likewise, shops that sell male clothes are located in a different region.

1208.   Online Banking: The credit cards of some Saudi banks do not work in shops abroad that offer traditionally inappropriate products.

1209.   Ordering: When ordering in Arabic, people say what is translated into *'give me this'*. This is why when Saudis order in English, they translate into English what they normally say in Arabic, therefore saying *'give me this'*, which some foreign salespeople find impolite.

1210.   Taxing: The *Value Added Tax* (a.k.a. VAT) system is introduced to Saudi society at the beginning of 2018. In other words, before this date, there was no VAT. That said, there are still no income taxes.

1211. Security: By the entrance of some shops (e.g. IKEA) and shopping malls, there is security checking shoppers by asking them to empty their pockets and then going through a metal detector (just as it is in airports). Near the exit gate of IKEA, there are illegal workers shouting, offering people to deliver or assemble what they have just bought from the shop.

1212.   Bargaining: <u>First</u>, bargaining is the norm, even if the price is written on the product. <u>Second</u>, people waste so much time negotiating the price of what they are wanting to buy.

1213.   Shop Names: The names of shops can be categorised into the following. First, shops are named after Arabic and non-Arabic cities and countries. For example, there are the *'German-Saudi Hospital'* or the *'British Bank'*, although hardly any German or British person works for these organisations. Using such countries (i.e. German and the UK) helps to attract customers, since citizens tend to trust the quality of such countries. Second, shops are named after Arabic and non-Arabic historical figures. Third, shops are named in the form of *'House of Something'*, such as *'the House of Love'*, *'the House of Strawberry'* or *'the Italian House'*. Fourth, shops are named after animals, such as 'The Green Barbershop'. Fifth, shops are named after colours, such as *'Golden Kangaroo Café'*. Sixth, shops are named after nature, such as *'the Flower of the Desert'*. Seventh, shops that have ambiguous names, such as *'the Red Circle'*. All such shops, most times, have nothing to do with the meaning of their names. To illustrate, the shop called *'Romance'* is a restaurant. Many names of shops are exaggerated and over the top. Such names are *'Life Maker'* and *'Through the Universe'*. Many names of shops are metaphoric. Such names are *'Pen Line School'* or *'The Shine of* [Name of City]'.

1214.   Saving: There are many small and large shops where everything costs only US$0.5 or US$1.5. These shops sell almost 'everything'.

1215.   Here are the main places where there is dependence on Asians:

1216.   Housekeeping: There is dependence on Asians concerning housekeeping. There is an office that is responsible for bringing maids to the country. If one wants a maid, one can simply go there and apply for a maid and specify the country from which the maid should come from. At times, there are three main social classes:

men, women and Asians. Outsourcing normally goes hierarchically down through these classes. Some men outsource domestic work to women, and some of these women outsource this work to Asian maids. These Saudi men and Saudi women consequently free themselves from domestic responsibilities. Some Saudi families have at least one maid (Asian or African) who helps them with domestic work, including raising their children and acting as babysitters. Maids normally become an integral part of the household, living and eating 'for free', travelling with them 'for free', going out for dinner with them 'for free', etc. Some mothers have maids even though their only 'job' is housewives. Even small families with medium income may have a maid (and moreover a driver).

1217.   Driving: There is dependence on Asians in terms of driving. Some Saudi male heads of households hire Asians to drive around women and children. At times, these drivers live with the household at a 'mini-house' that is located in the yard of the main house. This mini-house is, however, totally independent of the main house and has its own gate to the outside world. It is not physically possible to go directly from the mini-house to the main house without going out to the street. Whereas Asian maids normally live in a room inside the main house, Asian drivers live in a room that is independent of the main house since drivers are 'males' and therefore are seen as 'moral risks' to female household members. These drivers are, all the time, available and 'on-call' for driving any household members. They, at times, drive around not only households' immediate families but moreover households' extended families, neighbours and friends. Although having a driver is a necessity since women do not drive, having a maid is, at times, done only to show off and out of prestige. At times, a woman does not want to feel less than her female friends who have maids. It is common that one does not make their own decision *for* *themselves*, but *others* make decisions for them; hence, many lack responsibility and accountability. To illustrate, at times, men depend on women, who depend on Asians. Sometimes, Saudi culture forces one to outsource one's own matters. Ideally, one would drive oneself around, but because women do not drive, they are obligated to outsource such a task to men. Men hire Asians to drive their women around.

1218.   Laundry: There is dependence on Asians concerning laundry. Instead of men doing their laundry themselves, some used to outsource this task to women, and yet some of these women have outsourced this task to an external laundry service where Asians work. In almost every neighbourhood, there is, at least, one 'laundry shop' where some individuals leave their clothes to get them washed, dried and ironed by a third party (i.e. Asians or Yemenis). A quick laundry service takes a few hours. Many do not wear the traditional cloak unless it is ironed. Moreover, some of them wear jeans and t-shirts, but they do not wear them unless they are ironed.

1219.   Carrying Bags: There is dependence on Asians in terms of carrying bags. Here are some examples. <u>First</u>, at the airport or train station, some women outsource to Asian workers the tasks of picking up their luggage from conveyor belts and carrying their luggage. These Asians are more likely to accept these tasks in the hope of getting some small money in return. <u>Second</u>, some walk around at book fairs with Asian assistants who carry the books that these are buying. <u>Third</u>, a few students (who come from wealthy families) bring along to school their maids who carry or take care of their schoolbags and belongings.

1220.   Carwash: There is dependence on Asians in terms of carwash. Many do not wash their cars themselves. They get their cars washed for them by Asians. Many Asians illegally work as car cleaners, next to their normal jobs. They come around three times a week to wash cars. At times, some take their cars to washing services where cars are washed automatically or manually by Asians.

1221.   Shopping: There is dependence on Asians in terms of shopping. Some female household members send their Asian driver to get them certain items, take-away food or even just desserts. Once the driver is at the shop, these women will be on his phone, and he will pass the phone to the sale person, so that these women can tell the sale person directly what they particularly want to buy, so that the driver can buy and deliver the right thing.

1222.   Barbering: There is dependence on Asians regarding shaving and haircut. At times, not only cutting one's hair but moreover shaving one's beards and moustaches are outsourced to foreigners such as Asians. For this reason, the barbershop business is common, to the extent that, in almost every neighbourhood, there is, at least, one salon where male nationals get their hair, beards and moustaches shaved or cut. At a barbershop, some male nationals get their head messaged and their face cleaned using all different kinds of products. Turkish people are popular hair-cutters and considered to be the best.

1223.   Ridesharing: There is dependence on Asians concerning ridesharing. Since foreigners cannot work as ridesharing drivers, some nationals register themselves as ridesharing drivers and yet give their cars to Asians or Africans who do the job for them, and then, these nationals give these foreigners a share of the income and take the rest for themselves.

1224.   Catering: There is dependence on Asians concerning rubbish-collection and catering. Many nationals accept to do only white-collar work, leaving blue-collar work to foreigners (e.g. Asians). There are actually nationals working as cleaners or maids, but *only* in schools or offices not in houses. This kind of jobs is, however, slowly dying out. Working as a waiter is a job mostly done by foreigners (e.g. Asians). People collecting rubbish are normally Asians——no national does this job.

1225.   Construction: There is dependence on Asians concerning construction and building. Not the design but the manual construction of buildings is normally left to cheap, low-paid (at times, illegal) Asian workers. The 'magical' thing with some Asians is that they would not mind doing anything and would not mind working at the worst work conditions, such as bad weather, low safety standards, over-demand, low salaries and the like. Nationals tend to build their own houses, instead of buying already-built houses, for various reasons. First, many nationals do not trust that already-built houses are of good quality. Second, the Saudi population is growing fast; hence, more and more houses are needed to be built to respond to this need.

1226.   Service: There is dependence on Asians concerning service. Service (e.g. working as salespeople) in malls (particularly clothing stores) is mostly done by Asians. While traditional shops are taken care of mainly by nationals or other Arabs, big malls are dependent on Asians. Other service jobs that are mostly done by Asians are IT, secretary and nursing. Local electrical, plumbing and satellite TV shops are mostly run by Asians.

1227.   There are certain practices that are associated with Asians:

1228.   Breaks: Some Asians have limited or no weekly breaks. There are two types of maids. <u>First</u>, some maids have one day a week off. During this break, some of them break free, including having intercourse with strangers. Some maids use mobile communication apps to meet men and arrange dates, whether these men are Asian, Saudi or from other nationalities. Some Asian maids have intercourse with their dates for money or because of their own desire. <u>Second</u>, some maids have no day off at all and may do tricks to have intercourse. Some seduce their lord or secretly bring a stranger home to have intercourse with. To secretly bring a stranger home, the maid may first steal the lord's keys and ask her date to come in the morning when the lord is at work and the lord's wife is asleep. Some Asian maids have online private groups where they share erotic pictures and videos and talk about their intimate experiences with their dates.

1229.   Treatment: Some Asians are not treated well. Here are some examples. <u>First</u>, some nationals are too mean to Asians and talk to them in an angry voice, saying bad wording to them, such as *'you are stupid'*. <u>Second</u>, some Asians do not get paid on time or do not get paid without placing considerable pressure on their employers. <u>Third</u>, at times, eight Asians, for example, are transported in a car that has the capacity of five passengers. <u>Fourth</u>, at other times, Asians are transported in the open cargo deck of pick-up trucks. <u>Fifth</u>, although many Asians are brought to the country to do a particular kind of job, they are forced into a job that is totally different from what they have come for. <u>Sixth</u>, people of a certain race or nationality (e.g. Asians) are given a lower salary, less access to social services and worse working conditions. Maids' average salary is US$300——some maids ask their employer to remit part of their salary to their husband and families in Asia. Because nationals grow up seeing Asians as maids, drivers and the like, a lot of nationals have ended up seeing the whole Asian race as a working race. This has made them think less of Asians and reduced their emotional affection for this race. Asians with few or no qualifications are brought to the country, which has made some nationals have a negative image of Asians.

1230.   Language: Some Asians have come up with their own form of the Arabic language. Nationals speak using two forms of Arabic. One is the Saudi form of Arabic. The second is the Indian form of Arabic. When nationals talk to their fellow Saudis, they speak using the Saudi form of Arabic. Yet, when nationals talk to Indians, they speak using the Indian form of Arabia. Likewise, when Indians speak to nationals, they use the Indian form of Arabic. The Indian form of Arabic is a simplified version of Arabic, whereby the speaker simply puts together words with least grammar. That said, it is not that the Indian form of Arabic has no structure. Actually, speaking the Indian form of Arabic is a skill, which almost all nationals have gained as a result of the popularity of Indians in the country, and because the close interaction between nationals and Indians.

1231.   Asian Influence: Some Asians have influenced some nationals. There has been concern about the influence of Asian maids on Saudi children. This includes the influence over their attitudes towards Saudi culture and their Arabic language. Some nationals have an English-speaking maid, because they can practice English with her, and because their children can learn English through her.

1232.   Saudi Influence: Some Asians been influenced by some aspects of the culture. There are many centres that seek to encourage foreigners (particularly Asians) to convert. Some maids convert *not* necessarily because they are convinced but rather to trick their employed families into liking them, as some Saudi families treat their maids badly but when maids convert, these families start treating them well and showing them that all now share the same faith. Many converted maids officially change their first name to a name that is appropriate for the new faith.

1233. **Benefit:** Some Asians have benefited from some aspects of the culture. The unnecessary norms and practices of Saudi society have benefited Asians. If the culture has been rationalised its norms, and therefore many unnecessary practices are got rid of, many Asians will consequently lose their jobs. For example, if women were allowed to drive (which will happen soon), many Asians, who had come to the country to drive around women, would probably lose their jobs.

1234. **Male Driving:** Some male Asians are dangerous drivers. Here are some examples. Example 1, a problem with many Asian taxi drivers is that they are always on the phone with their family back home while driving, cruising around and having clients. For this calling, they use mobile phone apps that offer free international calls. They use headsets for this calling, which makes it difficult for the police to notice that they use their phone while driving. Example 2, many Asians are not really qualified as drivers or have hardly driven in their life, putting the life of passengers (who are normally women and children) at risks. Because some Asian drivers are not qualified or not comfortable (and confident) with driving, they drive so slow on highways, thus causing accidents. Example 3, on highways, some people drive in the left lane. Yet, when one flashes at them because one wants them to move right to the right lane so that one can overtake them, they do not respond and insists on being in the left lane. These drivers are normally old people, Indians or stubborn teenagers who do not want to be overtaken. Some Asians come to the country as drivers, although they may have never owned a car or hardly driven back home. This not only causes more accidents but moreover encourages nationals to dislike Asians. Because some Asian drivers do not know the rules or at least are not used to them, they drive slowly in the left lane, which is the fastest lane.

1235.   Female Driving: There has been a recent need for maids who can drive. Whereas in the past, many Saudi families employ a (female) maid and a (male) driver, they now (after allowing women to drive) want to employ a (female) maid who can drive. In this case, the workload of maids will increase dramatically, giving rise to many ethical issues. Whereas in the past, these families pay the maid US$400 and the driver US$400, they now do not mind paying the maid (who can drive) up to US$550 thus saving US$250 (and other expenses related to employing two people). If one wants to employ a maid or driver, one pays the agency the administrative fee of around US$5,300. This means that, whereas in the past, families used to pay the agency around US$10,600 (US$5,300 for a maid, and US$5,300 for a driver), they now pay only US$5,300 for a maid who can drive. Also, maids and drivers live with their employers and are provided with breakfast, lunch and dinner by their employers. So, now, employers will no longer have to accommodate and feed two people (a maid and driver), as they can have one person who acts as a maid and driver.

1236.   Concern: Some nationals are scared of Asians. There are certain human figures who claim to have direct connections with ghosts and to be able to ask a ghost to do certain things for them. These figures can ask a ghost to make a man fall in love with a woman or to make a man stop loving a woman. These figures normally have female clients who come to them for help, e.g. to make their husband stop loving his other wives. In order for the service to take place, these figures ask their clients to bring one single hair of the target woman. These figures use this single hair of the target woman to make her love or hate her man. For this reason, some women do not throw away any single hair of theirs. They rather burn it. Some wives are scared of their Asian maids, because such maids are known for collecting hairs. When these maids go home, they pass on these hairs to 'ghost whisperers' in their hometown to cause problems.

1237. **Services:** Some Asians offer some nationals virtual services. It is believed that a dream means something. It is not easy for the dreamer to know what his/her dream means. Hence, many individuals consult what are called 'dream-interpreters' who can tell one what it means. The job of a dream interpreter is similar in a way to the job of a palm reader, with the former reading dreams and the latter reading palms. There are live TV programmes wherein the dream interpreter sits in a studio and interprets the dreams of those who call him, on the basis of *'first call, first serve'*. A considerably large number of nationals (especially female nationals) are interested in getting their dreams interpreted. Dream interpretation is an acceptable, common and integral traditional practice. Nationals receive calls from international numbers. These callers are Asian or African dream-interpreters (or, 'ghost whisperers'), who offer their services to nationals.

1238. **Emotion:** Asian men are *not* seen by some male nationals as an erotic threat to their female family members. Here are two examples. Example 1, Asian single males are sometimes allowed to go to families' section, because of various reasons. One reason is that Asian single men are not seen by some nationals as 'male'. Another reason is that Asian single men cannot marry female nationals. An additional reason is that only Saudi single men (unlike Asian single men) are seen by some nationals as emotionally 'unsafe'. Example 2, a woman normally does not talk to her husband's best friend nor show her face to her brother-in-law, but she may spend a lot of alone-time with an Asian driver (a foreign man that she is not related to) while he is driving her around to all her errands. So, in a way, the husband trusts his Asian driver more than his best friend or even his brother-in-law. Men appear to grant their driver so much trust by allowing him to drive around their wife, with there being in the car only the wife and the driver.

1239.   Charity: Asians are the people whom nationals approach to give charities. It is common that some national drivers (when passing by an Asian) open the car window and give him charities (e.g. money or food). Many nationals give money (as charity) to Asians in certain places (i.e. by traffic lights). So, many Asian cleaners wish to work by traffic lights in the hope of being given charity. Although some Asians are supposed to clean whole streets, they clean only by traffic lights, expecting charity. Some Saudi visitors to restrooms give charity to restroom-keepers (i.e. Asians).

Interval

21 married female citizens were asked: '*Does your husband seek to satisfy you erotically?*' Some did not answer this question, because such answers are 'secrets of married life, which are not to be released even anonymously and for research purposes'. Four said that their husband did not satisfy them. They (except one) never talked about this to anyone. One added: 'He stops when he gets his orgasm and then falls into sleep, and I do not know why'. One said that her husband 'did sometimes; thank God'. Two hesitated: 'almost yes'. One participant 'was the one who seeks to please him erotically, because the Saudi man believes that he holds in his hand the guardianship, even in erotic matters. We talk about this problem, but the consequence of this talk occurs immediately but fades with the passage of time'. The rest said that their husband did 'through foreplay' or 'through talk and practice'.

42 Saudi male undergraduates were asked to write down if they would consider marrying an Indonesian. Four would consider it 'if she is Muslim'. If, however, 'she is not Muslim, I will invite her to Islam'. One would 'if she is academically and scholarly outstanding'. One 'would marry her temporarily while travelling'. The rest would not consider it, as 'I do not get along with them and do not like their food and country'. For one, 'there are no beautiful women, and I do not fancy short women'. For another, 'although their body can be pretty, their face is not pretty and makes me sick'. One is 'concerned that my children will look like their mother, and therefore people will make fun of them'. One complained about 'their lack of hygiene'. One 'would be up for only intercourse with Indonesians'. For one, 'their nation is immoral'. One sees 'them as merely cleaners and maids'. Saudi families and society 'do not allow me to do so'.

Closing

Some Saudi norms are among those few elements left essentially untouched and unaffected by modern ideologies over the last few centuries. This 'semi-academic' book has accordingly recorded these norms before they vanish. It has provided a realistic and observational portrayal of the lived experience of some Saudis. It has presented the Saudi context as a cultural 'landscape' full of distinct traditional norms, values, ideologies and, indeed, shocks, which many foreigners are uninformed about.

The book has taken non-Saudi readers 'backstage', to places within the country where foreign cameras and eyes have not been (and to which they can never go). It has delivered the voices of working-class and lower-middle-class nationals and expats. It has accessed many and diverse perspectives and experiences, revealing hidden realities, uncovering implicit contradictions and giving voice to the marginal and the excluded in the country. In doing so, the book has hopefully enabled the reader to explore rival visions of the Saudi Arabian context.

The book covers only what is *normal* (i.e. *norms* and long-established practices) in Saudi Arabia——it does *not* cover those *emerging* and *changing* liberal practices and outliers. Abnormal practices lie beyond the scope of the book. This book is associated mainly with the eastern and middle areas of Saudi Arabia. Besides, the Bro Code varies from one region to another; so its explanations do not apply to every single region in Saudi Arabia, but they *do* definitely constitute the norm in, at least, one region. This book is *not* intended to describe Saudi culture *in comparison with* other traditions, but rather to describe Saudi culture on its own.

Appendices (Methodology)

Data Collection

Many norms of Saudi culture remain obscure to non-Saudis. They have passed unnoticed by reformists and have slipped under the radar of the international media. Hence, there is a need to expose all of these norms to the outside world by providing a detailed description of these norms——the current book has provided such a description. This book is structured around the following research question: *To what extent has Saudi culture influenced the different parts of citizens' bodies?* This question has been addressed through a qualitative enquiry into Saudi society, conducting close observations of everyday activities and around 2,000 interviews with citizens and residents, over the past seven years. This is the first Saudi book to be based on such a generous number of interviews. This research has involved three main data collection methods:

- **Analysis of Documents**: This has included the analysis of relevant memos, announcements, guidelines, handbooks, leaflets, newspaper articles, reports, proposals, letters, large-scale policies and small-scale policies and almost everything.

- **Interviewing**: This has included interviewing citizens and residents. This technique has been chosen based on the belief that interviewing (as a data collection technique) should be promoted as a way into Saudi culture, for various reasons. *First*, publications on Saudi culture (with the exception of a few) are deficient in the presentation and delivery of 'voices' (especially the voices of normal Saudis, *not* the voices of Saudi and non-Saudi activists and elites). *Second*, qualitative data collection methods (here, interviewing) are still unwelcomed by many Saudi researchers and supervisors who consider these methods to be academically 'weak'. Hence, in an attempt to address this methodological limitation within the Saudi academic context, the current book has relied on a very large number of unstructured interviews with 'normal' Saudis (and moreover non-Saudis who have lived in Saudi Arabia) and with people from different social classes to report their voices. The author has seen every Saudi (or any resident in Saudi) as 'data', and therefore an interview has been conducted with almost anyone that the author has come across.

• **Observation**: The findings of the interviews have been informed and double-checked by an ongoing observation of day-to-day activities.

Methodological Challenges

Many Saudi decisions and opinions are based *not* on rational reasoning but rather on 'traditional reasoning'—this book has captured and documented this traditional reasoning. There are, however, certain challenges faced while conducting the research:

• **Cross-Gender Research:** Most qualitative studies in the country (especially those conducted by solo researchers) are carried out within gender lines, because of the Saudi norm of gender separation. Despite this challenge, the current study (which is conducted by a solo male) *did* include the female populations, through the application of roundabout data collection methods, such as recruiting female 'data-collectors'.

• **Female Privacy:** A qualitative enquiry into the female population (whether undertaken by men or even by women) is limited given the privacy and sheltered nature of its female members, making this population hard to reach. Despite these difficulties, however, the current study has encouraged the female data-collectors to establish 'peaceful relationships' with their potential female interviewees so as to make the interviewees feel comfortable talking about their female community despite its private nature.

- **Bold Information:** It is difficult to get Saudis to talk about certain parts of the human body (e.g. genitals), because questions about these parts are seen as 'bold, and our society does not like bold questions' (interviewee). Some of the data-collectors had to withdraw during the course of data collection because they had received so much criticism for asking 'bold interview questions' (interviewee) and seeking 'bold information' (interviewee). A Saudi woman agreed to secretly help the author by acting as a data-collector on the condition that he would not tell her husband, because she did not want to get into trouble with her husband owing to this 'collaboration against our culture' (in her words). Some data-collectors regretted conducting interviews, as they 'got noisy reactions for helping with such culturally inappropriate research' (date-collector).

- **Attitudes:** It is difficult to do attitude-based research in Saudi Arabia, as many Saudis do not tell what they sincerely believe in, and instead, they say what makes them all as a nation look perfect and united. For this reason, 'any survey or interview coming from a society that lacks freedom and is collective is worthless, and the western world not only knows this but moreover smiles contemptuously at whatever reports this society produces' (interviewee). Saudis want to show their society to be idealistic; hence the outcome of interviewing Saudis shows only the idealistic approach to Saudi society, not the reality of this society. Hence, Twitter, for example, represents merely an idealistic (and thus fake) picture of Saudi culture, to the extent that, 'if Saudis implement in their real daily life the nobility that they promote and write about in Twitter, angels will be honoured to shake hands with them' (interviewee). Bearing such a challenge in mind, interviewees are encouraged to talk about the reality of Saudi society, not about its idealistic image and not what the kind of society that Saudi society wishes to be.

Methodological Limitations

This book has, certainly, limitations and weaknesses, given that it is the effort of merely an individual (i.e. the author), and considering that it has no funding of any kind. The author does not represent through this book his own voice and instead represents the voices of the interviewees. The author is merely a messenger (whose *only* role is to deliver these voices) and therefore should not be 'shot'. The author does not expect the reader to agree with any of the interviewees' voices, but he *does* expect the reader to, at least, acknowledge and tolerate them.

Acknowledgements

Every book has more cooks than just the author. These cooks include the following, all of whom know how and why:

- Miriam Al Lily
- Juwaher Al Lily
- Omar Al Lily
- Lateefah Al Lily
- Alexis Michelle Garcia
- Muhammed Al Mowaidi
- Saleh Al Ablan
- Maher Al Sultan
- Saleh Alzahrani
- Ahmed Ali Alhazmi
- Kat Canfield
- Interviewees
- Translators and Interpreters
- Data Collectors

References

Al Lily, A. E. (2011). On line and under veil: Technology-facilitated communication and Saudi female experience within academia. *Technology in Society*, **33**(1-2), 119-127.

Al Lily, A. E., & Alhazmi, A. A. (2017). Passive conformism in academia: Saudi organization, education, and technology. *Digest of Middle East Studies*, 26(2), 340-361.

Al Rawaf, H. S., & Simmons, C. (1991). The education of women in Saudi Arabia. *Comparative Education*, **27**(3), 287-295.

Al-Adaileh, R. M., & Al-Atawi, M. S. (2011). Organizational culture impact on knowledge exchange: Saudi Telecom context. *Journal of knowledge Management*, **15**(2), 212-230.

Al-Aiban, K. M., & Pearce, J. L. (1993). The influence of values on management practices: a test in Saudi Arabia and the United States. *International Studies of Management & Organization*, **23**(3), 35-52.

Alamri, M. (2011). Higher education in Saudi Arabia. *Journal of Higher Education Theory and Practice*, **11**(4), 88-91.

Aldabas, R. A. (2015). Special education in Saudi Arabia: History and areas for reform. *Creative Education*, **6**(11), 1158.

Aldossary, A., While, A., & Barriball, L. (2008). Health care and nursing in Saudi Arabia. *International Nursing Review*, **55**(1), 125-128.

Aldraehim, M. S., Edwards, S. L., Watson, J. A., & Chan, T. (2012). Cultural impact on e-service use in Saudi Arabia: The role of nepotism. *International Journal for Infonomics (IJI)*, **5**(3/4), 655-662.

Al-Faisal, P. T. (2006). Saudi education in the global economy. *Vital Speeches of the Day*, 72(13), 414.

Al-Hariri, R. (1987). Islam's point of view on women's education in Saudi Arabia. *Comparative Education*, **23**(1), 51-57.

Alhazmi, A., & Nyland, B. (2013). The Saudi Arabian international student experience: From a gender-segregated society to studying in a mixed-gender environment. *Compare: A Journal of Comparative and International Education*, **43**(3), 346-365.

Ali, A. (2009). *Business and Management Environment in Saudi Arabia:*

Challenges and Opportunities for Multinational Corporations. Abingdon, UK: Routledge.

Ali, A. J., & Al-Aali, A. (2012). Corporate social responsibility in Saudi Arabia. *Middle East Policy*, **19**(4), 40-53.

Ali, A., & Al-Shakhis, M. (1991). Changing managerial values in Saudi Arabia. *Advances in International Comparative Management*, **6**(81), 102.

Al-Jabri, M. A. (2011). *Formation of Arab Reason: Text, Tradition and the Construction of Modernity in the Arab World (Vol. 5)*. London: IB Tauris.

Al-Khalifa, H. S., & Garcia, R. A. (2013). The state of social media in Saudi Arabia's higher education. *International Journal of Technology and Educational Marketing (IJTEM)*, **3**(1), 65-76.

Alkhazim, M. A. (2003). Higher education in Saudi Arabia: Challenges, solutions, and opportunities missed. *Higher Education Policy*, **16**(4), 479-486.

Al-Mazrou, Y. Y., Abouzeid, M. S., & Al-Jeffri, M. H. (2005). Impact of health education on knowledge and attitudes of Saudi paramedical students toward HIV/AIDS. *Saudi Medical Journal*, **26**(11), 1788-1795.

Al-Saggaf, Y. (2004). The effect of online community on offline community in Saudi Arabia. *The Electronic Journal of Information Systems in Developing Countries*, **16**(1), 1-16.

Al-Shahri, M. Z. (2002). Culturally sensitive caring for Saudi patients. *Journal of Transcultural Nursing*, **13**(2), 133-138.

Asiry, M. A., Albarakati, S. F., Al-Marwan, M. S., & Al-Shammari, R. R. (2014). Perception of pain and discomfort from elastomeric separators in Saudi adolescents. *Saudi Medical Journal*, **35**(5), 504-507.

Bosbait, M., & Wilson, R. (2005). Education, school to work transitions and unemployment in Saudi Arabia. *Middle Eastern Studies*, **41**(4), 533-546.

Bowen, W. H. (2008). *The History of Saudi Arabia*. London: Greenwood Press.

Commins, D. (2015). *Islam in Saudi Arabia*. London: I.B. Tauris.

Deady, K.W. (2005). *Saudi Arabia: A Question and Answer Book*. Mankato, Minnesota: Capstone Press.

Ebad, R. (2014). The role and impact of English as a language and a medium of instruction in Saudi higher education institutions: Students-instructors perspective. *Studies in English Language Teaching*, **2**(2), 140.

Eid, M. I. (2011). Determinants of e-commerce customer satisfaction, trust, and loyalty in Saudi Arabia. *Journal of Electronic Commerce Research*, **12**(1), 78.

El-Sanabary, N. (1993). The education and contribution of women health care professionals in Saudi Arabia: The case of nursing. *Social Science & Medicine*, **37**(11), 1331-1343.

El-Sanabary, N. A. G. A. T. (1994). Female education in Saudi Arabia and the reproduction of gender division. *Gender and Education*, **6**(2), 141-150.

Elyas, T. (2008). The attitude and the impact of the American English as a global language within the Saudi education system. *Novitas-Royal*, **2**(1), 28-48.

Elyas, T., & Picard, M. (2013). Critiquing of higher education policy in Saudi Arabia: towards a new neoliberalism. *Education, Business and Society: Contemporary Middle Eastern Issues*, **6**(1), 31-41.

Gallagher, E. B., & Searle, C. M. (1985). Health services and the political culture of Saudi Arabia. *Social Science & Medicine*, **21**(3), 251-262.

Hamady, S. (1956). *Temperament and Character of the Arabs*. PhD Thesis. University of Chicago, Department of International Relations.

Hamdan, A. (2005). Women and education in Saudi Arabia: Challenges and achievements. International Education Journal, 6(1), 42-64.

House, K.E. (2012). *On Saudi Arabia: Its People, Past, Religion, Fault Lines - and Future*. NY: Alfred A. Knopf.

Janin, H., & Besheer, M. (2003). *Cultures of the World: Saudi Arabia*. NY: Menchmark Books.

Jannadi, M. O. (1997). Reasons for construction business failures in Saudi Arabia. *Project Management Journal*, **28**(2), 32-36.

Kraidy, M. (2009). Reality television, gender, and authenticity in Saudi Arabia. *Journal of Communication*, **59**(2), 345-366.

Lawson, F. H. (2011). Keys to the kingdom: Current scholarship on Saudi Arabia. *International Journal of Middle East Studies*, **43**(4), 737-747.

Lefdahl-Davis, E. M., & Perrone-McGovern, K. M. (2015). The cultural adjustment of Saudi women international students: A qualitative examination. *Journal of Cross-Cultural Psychology*, **46**(3), 406-434.

Lippman, T. W. (2010). Saudi Arabia's quest for "food security". *Middle East Policy*, **17**(1), 90-98.

Lippman, T. W. (2012). *Saudi Arabia on the Edge: The Uncertain Future of an American Ally*. Potomac Books, Inc..

Lipsky, G. A. (1959). *Saudi Arabia: its People, its Society, its Culture*. New Haven, CT: Hraf Press.

Long, D. E. (1998). The Kingdom of Saudi Arabia. *International Journal*, **53**(1), 185.

Long, D. E. (2005). *Culture and Customs of Saudi Arabia*. Pennsylvania, US: Penn State Press.

Madini, A. A., & de Nooy, J. (2016). Cross-gender communication in a Saudi Arabian Internet discussion forum: Opportunities, attitudes, and reactions. *Convergence*, **22**(1), 54-70.

Mahboob, A., & Elyas, T. (2014). English in the kingdom of Saudi Arabia. *World Englishes*, **33**(1), 128-142.

Mahgoub, O. M., & Abdel-Hafeiz, H. B. (1991). Pattern of obsessive-compulsive disorder in eastern Saudi Arabia. *The British Journal of Psychiatry*, **158**(6), 840-842.

Mellahi, K. (2000). Human resource development through vocational education in Gulf Cooperation Countries: The case of Saudi Arabia. *Journal of Vocational Education and Training*, **52**(2), 329-344.

Moaddel, M. (2006). The Saudi public speaks: Religion, gender, and politics. *International Journal of Middle East Studies*, **38**(1), 79-108.

Nassuora, A. B. (2012). Students acceptance of mobile learning for higher education in Saudi Arabia. *American Academic & Scholarly Research Journal*, **4**(2), 24-30.

Niblock, T., & Malik, M. (2007). *The Political Economy of Saudi Arabia*. Abingdon, UK: Routledge.

Prokop, M. (2003). Saudi Arabia: The politics of education. *International Affairs*, **79**(1), 77-89.

Ramady, M. A. (2010). The Saudi Arabian economy: Policies, achievements, and challenges. Berlin, Germany: Springer.

Rice, G. (2004). Doing business in Saudi Arabia. *Thunderbird*

International Business Review, **46**(1), 59-84.

Roy, D. A. (1992). Saudi Arabian education: development policy. *Middle Eastern Studies*, **28**(3), 477-508.

Rugh, W. A. (2002). Education in Saudi Arabia: choices and constraints. *Middle East Policy*, **9**(2), 40-55.

Saleh, M. A. (1986). Development of higher education in Saudi Arabia. *Higher Education*, **15**(1-2), 17-23.

Salem, M. I. (2014). The role of business incubators in the economic development of Saudi Arabia. *The International Business & Economics Research Journal (Online)*, **13**(4), 853.

Smith, L., & Abouammoh, A. (2013). *Higher Education in Saudi Arabia*. Berlin, Germany: Springer.

Tuncalp, S. (1988). The marketing research scene in Saudi Arabia. *European Journal of Marketing*, **22**(5), 15-22.

Vassiliev, A. (2013). *The History of Saudi Arabia*. London: Saqi.

Wapler, F. (2001). Sponsors in Saudi Arabia: myths and realities. *Arab Law Quarterly*, **16**(4), 366-373.

Welsh, D. H., Memili, E., Kaciak, E., & Al Sadoon, A. (2014). Saudi women entrepreneurs: A growing economic segment. *Journal of Business Research*, **67**(5), 758-762.

Wilson, P. W., & Graham, D. F. (2016). *Saudi Arabia: The Coming Storm: The Coming Storm*. Abingdon, UK: Routledge.

Wright Jr, J. W. (Ed.). (2016). *Business and Economic Development in Saudi Arabia*. Berlin, Germany: Springer.

Wynbrandt, J. (2004). *A Brief History of Saudi Arabia*. Infobase Publishing.

Yackley-Franken, N. (2007). *Teens in Saudi Arabia*. Minneapolis, MN: Compass Point Books.

Index

Readers' Notes and Thoughts

....
....
....
....
....
....
....
....
....
....
....
....
....
....
....
....
....
....
....
....
....
....
....
....
....
....
....
....
....
....
....
....
....
....

....
....
....
....
....
....
....
....
....
....
....
....
....
....
....
....
....
....
....
....
....
....
....
....
....
....
....
....
....
....
....
....
....
....

About the Author

Professional Life

He is an Oxford graduate, active writer, associate professor & Saudi international consultant on Saudi culture. He has published with the largest academic publishers: Elsevier, Springer, Taylor & Francis, Wiley, SAGE, Palgrave, Nature Research & Oxford Press. His writings and interviews are translated into different languages: Chinese, Spanish, German, Italian, Arabic & English. He has co-coined 'the theory of multiple stupidities', 'the theory of retroactivism', 'the pedagogy of poverty', 'idiocy-dominated communities', 'crowd-reflecting' and 'crowd-authoring'. He is the initiator and first author of an article by 99 authors; the first article in the social sciences to be written by such a large number. He worked as a consultant for such organisations as Wikimedia Foundation (US), AlphaSights Ltd. (Dubai) and Oxford Strategic Consulting (UK).

Social Life

He is described as a sporty, 'cultured' & 'well-rounded' academic. He has been to 41 countries & visited Tibet. He scuba-dived 30m to see Underwater Museum and jumped from a cliff in Mexico. He is a cyclist, cycled on a safari trip in Kenya & mountain-biked in New Zealand. He flew in a helicopter, a hot balloon & a seaplane in the Maldives. He was on the Britannia cruise trip. He did rafting & wild-swam under Bali's largest waterfalls & in Mexico's caves. He dined at Dark Restaurant in Cologne. He went to an indoor pillow cinema & an open-air beanbag cinema. He went skiing in Kazakhstan & blowkarting in Holland. He saw, in the wild, pandas in China, penguins in South Africa, kangaroos in Australia & kiwis in New Zealand! He drove throughout Bali & Sri Lanka & in the desert by a 4*4 car. He snorkelled in the Philippines to watch turtles & explore Coral Garden. He floated on the Dead Sea in Jordan.

Address

Post:	Dr Abdulrahman Al Lily, Saudi Arabia, Al Ahsa, Post Code 31982, P.O. Box 346
Email:	allili55@hotmail.com
WhatsApp:	+966540015997
Twitter:	@abdulallily
Instagram:	allili55
Website:	https://abdulallily.wordpress.com

Hit me!

allili55@hotmail.com

+966540015997 (WhatsApp)

Printed in Poland
by Amazon Fulfillment
Poland Sp. z o.o., Wrocław

54095817R00199